WOMEN GARDENERS

WOMEN GARDENERS
A HISTORY

by

Yvonne Cuthbertson

Arden Press Inc.
Denver, Colorado

Library of Congress Cataloging-in-Publication Data

Cuthbertson, Yvonne, 1944-
  Women gardeners: a history/by Yvonne Cuthbertson.
    p. cm.
  Includes bibliographical references and index.
  ISBN 0-912869-21-6 (cl)
  1. Gardening—History. 2. Women gardeners—History. I. Title.
SB451.C88 1998
635'.082—dc21   98-25082
                                                               CIP

Jacket illustration, "July" by Eugene Grasset (1841-1917).
Private Collection/Bridgeman Art Library, London/New York.

Jacket design by Bookends.
Interior by Pearson Design and Bookends.

Published in the United States of America
Arden Press, Inc.
P.O. Box 418
Denver, Colorado 80201

For my daughter, Anna

The rate of exchange used throughout the book is $1.50 (U.S.) to 1 pound sterling.

Some of the plants used in the garden plans are no longer available. Consult your local garden center or nursery as to suggestions for replacements.

Warning:
Some of the plants mentioned in this book are poisonous. If you have any doubts about a particular plant, do not use it, touch it, or allow children to come into contact with it. When gardening, wear gloves at all times as some people are allergic to certain plants. Always seek advice from a gardening expert before selecting unfamiliar plants.

CONTENTS

ILLUSTRATIONS

ACKNOWLEDGEMENTS

I would like to thank and acknowledge the following for their help and advice:

Amateur Gardening Magazine, Poole, Dorset, England.

American Gardener (previously *American Horticulturist*), Alexandria, VA, USA.

Antique Collectors' Club Ltd., Woodbridge, Suffolk, England.

Antiques Magazine, New York, NY, USA.

The Association for Information Management (ASLIB), London, England.

The Book Trust, Book House, London, England.

The British Library, Wetherby, West Yorkshire, England.

Cassell plc, London, England.

Cherokee Garden Library, Atlanta, Georgia, USA.

Country Life Magazine, London, England.

J. M. Dent, London, England.

Dover Publications, Mineola, New York, USA.

Eric Glass Ltd., London, England.

The Fawcett Library, London Guildhall University, London, England.

Garden City Historical Society, Garden City, NY, USA.

Garden Design, New York, NY, USA.

HarperCollins Publishers, Hammersmith, London, England.

Her Majesty's Stationery Office, Norwich, Norfolk, England.

The Illustrated London News Picture Library, London, England.

Imperial War Museum, Lambeth Road, London, England.

Jill Hickson Associates, Woollahra, New South Wales, Australia.

John Johnson (author's agent) Limited, London, England.

Landscape Architecture Magazine, Washington, DC, USA.

The Library, University Of Reading, Berkshire, England.

The Loeb Classical Library and the Harvard University Press, Cambridge, MA, USA.

MacMillan Publishers Ltd., London, England.

Adam Massingham.

The Medici Society Limited, London, England.

John Murray, London, England.

National Federation of Women's Institutes, London, England.

Oxford University Press, Oxford, England.

Penguin UK, London, England.
Random House, London, England.
Richard Webb Limited, Dartmouth, Devon, England.
Routledge, Andover, Hampshire, England & New York, USA.
Royal Botanic Gardens, Kew, Richmond, Surrey, England.
The Royal Horticultural Society, Vincent Square, London,
    England.
The Royal National Rose Society, St. Albans, Herfordshire,
    England.
The Schlesinger Library, Cambridge, MA, USA.
Smithsonian Institution Libraries, Washington, DC, USA.
Margaret Tims, Brentham Press, St. Albans, Hertfordshire,
    England.
Veggie Life, Concord, California, USA.
WATCH Project, Reading, Berkshire, England.
Whitaker Bibliographic Services, London, England.
Women's Studies, Gordon and Breach Publishers, Langhorne,
    PA, USA.

My grateful thanks also go to the following for allowing me to
    reproduce copyrighted illustrations:

Mary Evans Picture Library, Blackheath, London, England.
Royal Botanic Gardens, Kew, Richmond, Surrey, England.
The Bridgeman Art Library, Garway Road, London, England.
Imperial War Museum, Lambeth Road, London, England.

Every effort has been made to trace and acknowledge copyright
holders. We regret any oversight, omission, or error.

INTRODUCTION

WOMEN HAVE ALWAYS TENDED THE LAND. Since the time that Eve picked the first forbidden apple, it seems that woman was preordained to be the gatherer. The centuries have witnessed a succession of industrious, though sadly forgotten, women whose place in gardening has often been a fluctuating and complex one, grossly underrated and neglected, and varying with the social and economic factors of the age in which they lived.

Historically, gardening has been a class-oriented activity, and a woman's place in the garden was dictated by her position in society. While the women of ancient Rome planned and cultivated kitchen gardens and those of ancient Greece grew vines and herbs, thousands of slaves, some of whom were women, toiled to establish fragrant flowers and exotic fruits in the gardens at Luxor and Thebes. Pliny reflected the chauvinistic ethos of the age by stating that "garden work is women's work." Arguably, this may have been so, for, by tradition, women, as second-class citizens, have always toiled on the land, tending flower beds, cultivating vegetables and herbs, sowing seed, and weeding. In fact, they have performed every menial task considered suitable to the male concept of their lowly status, thus establishing for themselves a set pattern that was to hold good throughout the centuries.

With the advent of the Dark and Middle Ages, the primary concern of gardening became that of producing food. The cottage wife planted staples of peas and beans and occasionally cultivated a plum or pear tree. Gentlewomen, on the other hand, planted rose trees in the wider spaces of castle battlements along with medicinal herbs and flowers, so creating miniature gardens where they could stroll on warm summer evenings.

It was not until the dawn of the Georgian era that gardening patterns began to change; the formality of the sixteenth century was replaced by a more easily managed, natural style. But, while the cottage housewife's garden continued to thrive and expand, and peasant women, motivated largely by hunger, were employed as humble weeders, society in general refused to recognize gardening as a suitable recreation for "ladies of quality."

By the nineteenth century, however, gardening had started to emerge as a family activity. Middle-class matrons discovered its delights as a satisfying hobby. Skillful female horticulturists began to make their mark, Gertrude Jekyll and Jane Loudon pioneering the way forward. And, for the first time, girls were employed in the Botanic Gardens at Kew. Women were at last emerging as a force to be reckoned with, as independent individuals capable of choosing a career for themselves, a fact that is reflected in the founding of horticultural colleges, at Swanley in 1900 and Studley in 1910, both of which offered professional training courses to women.

The concept of gardening has always been part of a common culture that began at different times in different parts of the world. Initially utilitarian, a means of providing our ancestors with sustenance, it gradually developed into the decorative art form we know and recognize today. Ordinary women played a large part in this development, as tirelessly and diligently they set about helping their menfolk, performing such tedious tasks as weeding corn, ploughing, sowing, and harvesting, in addition to cultivating the kitchen garden and tending the flower beds. Eventually, they earned for themselves the right to be free to choose, regardless of their social standing, what they were prepared to do and just how much they were willing to contribute.

This book begins with an overview of women's role in the garden in biblical times and in Egypt, Greece, and Rome. Then it focuses on women's evolving social status and role as gardeners in Great Britain and the United States, because, during the earlier centuries, innovations in gardening and agriculture were inevitably brought to England—whether by way of the Roman occupation or, later, from countries such as the Netherlands and France—then passed on by the early settlers in America. Since then, gardening innovations, as well as advances in women's rights, have most often originated in these two countries. The book tells the story of how these women, these "worthless creatures of sin," living in a male-dominated world, struggled for emancipation from the shackles of drudgery and chauvinism. It traces women's long, hard-won fight for freedom, equality, the right to vote, the right of free speech, and the right to be treated without prejudice in the home, in the workplace, and, not least, in the garden.

CHAPTER ONE

BIBLICAL, EGYPTIAN, GREEK, AND ROMAN GARDENS

The First Gardens of Necessity

EVE SPENT HER EARLY DAYS in "a garden eastward in Eden."[1] It was a garden of pleasure, a paradise of plenty, and she shared it with her husband Adam. And it was here, in the idyll that God had created, that this first woman picked the forbidden fruit. In so doing, she dared to defy the wrath of God, as many thousands of her female descendants would later risk defying the wrath of the unknown by venturing into forests and fields filled with hidden dangers to fulfill their role as gatherers of wild plants to feed their families. Those plants were the objects of awe, part of the supernatural world. They possessed certain properties, the elements of which composed revered deities, and the first cultivators would ultimately domesticate and nurture these plants in the first gardens of necessity.

God's punishment was swift. He turned Adam out of Paradise so that he might till the ground and eat of it in sorrow for the rest of his days. Thus, man's first vocation, that of manual laborer, was chosen for him. It was a vocation which, as a more systematic form of husbandry replaced casual cultivation, he was to share with his wife, and one that was constantly prompted by his need for food and drink. It was a labor that eventually, in part, would be taken over by women in the millenniums to come.

Women of the Bible thereafter had a continuing role to fulfill in planting the land and in tending and harvesting its produce. When the widow Ruth and her mother-in-law Naomi reached Bethlehem at the start of the barley harvest, Ruth found employment in the field of Boaz, gleaning after the reapers among the sheaves. Barley loaves were the food of the poor, and it was customary in ancient

Israel to remember those in need at harvest time. The reaper never went over his field twice. Instead, he permitted the poor, the fatherless, and the widow to share in Nature's bounty by gleaning after him.

In the Book of Isaiah there is a reference to the women of Jerusalem working on the land and an exhortation to them to "Rise up, ye women that are at ease...for the vintage shall fail, the gathering shall not come." They are referred to as "careless women" and ordered to "tremble and be troubled."[2] The Book of Proverbs, however, speaks of the "good wife" who "bringeth her food from afar." She also "considereth a field, and buyeth it" and "with the fruit of her hands—planteth a vineyard,"[3] a point that illustrates the amount of authority and freedom Israelite women enjoyed at that time and the energy they expended on their gardens. But the "real work" of the good wife was her husband and family, and her reward was their complete trust in her. "She looketh well to the ways of her household, and eateth not the bread of idleness. Her children arise up, and call her blessed; her husband also...."[4]

Biblical women grew flax, with the wife laying "her hands to the spindle."[5] The plants were harvested when fully ripe and then laid out to dry on a flat surface, a process that was underway at Rahab's house when Joshua's spies came to lodge with her and when she "brought them up to the roof of the house, and hid them with the stalks of flax, which she had laid in order upon the roof."[6]

In ancient Babylon, the housewife was known to tend the flower garden, which was situated in the vicinity of the house. So cool and shady were the vine arbors contained within it that they were frequently used by the whole family when dining out of doors. And it was a woman, moreover, who inspired the Hanging Gardens of Babylon, one of the celebrated Seven Wonders of the World. When the Median Princess Amytis married King Nebuchadnezzar, she left behind her the green hills of her childhood home and exchanged them for the flat, gloomy Euphrates valley of Mesopotamia. She was so homesick that her husband, an indefatigable builder, "had a so-called pensile paradise planted because his wife...longed for such...."[7]

From the writings of Philo of Byzantium it is learned that the Hanging Gardens had "plants cultivated at a height above ground level, and the roots of the trees are embedded in an upper terrace rather than in the earth." Added to which, "The whole mass is supported on stone columns, so that the entire underlying space is occupied by carved column bases. The columns carry beams set at very narrow intervals....This structure supports an extensive and deep mass of earth, in which are planted broadleaved trees of the sort that are commonly found in gardens, a wide variety of flowers of all species and, in brief, everything that is most agreeable to the eye and conducive to the enjoyment of pleasure."[8]

Covering an area of approximately three acres, these gardens were an impressive sight, with stairs and paths connecting each terrace. They were irrigated by means of water from the Euphrates "emerging from elevated sources" and "partly forced upwards through bends and spirals to gush out higher up, being impelled through the twists of these devices by mechanical forces."[9] Queen Amytis and her handmaidens no doubt enjoyed countless hours of pleasure walking and resting in this dazzling, man-made Utopia.

The role and duty of early woman, however, was far removed from the delight and splendor of such a paradise. To her fell the tasks of mothering her young and tending to her husband's needs. If early man was the hunter, then early woman was the provider of succor and care in a female-centered society, spending her days in intense occupations that would ensure the survival of both her family and her tribe. Her main task was that of foraging and, later on, of scratching the earth with a pointed, fire-dried stick and planting the seeds she had gathered in the wild.

With the evolution of the village came the cultivation of plants and the abandonment of wild vegetable subsistence. Agriculture largely consisted of growing cereal grains and wild fruits such as figs, pomegranates, and grapes. The Bible tells of every man, and presumably every woman, sitting in the shade under "his fig tree"[10] and of the wise and learned King Solomon, who planted a vineyard at Baal-hamon. King Solomon's garden was a joy to behold; surrounded by a wall, it was filled with a wide variety of plants, including hyssop, camphire, saffron, spikenard, lily of the valley, and cinnamon, in addition to magnificent cedar, pine, and fir trees and succulent apples and figs. Egyptian hieroglyphics relate how the Queen of Sheba, a great user of herbs, presented a gift of herb seeds to the king so that he might plant them in his wondrous garden.

Shady trees were very important to the ancient cultures. The people of Israel used poplars in their worshipping groves. Hagar laid her baby Ishmael "under one of the shrubs" to keep him cool.[11] Deborah, the prophetess and judge, sat under a palm tree "between Ramah and Bethel in mount Ephraim, and the children of Israel came up to her for judgement."[12]

Egypt

*A*ll gardens have their origins in agriculture, and from the days of antiquity garden construction was governed by religious and mythical symbolism, with water and shade as two of the main features. Early Egyptian farming dates back to 5000 B.C. and is the foundation of the country's civilization. By 1500 B.C., the first decorative utility garden had been established in Egypt. In the Nile valley the land and river were interdependent, the Nile supplying "all men with nourishment and food."[13] Indeed, after the children of Israel had journeyed out of the wilderness of Sinai and the cloud had come to rest in the wilderness of Paran, they began to complain, saying: "We remember the fish, which we did eat in Egypt freely; the cucumbers, and the melons, and the leeks, and the onions, and the garlick."[14]

The ploughing of the land and the planting of staple crops began in October after the waters of the Nile had subsided. Because most of the food crops grown needed constant irrigation, a network of canals criss-crossed all arable land. Peasant women helped in the fields, particularly at harvest time, performing such tasks as weeding, winnowing, and gleaning. The corn was cut with a short sickle and then bound into sheaves, after which the women gleaners collected the residual ears in small bags. Women also separated the corn from the chaff after it had been threshed, sometimes piling up a heap of grain and placing a little bowl on top as an offering to Renenutet, the snake goddess. And it was, moreover, female servants who performed the daily task of grinding the grain by hand.

Fruits and vegetables were grown in early Egypt, and kitchen gardens were laid out in a chessboard pattern, which allowed irrigation water to run between the squares. Chicory, melons, dates, figs, bananas, lemons, and pomegranates were cultivated, in addition to onions and lentils, which, together with a wide variety of bread, formed the staple diet of the population. The jujube tree (*zizyphus spina Christi*), the date palm, and the sycamore fig provided both fruit and shade, and grapes were grown in abundance. It was common practice to train the grape vines into round arbors or arches, and the grapes were hand-picked and placed in rush baskets often woven by females. Peasant women went to market carrying these baskets, full of produce, on their heads.

On the outskirts of the towns, which sprang up at regular intervals along the banks of the Nile, could be found the villas of the wealthy, surrounded by mud brick walls. And it was in the riverbank gardens of eighteen thousand years ago that women first planted the seeds of wheat and barley that flourished in the fertile mud and silt.

The Egyptians were keen gardeners, believing that when they entered the world of the dead the first thing they would see would be a shady tree and a goddess welcoming them with the fruit of that tree. They made their gardens not only to delight in while they were living but so that their spirits might rest in them upon death, coming out in the cool of the evening to relish the refreshing shade and water they offered. The earliest gardens, in which women grew flowers and vegetables, took the form of the four-fold field plot surrounded by a wall, the inner side of which was planted with trees—palms, sycamores, figs, and pomegranates—that provided shady avenues in the heat of the sun. Here could be found orchards and decorative water gardens, summerhouses, pergolas, and shrines. Grape vines planted along vine walks grew up stone-mounted trellis work, there was a fish pond encircled by shrubs and palms, and a double row of palm trees encompassed the house itself.

Egyptian gardens were very formal, and planting was done in a systematic manner in straight lines. Poppies and cornflowers were placed in blocks of color. Blue lotus flowers were a favorite plant because of their powerful scent, and ladies wore garlands of them around their heads. Papyrus was also cultivated, and multitudes of brilliant flowers and shrubs abounded in pots and boxes along the walks. Many gardeners, including a number of women, were employed not only to tend the gardens but to make garlands of cut flowers for use in religious ceremonies.

Roses were grown in profusion, many being shipped to Rome, and topiary was a popular garden feature. The Egyptian housewife filled the rooms of her home with cut flowers, both for decorative purposes and for their scent. The Egyptians took great pleasure in flowers of all kinds, chrysanthemums, water-lilies, and anemones being particular favorites, while herbs and aromatic plants were cultivated for medicinal and culinary use as well as for their oftimes pungent perfume. Indeed, legend has it that Osiris, the Egyptian god of plants and trees, was restored to life by his wife, Isis, with herbs after his body had been dismembered by his brother Set.

Egyptian society was based on servitude, all members owing allegiance to someone higher than themselves in the social hierarchy all the way up to the Pharaoh. The lowest class of this society was comprised of slaves, the majority of whom were female and who could be bought and sold at will. All landed property of the well-to-do was passed down through the female line, giving women some influence beyond domesticity, although they received no formal education to equip them for a career outside the home. Nevertheless, women enjoyed a large amount of social freedom, taking part in their husbands' business transactions, and there were several professions open to them, dancing, music, mourning, midwifery, and the priesthood being the main ones.

Religion played a vital role in ancient Egypt, and women who took an active part in religious affairs could gain for themselves a certain prestigious position. There were both male and female deities, and goddesses were often cast in the role of protectress. Women also had the same rights as men to a life after death, although private tomb holders were usually men, and women were buried with their closest male relation.

The husband was the head of the household in a closely knit family where husbands and wives were usually affectionate and faithful. Women held no position in public life, however, and their role was that of wife and mother. They were responsible for running the household but were their own mistresses and could conduct their own legal transactions rather than relying on a guardian to act for them. The more fortunate female members of the higher orders led a life of luxury and ease, sharing an equality with their menfolk in law and in owning, managing, and receiving property. Marriages were usually within the same level of society and sometimes within the same family. Many marriages were arranged, although love matches were not unknown, but parental consent was always sought. Marriage contracts were drawn up, and if the union ended in divorce, the woman had her rights protected and was entitled to financial support from her husband, even if she was the guilty party.

Greece

Greek women, on the other hand, enjoyed far less freedom. They were denied citizenship, played no part in public life, and had no role in political activities because of their alleged inferior intellect that was debased even more by the paucity of their education. They lived their lives under the control of a male guardian, according to the laws of the country, and could neither legally own nor dispose of property. Their guardian was their father and then, after marriage, their husband. Their function in life was purely biological—that of producing legitimate heirs.

While their menfolk indulged freely in pederasty, women of all classes were confined to a part of the house known as the gynaeceum, which was usually situated on the upper floor and set aside for their use. Male-dominated Greek society dictated that women live in seclusion, keep their own counsel, manage the household, and adhere to the popular masculine concept of them as voiced by Demosthenes: "Mistresses we keep for the sake of pleasure, concubines for the daily care of our persons, but wives to bear us legitimate children and to be faithful guardians of our households."[15] Thus, women pursued their pre-ordained role and men followed theirs, although the woman's tasks, while dull and monotonous, were crucial to the smooth running of the household.

Greek literature abounds with obliging, suppliant women. In *The Odyssey*, Homer uses Nausicaa to represent the glory of virginal womanhood, and her mother, Queen Arete, is chosen by King Alcinous as his wife for her faithfulness and domesticity, the king honoring her "as no other woman in the world is honoured."[16] Penelope, the wife of Odysseus, is also portrayed as faithful, diligent, and noble, in keeping with the poet's idealized view of the position that women held in Greek society rather than the realistic one of the neglect they were made to suffer at the hands of their husbands. Euripedes, however, by way of contrast, delineates the female character, but this may have been because he did in fact realize women's latent possibilities, possibilities which, in turn, allowed him to criticize their shortcomings and which led to certain factions hailing him as a champion of feminism.

By the end of the fifth century B.C., a new interest in the rights of Greek women was beginning to emerge and attitudes toward them were becoming more sympathetic, prompted, no doubt, by the political power wielded by the queens of the Ptolemies of Egypt. Many female precedents created at that time reached all levels of society.

The Hellenistic Age, the three centuries following the death of Alexander the Great in 323 B.C. when Greek civilization spread throughout the known world, witnessed Ptolemaic expansion overseas. Consequently, the male rulers of the vast Hellenistic states needed the help of the female members of their families—their wives, if married; their mothers, if not—to retain control over their dominions. Thus, the queens of the Ptolemies invaded the traditional masculine bastions of politics to become powerful leaders, although they still did not rule alone. And because the city and seaport of Alexandria was the capital of Egypt under the Ptolemies and the center of Greek culture until the Roman conquest, the power and freedom of these Ptolemaic queens percolated through the social orders in Greece until ordinary women eventually gained a lot more freedom.

There was less hostility between the sexes, and women began at last to be treated with more respect and equality as female education improved and women gained more control over their property. This became apparent in the Greek literature of Hellenistic Alexandria (Alexandria was the chief center of Hellenistic literature), with the writers of the time being less biased in their approach to women. Ordinary Hellenistic women were given more freedom—to such an extent, in fact, that some of them took up writing themselves. Alexandrian women poets, sculptors, and painters also began to emerge, and women's improved education gave women greater status, a better social life, and more control over their inheritances. Added to which, Solon, the Athenian statesman, issued regulations giving women without brothers the legal right to inherit their father's property, which also enhanced their position.

In the late fifth century B.C., interest began to be shown in the female body, in naked girls, and in what women really looked like. This upsurge of curiosity in the realistic depiction of the female body, particularly in the visual arts, led to a much greater interest in women generally and a much more sympathetic attitude toward them. Previously, homosexuality had been greatly exploited, and women were kept very much in the background. This was now beginning to change, as the Greek literature of Hellenistic Alexandria began to refer to intimacy rather than hostility between the two sexes.

In ancient Greece, it was customary for the housewife to undertake the planning of the garden, not only the garden in the women's court but the orchard as well. She also tended the numerous potted plants in the open court of the house, where she cultivated vegetables and flowers such as hyacinths, larkspur, gillyflowers, irises, and white lilies. In the beds between the trees outside this court, roses, lilies, crocuses, and violets were universally grown. Violets were in great demand for their perfume and ultimately became the symbol of the city of Athens, where they were commercially raised and sold in the public markets.

The gardens themselves were formal, and fragrant flowers were planted close to the living rooms as their scent was thought to make the house wholesome and healthy. Container gardening was also a popular female pastime, and the women arranged pots of decorative plants along the flat rooftops of their houses.

The architecture and the gardens of ancient Greece were copied from the Persians, and both cultures were fond of brilliantly colored, fragrantly perfumed flowers. The Greeks covered their tables with flowers and wore them during mealtimes because they believed that the blooms would prevent them from succumbing to the fumes of wine, refresh their minds, and help them to maintain their high spirits. Greek altars were strewn with flowers, and flowers were planted under trees and on elevated sites. Greek housewives scattered rose petals and black hellebore on the floors of their rooms, the former adding perfume and the latter acting as a protection against evil spirits.

In Athens, baskets of flowers sold quickly at the flower market, with housewives buying them for indoor decorations and young men procuring them for their loved ones. The Greeks used flowers lavishly: garlands were suspended from gates during celebrations, philosophers wore crowns of flowers on their heads, warriors decorated their foreheads with them, and the young people crowned themselves with flowers at fetes. Brides wore garlands of hawthorn blossom, bodies were made fragrant with floral lotions, and myrtle was worn by magistrates as a symbol of authority.

Public gardens evolved in many of the larger Greek towns and were generally frequented by philosophers and men of leisure. The gardens were planted with trees and shrubs, and there were walkways, benches, colonades, pavilions, altars, and small temples to be found within them. The public gardens of Athens, however, remained uncultivated until Cimon planted them with shady groves of olives, planes, and elms and added streams of water, gymnasia, and philosophic walks. In addition to these public gardens there were temple groves, which were sacred places reserved for worship and where specimen trees and flowers associated with just one god were cultivated.

Herbs were in widespread use throughout Greece; Hippocrates is known to have listed several hundreds of the medicinal kind, and Dioscorides recorded herbal cures in his *De Materia Medica* of A.D. 77. Although housewives cultivated herbs in their gardens, the majority of herbs were grown in large, neat areas outside the city boundaries to be sold in the city markets, where women worked as herb sellers. The herbs were used in medicines, in religious ceremonies, and in the making of chaplets and garlands, another female occupation.

Greek horticulture and agriculture were often combined, as many affluent Athenians owned both a town villa and a country farm. Different regions favored different types of farming, but the cultivation of vines, olives, and fig trees formed the standard economic base. The growing of corn assumed a lesser importance, mainly because of the hot summers and the poor condition of the soil, with the result that Athens imported a high percentage of its grain from regions such as the Black Sea. Some barley was grown, however, in the fertile plains, in small fields, or between fruit trees and vines, and even the small estate owner was able to cultivate all the popular fruits of the time within an exiguous area. Lupins and cytisus were grown as fodder, and beans, chick-peas, vetches, and a few varieties of clover were also raised. Landholding differed according to place and time, although, during the classical and Hellenistic periods, land was usually privately held.

During the fourth and fifth centuries, Attica comprised a large number of small farms, and market gardening thrived in rural areas, where yeomen burgesses grew flowers and fruit in the mild climate to sell at the local markets. Attican farmers led the life of the bourgeoisie, most of them keeping at least two slaves or farmhands. Some farms were run by bailiffs, particularly those owned by men who spent much of their time in Athens. Seasonal workers, who were usually wage-earning freemen, were employed at harvest time, and mower-women found work as day laborers. And, while there was a social and economic contrast between country and town, the one depended greatly upon the other.

Ancient Rome

*A*griculture, as in so many ancient civilizations, was the primary industry of ancient Rome. Although early Roman history was politically dominated by land hunger, agriculture was a family matter. The Roman farmer worked his plot of land, where he grew spelt and oats, as well as beans, with the help of his sons and, in some instances, his slaves. After the Roman conquest of the Mediterranean, conditions in rural areas changed very little, but the Hannibalic Wars witnessed a gradual revolution whereby land became a speculative proposition and a source of financial gain. The State leased packages of land to those who could afford it, which led to the cult of absentee landlords, wealthy owners no longer living on their estates but employing stewards to manage them while they themselves resided in Rome. A single man, however, could not manage a farm on his own; it had to be run by a married couple. The duties of the wife were specific and included keeping a supply of cooked food, hanging a garland over the hearth on holy days, keeping a substantial number of hens, and having a large store of dried pears, sorbs, figs, and raisins and a quantity of preserved pears, grapes, and quinces, which "she must store away diligently every year."[17]

The Roman scholar Varro advised farm owners to "be careful to place the farmhouse at the base of a well-wooded mountain—the best situation—where there are wide pastures, and see that it face the healthiest winds which blow in the district."[18] He also advocated that stables and cowsheds be made for winter warmth, that wine and oil be housed in storehouses on the ground floor, and that beans and hay be stored in raised barns. He suggested economic prudence at the end of harvesting, advising the farmer to "sell the gleaning, or pull the stalks yourself....For you must look to the main chance lest in this matter the cost exceed the return."[19]

Vast amounts of money were lavished on these estates. Some of the more affluent Romans owned several rural retreats in areas such as the coast of Antium, on the slopes of the Alban Mountains, and at Baiae, each one with its own surrounding garden. A variety of produce was grown, and olives, vines, and fruit trees were extensively cultivated. Clover, vetch, fenugreek, beans, and bitter-vetch were raised as forage for cattle as capitalist farming, great and small, replaced peasant husbandry, with a shift toward pasturage because of the greater profits to be realized.

The Roman Empire was widespread, and practical farming varied considerably throughout its occupied territory. The Roman conquest of Great Britain, however, did not greatly change the pattern of the countryside, nor did it alter the lives of rural peasant women who continued to gather food and grow and harvest crops. While the majority of farmers were native Britons, a considerable acreage of agricultural land was given over to the model towns (coloniae) to be farmed by legionary veterans and their families. Other areas of land became part of the imperial estates and were either worked by slave labor or leased to tenant farmers. The villa system, villa covering a wide range of dwellings from humble farm cottages to substantial country houses, was entirely concerned with agriculture, and a high percentage of the farmhouses were occupied by native Britons.

Throughout the four centuries of Roman occupation, a variety of villas were built, some of the more elaborate ones run by large numbers of servants. Slave women were employed to carry out various domestic tasks, such as looking after the hens and attending to the laundry, under the supervision of a housekeeper or steward. The mistress of the house merely issued orders, because, like her husband, she was often away from home for periods of time.

Among women in all the ancient cultures, Roman women of the upper classes probably enjoyed the greatest legal and economic autonomy, and yet the position of such women in Roman society was a complex one. While they led an active social life and enjoyed comparative freedom, they had no unique identity. Before marriage they were under the guardianship of their father, and upon marriage their husband became their protector.

Roman women, moreover, experienced no political freedom, could not participate in public life, and had no vote. They did, however, have the right to inherit and bequeath property, and, during the last century of the republic, they acquired an economic and legal independence, the two conditions necessary for social and moral equality with men. It was also at this time that unmarried women became free to choose their own general guardian, although they still could not make a will.

Despite the amount of freedom and privileges accorded to Roman women, no gentlewoman was permitted to choose her own husband. Marriage was used to establish and increase the power of the upper classes and to strengthen the aristocratic families, many of which were already inextricably linked by political power. Marriage itself took two forms: marriage with *manus*, when the husband took control of the wife's possessions, and marriage without *manus*, whereby she remained mistress of all that she owned, apart from her dowry, which automatically became the property of her husband.

The popular ideal of the Roman woman was the embodiment of feminine domestic virtues. The Roman scholar Pliny writes of the state of health of Fannia, wife of Helvidius, speaking of her in glowing terms: "How consummate is her virtue, her sanctity, her sobriety, her courage!"[20] Indeed, the *mater familias* was very important in the life of the family and wielded great influence. Her role was further enhanced by deities such as Juno, who supervised female lives, and in the home she was the mistress on an equal footing with her husband as the master.

While the general education of a lady of gentle birth was of a relatively high standard, great emphasis was always placed on the skills of good housewifery, and to her fell the task of planning the garden. Both she and her maids were greatly involved in the cultivation of the kitchen garden, in addition to growing and gathering flowers, although Democritus was of the opinion that "green things languish and are checked in their growth" when handled by women.[21]

Roman gardens were basically formal and were always surrounded by a wall or hedge, which allowed the women, as the main cultivators, to work in peace and seclusion. The produce of the kitchen garden was mainly staple vegetables such as beans, peas, cucumbers, marrows, lettuce, and leeks. Pliny tells us that a husbandman referred to the kitchen garden as a second dessert or a flitch of bacon, always ready to be cut, and that any unkempt, unproductive garden must be under the care of a bad housewife. On the other hand, Martial, the Roman epigrammatist, was clearly delighted with the labors of his housekeeper and was relishing the prospect of the culinary delights to come:

> My bailiff's wife has brought me mallows
> that will unload the stomach
> and the various wealth the garden bears;
> amongst which is squat lettuce and clipped leek,
> and flatulent mint is not wanting nor the
> salacious herb [22]
> [the salacious herb is eruca or rocket].

Epicureans by design, the Romans delighted in the choicest, most succulent of produce. The fruits they introduced into Italy included figs, citrons, pomegranates, apricots, apples, pears, plums, and cherries. They had at least twenty-two varieties of apples; thirty-six of summer and winter pears; three sorts of quinces; four kinds of peaches, including nectarines, apricots, and almonds; black, white, and variegated plums; eight kinds of cherries; many sorts of thick- and thin-skinned grapes; and strawberries, which were not so highly prized. Olives and grapes were grown commercially, and it is said that the Roman statesman Cato wrote *De Re Rustica,* in which, incidentally, he gives detailed instructions on grafting, to teach his wife, among other things, the various methods of fruit cultivation.

Roman gardening was based upon observation and experimentation, superstition, and the worship of various gods. Virtually every horticultural process had its own deity whom it was necessary either to consult or appease at all times. Varro speaks of "adoring Venus as the patroness of the garden, and offering my entreaties to Lympha, because culture is drought and misery without water."[23] Certain tasks were performed upon the waxing or waning of the moon, and Democritus was of the belief that caterpillars could be destroyed by a bare-footed woman with loose hair walking three times around the beds that contained them. Despite their lack of scientific knowledge, the Romans propagated plants using similar methods to those of today. They also thinned, pruned, and forced as necessary, having hothouses and possibly hot walls in addition to hot beds to induce early produce. The Emperor Tiberius is known to have had cucumbers growing in his garden throughout the year.

Initially regarded as a luxury in the Roman republic, flowers such as roses, nigella, wallflowers, asters, and narcissus were gradually introduced, and the passion for them grew so rapidly that a law regulating expenditure on the plants had to be enacted. Roses were universally prized for their fragrance, and their petals were variously used for marriage beds, to stuff cushions, scent wine, trample underfoot, and in rituals and religious observances. Rose pudding was considered a delicacy, rose water perfumed the body, roses were woven into garlands, and Cleopatra covered the floor of her banqueting hall with rose petals to a depth of one cubit (18–22 in./45–55 cm.) to welcome Mark Antony. Columella advocated that part of the garden be set aside for the production of late roses, which, incidentally, were also grown in vast nurseries equipped with heating pipes, and talked of the gillyflower, the lily, the hyacinth, and the rose as adjuncts of the kitchen garden.

PLINY'S TUSCAN GARDEN

*P*liny writes of the gardens at both his Laurentine and Tuscan villas. The larger, horse-shoe shaped Tuscan garden, situated some 150 miles from Rome, is thought to have covered between three and four acres, with a terrace edged with box and scented with violets in front of the wide portico, from which descended a lawn covered with acanthus. Here could be found fantastically shaped animals cut from box trees by the tree-barber or *topiarius*, and a lawn was surrounded by a walk enclosed with tonsil evergreens shaped in a variety of forms. Beyond this was a circular exercise area, with boxwood topiary figures and low clipped shrubs at its center, the whole area being fenced in by a wall covered with box rising in tiers to the top. In another direction from the house was a small area of ground shaded by

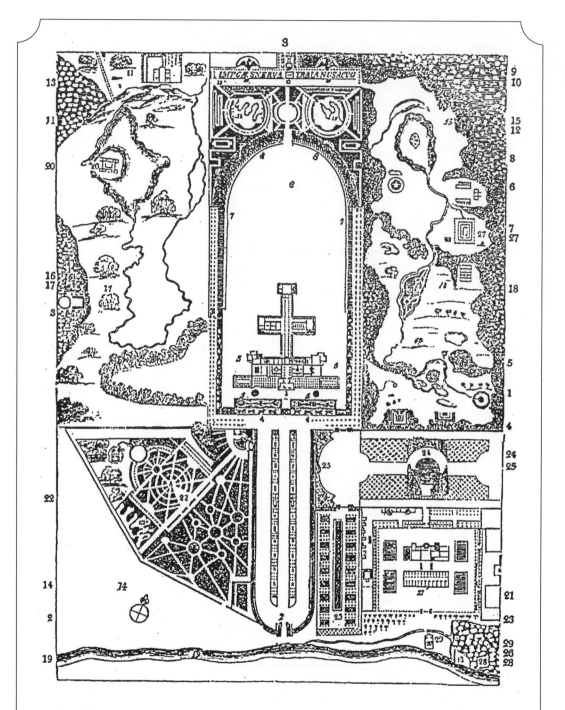

A detailed plan of Pliny's Tusculan villa situated in a natural amphitheatre of the
Appenine Mountains (from Castell's "Villas of the Ancients" cited in J. C. Loudon,
An Encyclopaedia of Gardening, 1827).

four plane trees, in the center of which was a fountain overflow-
ing a marble basin and used to water both the trees and the grass.
There was also a hippodrome constructed of alternately planted
plane and box trees and linked by festoons of ivy. And, behind
the hippodrome, with its semi-circular ends of cypress, bay trees
were planted.

Winding internal walks lined with rose trees could also be
seen. These ended in a straight path that branched into several
other allees, or walkways, all of which were divided by box
hedges clipped into an array of wonderful shapes and letters,
some depicting the name of the master himself, others of the
topiarist responsible, while obelisks, intermingled with fruit
trees trained espalier-fashion, were placed at random. At the
upper end of another walk, ornamented with clipped trees, was
a white marble alcove, shaded with vines and supported by marble pillars.

> Water gushing through several little pipes from under
> this bench, as if it were pressed out by the weight of the per-
> sons who repose themselves upon it, falls into a stone cistern
> underneath, from whence it is received into a fine polished
> marble basin, so artfully contrived that it is always full
> without ever overflowing. When I sup here, the tray of
> whets [hors d'oeuvres] and larger dishes are placed round
> the margin, while the smaller ones swim about in the form
> of little ships and water-fowl.[24]

In addition to this decorative water feature, there was a fountain that issued water of some considerable height and an elegant
marble summerhouse. Placed at intervals along the walks were
marble seats, each seat with its own fountain close by, and
throughout the whole garden small rills of water could be heard
murmuring.

---

(1) Villa, or house.
(2) Gestatio, or place of exercise for chariots.
(3) Ambulatio, or walk surrounding the terraces.
(4) The slope, with the forms of beasts cut in box.
(5) The xystus, or terrace, before the porticus, and on the sides of the house.
(6) The hippodrome, or plain so called, on the north side of the house.
(7) Plane trees on the straight bounds of the hippodrome.
(8) Cypress trees on the semicircular bounds of the hippo-drome.
(9) The stibadium and other buildings in the garden.
(10) Box cut into names and other forms.
(11) The pratulum, or little meadow in the garden.
(12) The imitation of the natural face of some country in the garden.
(13) The walk, covered with acanthus or moss.
(14) The meadows before the gestatio.
(15) The tops of the hills, covered with aged trees.
(16) The underwood on the declivities of the hills.
(17) Vineyards below the underwood.
(18) Corn-fields.
(19) The river Tiber.
(20) The temple of Ceres, built by Mustius.
(21) The farmery.
(22) Vivarium, or park.
(23) Kitchen-garden.
(24) Orchard.
(25) Apiary.
(26) Cochlearium, or snailery.
(27) Glirarium, or place for dormice.
(28) Osier-ground.
(29) Aqueduct.

By way of contrast, urban gardens took the form of the Greek peristyle, with the flower-filled atrium, generally used by the women and surrounded by the living rooms, situated in front of the house and the peristyle garden at the back. The courtyard was laid out in small, formal flower beds with altars, sculptures, and miniature temples, and with vines growing up the columns and along the walls. To make these areas appear bigger, garden scenes depicting pergolas, trellises, statues, and fountains were painted on the walls. There might also be another garden at the rear of the house where fruit trees and vines were cultivated.

Roman women grew herbs in open beds, but herbs were also grown in pots, urns, and vases on balconies and windowsills in the crowded tenements of the city. Every class of society was determined to take part in some form of gardening. In smaller gardens, flower boxes two to three feet in height (60–90 cm.), placed between the pillars of the peristyle and planted with flowers, were a popular feature and were tended by the Roman housewife, who took great pride in the profusion of irises, poppies, pansies, lilies, and violets she had grown. Roof gardens were developed by middle-class citizens, with pergolas, trees and flowers, and lead and stone vases adding shape, color, and perfume to the flat rooftops.

With the internal decay of Rome and the decline of her empire, coupled with the menace of invading barbarians and the rise of Christianity, there followed the dismal period of the Dark Ages when gardening stagnated. It was a period during which virtually all knowledge of horticulture appears to have died out. The estates of the aristocracy were pillaged and razed to the ground, and the soil was once again cultivated only from necessity. Forts and castles rested cheek-by-jowl with churches and chapels, with the monks being the only class of society to occupy themselves with gardening and the only people to preserve any form of existing culture. The Dark Ages, which are generally supposed to have extended from 500 A.D., followed the fall of Rome. Romano–British culture was virtually wiped out by the invading Saxons; villas were left in ruins, and, in the main, herb gardens and orchards returned to the wild.

The role and duty of women, however, remained constant throughout the turmoil, revolving, as always, around the family unit. Any new frontiers that may have been open to women were greatly curtailed, and, with the breakdown of the Roman legal system, women became even more subservient to their menfolk. During the fifth century, Romanization quickly disintegrated, trade routes closed, and Great Britain reverted to her former insularity, with the population returning to the ideas and methods of its ancestors. It was to be many years before women would once again have any knowledge of the world outside domesticity, and even longer before they would regain either the motivation or the confidence to forge for themselves a place within it.

CHAPTER TWO

MEDIEVAL AND TUDOR TIMES

From Feudalism to Ploughing for Profit

DURING THE MIDDLE AGES, ninety percent of the population were peasants, who lived in the countryside and traveled no further than the nearest market town. Their very immobility forced them to eke out an existence toiling on the land, cultivating crops, and rearing animals to provide for themselves and their families. Agriculture was a way of life that was governed by the seasons, a social economy that formed the backbone of Medieval England.

During Norman times, Great Britain consisted of vast acres of woodland, marsh, and moorland, punctuated by village settlements. The few towns that existed were only slightly larger than the villages, although there were ports through which trade with the Continent was conducted.

In 1086, William I ordered a detailed survey of the country, the findings of which were collated in *Domesday Book*. While the object of *Domesday* was to simplify the collection of taxes, from it there emerged not only a comprehensive study of medieval society but also the passport to that society: tenure of land and lordship. William, as owner of all land, bestowed large parcels of it both on the Church and on his barons in return for fighting knights. These men then granted landholdings to their social inferiors in return for certain services, from which evolved the system of feudalism.

Domesday reveals that over thirty percent (indeed, over fifty percent in some areas of the country) of the rural population were *villeins*, or unfree tenants, who had a land allocation or *virgate* of between ten and sixty acres. (Technically, a virgate was between twenty and forty acres, but land allocation varied from place to place.) Above the villeins in rank were the freemen who rented their land, and below them the humble cottagers who held land of up to five acres. At the very bottom of the social and economic scale were the serfs, non-landholders who worked on the *demesne,* a manor house and adjacent lands used solely by the lord of the manor. The villeins were granted land in return for a stipulated number of days' labor and were divided into two groups: regularly employed laborers and seasonal workers. Those in regular employment, the plough-men, carters (drivers of horse-drawn carts carrying farm pro-duce), and dairymaids, worked 310 days a year and, according to the tasks they performed, could receive up to 6s. (shillings) (45¢) in wages plus a grain allowance. Occasional laborers were paid 6d. (6 old pence/3¢) for an acre of ploughing, 1d. for hoeing, and 2 1/2d. for mowing, with women earning 1d. a day. Women were also employed at harvest time and for winnowing grain during the winter months.

During the fourteenth century, land was usually divided into three parts: the lord's demesne, the village farm, and the wood-lands, wastelands, and commons. The demesne was cultivated as a separate entity by the manorial tenants. Over a period of time, the labor rents, payments in labor to manorial landlords, ceased and were commuted into payments of money. This money was then used by the landlords to hire laborers at either annual or daily rates of pay. When the Black Death resulted in labor short-ages, wages doubled, which meant increased expenditure for the feudal lords who, when they failed to secure a fixed level of wages, divided their demesne into smaller landholdings that they then let to tenants.

Tenancies continued to increase as lords enclosed and rent-ed out parts of wasteland or withdrew their own land from the common-field system and leased it out. By the beginning of the Tudor Age, a large number of tenants held arable land of, on average, eighteen acres, with two acres of meadow land and com-mon rights to unlimited livestock. Rye, barley, oats, beans, and vetches were sown, and flax, hemp, and nettles widely grown, the latter for use in the manufacture of linen. Saffron was culti-vated by housewives, who also harvested and peeled rushes to make candle wicks.

A series of labor statutes from the reign of Edward III to Elizabeth I witnessed the end of the manorial system; a free laboring class evolved with wages set by justices of the peace, and new markets emerged for agricultural produce. While medieval farmers had been content merely to raise the food they needed, Tudor tenant farmers ploughed the land for profit. The Hundred Years' War, moreover, saw a rise in the wealth of the nobility from ransoms and gratuities, the bigger landlords turning to sheep and cattle farming. Because the population was smaller, they were forced to lower rents and lengthen leases, the result of which was rising wages for the lower classes. Serfdom had all but disappeared, and women were able to find employment. Female agricultural laborers occasionally earned as much as men, and widows found themselves in control of their own holdings, some of them ploughing their own land.

A Hint of an Emerging Feminism

Throughout both Medieval and Tudor times, women were highly valued on the land, even though their value lay only in the fact that they were generally far cheaper to employ than men. From driving the plough to reaping and binding, the unchanging pattern of their lives was closely linked to the soil and the agrarian calendar. In medieval society, women were looked upon as second-class citizens, inferior to men in every way, their position being very specific and defined by their relationship to men. Socially restricted, once married they showed unquestioning obedience to their husbands, who were permitted by Canon Law to beat them, a form of chastisement that was frequently practiced. Marriages were arranged in both the upper and lower orders to suit the families rather than the individuals concerned, the key factor being tenure of land. The services of a marriage broker were employed by all classes and bargains struck regarding money and land settlements.

From the earliest period of Church history, women were viewed as instruments of the Devil. Much of medieval thinking about women was expressed by the clergy, who regarded them as a threat to their celibacy; most of Europe was, by the twelfth century, Christian in both its beliefs and codes of behavior. Eve, argued the theologians, had introduced sin into the world, and women, because of the guilt they bore as a result, were naturally the inferior sex, a fact of life that they had always accepted without question.

During the twelfth and thirteenth centuries, the cult of chivalry grew up among the nobility. Courtly love was sought outside marriage, the gentlewoman being the object of a knight's adoration, the all-important being for whom heroic deeds were performed. Romantic worship of an aristocratic lady played a vital role in the manifestation of a knight's valor and in the idealized concept of love. Many great ladies welcomed the elaborate deference and homage paid to them, delighted to be the subject of some of the finest literature courtly love inspired.

The medieval concept of womanhood was also placed on a higher plain by the Cult of the Virgin. Worship of the Virgin Mary was widespread; pilgrimages were made to her shrines, wildflowers were named after her, and Lady Chapels were established in churches. Miracles were spoken of and recorded in books and manuscripts, and feasts were held in her honor. Both the devotion accorded to the Virgin and the divine reverence shown to noble ladies went someway toward counteracting women's lowly position in society.

Medieval chivalry, however, applied only to a small minority of the female population, namely, those of gentle birth, and was sanctified solely by the knight, the champion of God. Those excluded from this small, select group were accorded no such considerations or privileges. Indeed, by the end of the thirteenth century, women were the subject of anti-feminist literature as the new bourgeoisie encouraged the *fabliaux*, rhymed verses that expounded the contempt of woman and her depravity and deceit. Cruel though these anecdotes were, they reflected to some extent the sexual equality that prevailed on a practical level between male and female members of the middle classes.

While the women of the fabliaux were depicted as being depraved and deceitful, it was often in a free and easy style. The husbands, on the other hand, were portrayed as being henpecked and downtrodden by their wives. Medieval women were known to have sharp tongues that were used to good effect, discomfiting their husbands and deflating their egos. Accordingly, the man who wanted a quiet, patient wife often found himself married to a veritable virago who had more say in the marriage than he had because he was too much under her thumb to argue. Nevertheless, even though there were some dominant wives, there was often real affection between married couples. Added to which, many women shared in the work of men, as human resources were scarce and could not be restricted to one sex; thus, women could be active partners. They could also find work in trade; the silk trade at this time was run almost exclusively by women. These were the practical levels of sexual equality.

Social position was important to women during the Middle Ages because it dictated the quality and pattern of their lives. The gentlewoman as a landowner was a person of great prestige. Inferior she might be, but such was the organization of feudal society that an aristocratic widow or unmarried lady holding land wielded great personal power; she could make a will or enter into a contract and enjoy a very favorable legal status in addition to being of rarity value.

Women formed the minority of the population at this time and so they were prized for their scarcity value. The feudal and political organization of the feudal system was based on tenure of land; as a result, women landowners were even scarcer and so even more highly prized for the land and money they could bring to a marriage. Once married or remarried, however, a woman's land and rights became those of her husband for the length of the marriage, although, upon his death, she regained part of her land as her right of dower (with which she was endowed by her husband, usually one-third of his lands).

Medieval nunneries were houses of power and importance where social class dictated the pattern of religious life for women. Originally founded by kings and nobles for dependent female relatives, convents enjoyed the patronage of the aristocracy, whose influence was brought to bear upon all aspects of life within their cloistered walls, particularly the appointment of the abbess or prioress, a most influential person both within her own religious calling and in the world outside.

Some of the mother superiors were ladies of royal birth who enjoyed a life of luxury in separate accomodation. As autocratic rulers, they controlled the finances of the establishment, which amounted to considerable sums of money in many instances. Entry into these established nunneries was denied to all but those of noble birth, and many girls were placed within their walls at an early age to allow them to become accustomed to the life of the religious order they would eventually enter.

Records of the twelfth and thirteenth centuries disclose details of the periodic visitations of the bishops to the convents within their diocese. They reveal the independence and freedom enjoyed by the nuns, who, in the eyes of the bishops, should have been quiet and submissive.

Nunneries or convents came under the jurisdiction of bishops, and inspection visitations were periodically made by them so that they could report on any deficiencies they discovered. During such visitations, the bishops scrutinized the behavior of the nuns, their morals, their private property, their clothing, money, travel outside the convent, and whether they had too much contact with local people. As a result of these visitations, changes were often made and punishments given such as penances, transference to another convent, curtailment of movements, and even dismissal. Efforts were made to keep the nuns enclosed and prevent them from going out into the outside world, and in 1298 Pope Boniface VIII made a strict regulation of enclosure. Records suggest that the nuns fought a continuous battle against austerity on the one hand and worldly pleasures on the other.

Hildegard of Bingen was a nun of tremendous ability, good sense, and independence. An intellectual and a mystic, qualities highly respected during the Middle Ages, she was also a feminist in that she was aware of woman's rightful place in society and strong in her conviction that men and women complemented each other.

Women's role remained unchanged for centuries: peasant wives worked with their husbands on the land, ladies of aristocratic birth organized household affairs during their lords' frequent absences from home, and middle-class women competed with their menfolk in trade. Not all medieval and Tudor women fit the stereotyped mold into which they were cast, however, a situation which, at the beginning of the fifteenth century, led to the birth of the feminist movement.

This movement was championed by Christine de Pizan, the French poetess, in her writings. By the use of allegoric references in *The Book of the City of Ladies*, de Pizan was able to illustrate the virtues of women and to conclude that it was the poor quality of education and training that made women appear inferior to men. Among one of the first women authors to participate in the ongoing debate, "querelles des femmes" concerning the value of women, she passionately defended the female sex, speaking out against its denigration and degradation.

Throughout the Tudor period, two themes—the disparagement of women and the question "Do women have souls?"—continued to be debated and elaborated upon in the large number of books written by anti-feminists. There was much discourse on the subject, and, while during the reign of Elizabeth I women were still considered subordinate to men, they began to play a more clearly defined role in society.

There were, of course, those who decried the satirists and wrote in praise of women, allowing them the characteristics of intelligence and reason and illustrating these virtues with tales of women historically regarded as glorious examples of their sex. But it was Elizabeth I who did the most to improve female status by promoting cultural interests and, in view of her own scholarly inclinations, setting the vogue for upholding the educated woman as an ideal. Thereafter, a formal education for females was considered essential.

Strong female personalities began to surface in England, and during the years 1524-1640, more than fifty women wrote books, fifty-eight of which were printed separately. The rise of the middle classes, together with changing social attitudes, resulted in a new kind of woman who was not as malleable as her medieval predecessor. The world was expanding rapidly during the Elizabethan era, and a new way of viewing women began to emerge as an attempt was made to evaluate their status and position in a less restricted society.

Castle Gardens

Throughout medieval and Tudor times, gardening was regarded as a female duty and pastime. Medieval castles and large houses were made up of a variety of buildings, some of which were separate, with gardens enclosed between them, while others were joined by covered walks. These castle gardens were often herb gardens and pleasances, with orchards and vineyards situated outside the castle walls. Gentlewomen grew pansies in pots on the battlements and cultivated utilitarian herbs, for every plant earned its keep and was grown for its usefulness rather than its beauty. Culinary herbs were grown to flavor fish and disguise the taste of tainted meat. Chervil roots were candied as sweetmeats (safe to eat only if boiled first), rosemary clippings were burned to scent musty chambers, and the perfumed oil of angelica seeds and roots flavored drinks and made cordials.

Every lady had her own stillroom where she decocted perfumes, ointments, salves, and medicines for the use of the household, for medieval gentlewomen were well versed in the medicinal properties of herbs. Literature of the time contains many references to female herbalists whose knowledge was acquired from the nuns, handed down by word of mouth, or simply accrued from personal experience. Their lords, upon their return from the crusades, brought with them new herbs and flowers, and medieval privy gardens were divided into many small areas to house them. These gardens were enclosed by high stone walls covered with rosemary, with fencing, or with wattle and daub, a strong gate often reinforced with iron bars and securely locked, forming the entrance.

Honeysuckle and rose-covered trellises and arbors, many of which had roofs, surrounded the gardens, and lime trees trained to form tree arbors two or three stories in height became a popular feature. Turfed seats planted with daisies, camomile, and violets were common, situated along the walls or encircling trees. There were alleyways and herbal lawns, paths, and ornate fountains, the whole garden being made to represent the enclosed realm of Paradise, an idyllic sanctuary from the outside world. Here, medieval ladies tended beds of herbs and flowers, weeding, hoeing, staking, and trimming plants. They grew lavender and rosemary in pots and in narrow beds surrounded by low fences. Irises, lilies, gilliflowers, and columbines were also cultivated, as were honeysuckle, thyme, parsley, and fennel.

Town and City Gardens

*T*he town and city gardens of the later Middle Ages were a bourgeois fashion that became popular with the wives of tradesmen. Enclosed by brick walls or thick thorn hedges, utilitarian flowers and herbs were grown in rectangular beds, with plots of thyme and camomile bordering them and serving as ground cover. There were paths of gravel and sand, a central fountain, and corner arbor, and fruit trees were cultivated for both their fruit and the shade they provided. Banks of earth planted with aromatic herbs were placed against the enclosing walls, walls into which recesses were cut to house turfed seats where the ladies of the establishment retired to ply their needle or to chat with friends.

In the fourteenth century, the Menagier of Paris wrote a manual for his fifteen-year-old wife, instructing her upon household management. A keen gardener, he taught her the finer points of horticulture, advising her to "take pleasure and have some little skill in the care and cultivation of a garden, grafting in due season and keeping roses in winter." He also made various suggestions for the benefit of the household: "And in summer take heed that there be no fleas in your chamber—if the room is strewn with alder leaves, the fleas will be caught on them."[1]

Cottage and Kitchen Gardens

Vegetables were not popular in Medieval England except, perhaps, for those containing starch. Cottagers usually had yards attached to their dwellings (thousands of yards and gardens attached to cottages can be found listed in *Domesday*), part of which they used to grow necessary vegetables such as grass peas, chick-peas, and beans. Beans were a staple, and planting them seems to have been a solely female occupation. Onions and cabbages had been cultivated in cottage gardens since the reign of Henry III, and even the poorest cottager would have a plum, cherry, apple, or pear tree, because fruit was grown extensively during the Middle Ages. Before the reign of Henry VIII, however, good quality fruit and vegetables were rare, and both the royal households and others of affluent means purchased fruit and vegetables imported from France and the Low Countries.

The cottager's wife also grew wild herbs for culinary and medicinal purposes, roots of which she would have dug up from the surrounding woodlands, sometimes transplanting wild strawberries as well:

> *Wife unto the garden and set me a plot*
> *With strawberry roots of the best to be got.*

Early garden plants were used in all sorts of ways; leaves, roots, flowers, and seeds all had a part to play in medicinal, culinary, or perfumery usage. One of the most important plants of the Middle Ages was the sweet violet, which women wove into garlands, chopped into salads, made into syrups, and strewed over the floors of damp, dark rooms to discourage fleas.

In his *Boke of Husbandrie* (1523), Sir Anthony Fitzherbert wrote of the tasks performed by husband and wife, gardening being named specifically as woman's work:

> And in the beginning of March, or a little before, is the time for a wife to make her garden, and to get as many good sedes and herbes as she can, and specially good for the pot, and to eat, and as oft as may need shall require it must be weded, for else wedes will overgrow the herbes.

Women were often in charge of the kitchen garden, working in it when they were not laboring in the fields. Peasant women were paid by the well-to-do to plant and weed vegetables, but women's wages were usually far lower than those of men, a fact of medieval life that was accepted and considered fair because women did not have the physical strength of men. Nevertheless, a wife belonged to her husband according to the law of the land and by her own acquiescence, so the financial fruits of her labor were his also.

Herb Gardens

*H*erbs were very popular in medieval London, where herb women could be found selling the wild herbs they had gathered from the fields beyond the city. The gateway to St. Paul's churchyard housed an herb market where the gardeners to the wealthy members of society sold their produce, for few citizens ventured abroad without a nosegay or posy of aromatic herbs to offset the evil odors of streets that ran with raw sewage and where refuse was heaped in piles.

Gardens and religious houses have always been closely linked. Monasteries traditionally treated those who were sick, with the infirmarer's medicinal herb garden sited close to the infirmary. Monastic medicine was almost totally herbal, with the infirmaries dispensing herbal cures and monastic physicians teaching their uses. Medieval monastic hospitals were run by priests, but nuns often worked in them.

Nuns were skilled medical practitioners and were the first professional nurses. There was a considerable amount of medical knowledge within the convents, each one having formal rules for the care of the sick. These rules comprised of changing beds and clothing regularly, giving medicines, caring for the patients night and day, and giving out food and drink. These rules referred to caring for their own sick sisters; nuns were not allowed to undertake public nursing. They did, however, give their nursing services to the local monasteries.

Nuns also had a good working knowledge of growing and using medicinal herbs, keeping gardens of flowers and herbs that they tended themselves, although they hired outside help for heavy work such as wall building, tree lopping, and digging herb beds. The skill of horticulture was widely studied, practiced, and advanced by these convent women. Many monastic gardens contained flower beds, and these supplied the churches with flowers for decoration, roses and lilies being the two most important devotional flowers. The nuns encouraged flower growing for medicinal purposes. They also gave lessons on herb cultivation, particularly to the ladies of the great houses.

The Flower Garden

Flowers were employed more widely in medieval times than they are today both in sacred festivals and for personal use. A major pastime for medieval women was the making of floral garlands (periwinkle was popular), the drying and strewing of flowers, and the decoction of floral perfumes, ointments, cosmetics, and air fresheners.

The abolition of feudalism, an increase in wealth, and a settled system of government during the Tudor Age led to the flower garden assuming a new importance. Previously, it had been an adjunct to royal palaces, great houses, and religious establishments, where it was considered largely insignificant when compared to the kitchen and fruit garden. This was to slowly change, however, until, by the reign of Elizabeth Tudor, the flower garden was sited in a central position in full view of the house with the orchard and kitchen gardens on either side.

Gardens started to become places of beauty as well as utility. Flower gardens often were formally arranged in a cruciform pattern with two walks dividing the plot into four equal beds for planting the more ornamental flowers being brought back from foreign parts. It was here that gentlewomen walked and gathered scented blooms to arrange indoors to add perfume and color to musty chambers, although William Coles comments wryly that "Gentlewomen if the ground be not too wet may doe themselves much good by kneeling upon a Cushion and weeding." In summer, these ladies also carried "in their hands nosegays and posies of flowers to smell at, and which is more, two or three nosegays sticked in their breasts before."[2]

Gardening Innovations in Tudor England

With its new ideas and philosophies, Tudor England witnessed an upsurge in the use of herbs. Housewives grew vast quantities of medicinal herbs, the majority of which were surrounded by superstition and lore. They also cultivated plants for use in their stillrooms where they would prepare ointments, syrups, wines, conserves, cosmetics, perfumed sachets, candles, and the like. Old women would compound *simples*, remedies decocted from the wild herbs gathered by young girls who went "simpling."

Cardinal Thomas Wolsey introduced the Italian style of garden with its hedged parterres to both Henry VII and Henry VIII. While the turfed seats, arbors, and raised beds of the medieval garden remained, numerous novel ideas were added, including statues of heraldic animals—dragons, tigers, griffins, antelopes, and leopards—and figured flower beds edged with railings of green woodwork. In 1533, Henry VIII built his famous mount at Hampton Court upon a foundation of over a quarter million bricks. Mounts were to remain a garden feature until the late seventeenth century.

From 1540 onwards, Flemish, Walloon, and French refugees came to England, many of them, including women, skilled horticulturists who brought with them their knowledge of market gardening. Settling initially in East Anglia and southeast England, many eventually moved to London where they cultivated vegetables on the fertile banks of the River Thames. Floristry was also introduced by the French and Flemish refugees, who were experts in growing "florists' flowers," specimen blooms of perfect shape and size that soon became an important part of the cottage garden.

Thomas Tusser's *Hundred Good Points of Husbandry* (1557) is a practical gardening book originally written in rhymed couplets for tenant farmers and their wives. Later to become *Five Hundred Points of Good Husbandry* (1573), it deals with farming on a month-to-month basis, with information on horticulture and lists of plants presumably grown in Elizabethan gardens. Tusser believed that the orchard was the man's domain, while the kitchen, flower, and herb gardens were the responsibility of the wife:

> *In March and in April, from morning to night*
> *In sowing and setting, good housewives delight;*
> *To have in a garden, or other like plot,*
> *To trim up their house, and to furnish their pot.*

The wife had a surprisingly wide range of plants from which to choose: forty-three seeds and herbs for the kitchen, including violets, primroses, and pot marigolds; twenty-one herbs for salads and sauces, among which were radish, endive, tarragon, mint, and cucumber; nine herbs to boil and butter, pumpkins and carrots, for example; twenty-one strewing herbs, lavender and tansy in particular; and seventeen herbs for the stillroom, two of which were sorrel and roses. Tusser also suggests thirty-nine herbs and flowers to grow indoors on windowsills and in pots, to include sweet Williams, nigella, and roses. In the herbs to be grown for "physicke," he recommends rhubarb, not then used in cookery.

Elizabethan gardeners believed that all plants derived their good or evil qualities from their neighbors. Strawberries were the exception; nothing could invade their purity even though they were exposed to a variety of evils as they crept along the ground. It was common practice at that time to plant strawberries between bush fruit trees and paths. Thomas Tusser maintained that they would grow more successfully under raspberry, gooseberry, and rose bushes. Strawberries were usually raised from wild stock, and Tusser urged the housewife to choose her roots from those growing under thorn trees in the woods, to plant them in September, and to cover them with straw in December. Seeds were scarce and seedsmen a rare commodity, so it was the wife's duty to collect her own and to exchange seeds with neighbors:

Good huswifes in Sommer will save their owne seedes
against the next yere, as occasion nedes.
One seede for another, to make an exchange
with fellowlie neighbourhood seemeth not strange.

Many plants were introduced from the East during Tudor times, but there were notable absentees from the Elizabethan garden: asparagus, horseradish, kidney beans, but most noticeably, potatoes. These were very slow to find their way into the kitchen garden after their arrival from the Pacific slopes of South America around 1580, although the sweet potato had been grown in Europe for the past hundred years. Curiously, the first potatoes were cultivated for their flowers, which were picked by ladies and woven into garlands for their hair.

Farming and Gardening in the New World

The Elizabethan era was a period of great progress, an age of geographical discovery, expansion of trade, and the foundation of private trading companies. Many years before Sir Walter Raleigh founded a colony in Virginia, English sailors had been sailing the Western seas and hearing tales of the riches already discovered by the Spaniards in the New World. Sir Francis Drake, during his circumnavigation of the globe in 1577–1580, explored the west coast of the land that one day would become the United States of America. His journey took him as far as Oregon, where he nailed a brass plate to a tree in the country he called New Albion.

In a report made by Drake in Florida in 1583 can be found the first record of Indian gardens. Written after a retaliatory attack on Indian villages, it states that he "burned their buildings and destroyed their gardens."[3] These "gardens" are thought to have been corn and bean patches and possibly peach groves. The Indian braves did not garden as such; they were more concerned with fishing, hunting, and trapping. So it was left to the squaws to labor on the land.

Agriculture was crude and haphazard, although productive. Corn was planted in rows of hills about 3 ft. (90 cm.) apart, with beans sown in the same hole and the vines trained up the corn.

Pumpkins and squash were cultivated between the hills, and the squaws and children weeded and tended the plots. The children also scared off crows that decimated the corn. The women harvested and stored the produce in caves, stockpiling the charred corn, beans, and dried berries for winter use.

In forest regions, the Indians burned down trees they had first girdled with stone hatchets, after which the ground was tilled with wooden mattocks. Here the squaws planted two kinds of maize, white dent and white flint, in addition to wild onions and Jerusalem artichokes. They cultivated tobacco for smoking, sunflowers for oil, and gourds from which they made vessels. These women also collected wild plants, not only for food but for making ropes, baskets, and dyes.

The northern Indian squaws grew small, black plums that they dried for prunes, while the women of the southern Cherokee, Choctaw, and Creek tribes cultivated the peach, distributing its kernel as far north as Rhode Island. The Indians traded in crops among their own tribes and with the settlers, who soon came to enjoy the delicious mixture of corn and beans and who learned and adopted many of the tribal methods of agriculture.

Elizabethan Gardens

The formal gardens of the Elizabethan nobility were a status symbol, an outward manifestation of wealth and power, as were the magnificent great houses they built and the garments they wore. During the summer months the Elizabethans indulged their passion for outdoor living, their favorite entertainments, music and dancing, taking place in some style in these splendid surroundings. For gardening was an accomplishment, a creative joy to be freely indulged by the wealthy. Accordingly, a quantity of gardening books began to appear, written by a brilliant array of talented writers—Thomas Tusser, John Gerard, Thomas Hill, and Henry Lythe, learned and dedicated men who inspired the horticulturist.

Sir Thomas More, English statesman and Lord Chancellor to King Henry VIII from 1529 to 1532, had an exceptionally beautiful and famous garden that sloped down to the River Thames at Chelsea, where he would often walk with the king. His garden was filled with lovely flowers and fruit trees and was surrounded by green meadows and wooded hills. More, who was a great humanist, wrote in 1519: "They [horticulturists] set great store by their gardens. In them they have vineyards, all manner of fruit, herbes and flowers, so pleasant, well-furnished and fynely kept," an apt description of the gardens of the time, which had developed systematically from the modest medieval layout to the dramatic parterres or knots of Elizabethan England.

The first English knot gardens were recorded in the fifteenth century, and knot designs began to appear in sixteenth-century gardening books. In *The Gardener's Labyrinth* (1577), Thomas Hill provides designs for knots and mazes and also discusses garden flowers in great detail, giving practical instructions for their cultivation, including soaking seeds in perfumed water to make them fragrant. Greatly influenced by astronomical gardening, he believed that all plants should be planted and harvested according to the phases of the moon.

The "curious-knotted" gardens were laid out in geometric beds, squares or rectangles, or adapted from family crests, heraldic devices, or even the entwined initials of the lord and lady of the manor, and the beds were divided into sections to form decorative patterns and planted with clipped box or yew.[4] The interstices were usually filled with spring flowers, cowslips, daffodils, and primroses, and the beds were either raised or level with the path. They were traditionally placed below a window or terrace so that the intricate design could be fully appreciated from above. Open knots left space for herbs and flowers or, if desired, colored sands and gravels, while closed knots were tightly interlaced. Mazes were also popular, traced in clipped, perfumed hedges of lavender or rosemary. They were either "penitential," to be gone through on the knees, or used merely as puzzles and, of course, as places for illicit dalliance.

THE KNOT GARDEN

*T*he keynote of a knot garden is its traditional uniformity, the result of the types of hedging chosen and the way it is clipped. Dwarf herbs can be used and clipped to the ground, or larger herbs can be grown to about 24 in. (60 cm.) high and cut smooth and flat on the top and clipped straight at the sides, allowing today's modern herb garden to recall the delights of the Renaissance.

The knot itself may be planted with just one kind of hedging herb, but a combination of several varieties, each having its own different color and texture, can be used. The foliage of either hyssop or germander, for example, makes a striking contrast to both the green and silver-leaf santolina. Knot gardens lend themselves to the cultivation of fennel, parsley, and dill, as well as basil, feverfew, and thyme, all of which may be grown to fill their own geometrical compartments. Care should be taken in positioning the herbs so that the overall pattern and neatness of the knot are preserved.

Tall plants, lovage, angelica, fennel, and sweet cicely should take the corner beds, while more compact varieties fill in the center space so that the symmetry of the design is not spoiled. The amount of space each plant will take up in width and height should be considered, and herbs that enjoy the same growing conditions cultivated together. Herbs vary in appearance from species to species, and spiky needles next to soft, round leaves, and shiny purples and bronzes near silvery grey make a spectacular display. Some herbs die down in winter, some have bright, attractive flowers, and others are evergreens, all of which should be taken into account when planning the knot.

Siting the garden is very important; a warm, sheltered spot that catches the sun for a few hours each day is ideal, since all herbs need sunshine to thrive, and many dislike persistent, chilly winds. The garden should be planned on paper first so that the colors of foliage and flowers can be blended aesthetically and the mistake of planting tall herbs in front of shorter varieties avoided. The plan should be drawn to scale in order to visualize the size of the beds, assess the proper placement of the plants, and get a good, overall image of the knot.

Once the design has been committed to paper, the soil should be assessed to determine its composition: is it well drained, primarily clay or silt, dusty and dry, or retentive to frost and snow in winter? The area then needs to be prepared by digging or tilling to a depth of 12-18 in. (30-45 cm.), mixing in compost, aged manure, or other nutrients as the work progresses. Any large pieces of earth should be broken up with a fork and the plot raked to a fine tilth, free from debris and rocks.

To transfer the knot design to the selected site it will be necessary to use: short stakes; a squeezable bottle of chalk dust; a 90-degree angled piece of wood to make sure that the corners remain square; stakes or bamboo canes of different lengths to

Elizabethan knot garden designs (artwork reprinted by permission from Veggie Life magazine © 1993).

mark the height of the herbs in the finished garden. The area should then be carefully marked using the string and stakes and the details of the knot filled in with the chalk.

Begin by planting the hedging herbs that will outline and define the knot 12 in. (30 cm.) apart. When the plants begin to spread, clip their tops and the sides facing the walks or beds so that they are encouraged to grow more quickly. Once the hedging plants are in place, the beds can then be planted and the pathways laid. The perennial herbs should be planted first, with careful thought given to their foliage or flower color. A sundial or birdbath may be placed in the center if desired, with the smaller, more uniform herbs positioned around it.

The pleasure gardens of the early Tudors eventually developed into the elaborate ones of the Elizabethan era. These gardens were to remain popular throughout the following century both in England and in Virginia, where they were introduced by the settlers. The gardens, cruciform in shape, contained a strong Italian influence, and those belonging to the wealthy were usually approached from terraces at the front of the house with flights of steps leading down and walks at right angles from the terrace leading across the garden. Other walks parallel with the terrace led from the straight ones, the four plots between laid out in knots, flower beds, mazes, and topiary. Arbors were a prominent feature, the more splendid of which were used as the centerpieces of pageants and masques. There were turfed seats with roses entwining upright poles to form bowers as well as vases of lead and stone placed between the flower beds and along the terraces. Rows of cypresses, yews, and privets were fashioned into elegant shapes, and sundials and fountains could be found in the open spaces where the main pathways met.

Gardening gradually evolved from a charming, modest medieval concept into the embodiment of Elizabethan sophistication and artifice. In a similar way, the unyielding viewpoint of the Middle Ages blossomed into the challenging, enquiring age of the Renaissance. The inflexibility surrounding medieval obeisance to the monarchy relaxed, to be replaced by the innovative philosophy that sovereigns were mortal and, as such, fallible. People of all classes believed in witchcraft and the supernatural in a religiously divided society of Protestant, Catholic, and

Puritan, of new and established nobility, of a rising bourgeoisie, and an impoverished peasantry.

The Seeds Are Sown

The status of women also began to improve after their degradation by the Church, which had always viewed women as temptresses and the biggest hindrance to salvation, and by the aristocracy, who, while looking upon women as decorative assets, subjugated them in the interests of land. Katherine of Aragon started the vogue for scholarly women that was continued by Elizabeth Tudor. Gradually, women began to emerge as people rather than just females, a fact that forced the social attitudes of the time into disarray. A new way of thinking arose and, with it, a new attempt to evaluate women's position in a world that was constantly changing. The seeds of feminism had been sown and, through the centuries to come, would be carefully nurtured as women gained the confidence and desire to shake off the shackles of subordination and inferiority with which their medieval sisters had been so unfairly cursed.

CHAPTER THREE

THE STUART PERIOD

Poverty and Splendor

WHEN SIR ROBERT CAREY left the Royal Palace of Sheen in the early hours of 24 March 1603, he little realized that the news he was carrying was about to change the course of English and Scottish history. Queen Elizabeth I was dead at last, unwillingly vacating a throne she had so jealously guarded for forty-five long years, reluctantly yielding it to her cousin King James VI of Scotland (who became James I of England). It was done grudgingly and not without rancor, almost as if her hands reached out from the grave in a last desperate bid to claw back that which she had so resolutely coveted. It was not to be; and on that grey, dank, spring morning, as the English courtier began his long and hazardous ride north to pay homage to England's new monarch, the protracted, eventful, and turbulent rule of the House of Stuart was about to begin.

The English throne was once again unstable; James I was not trained for the position he now held. Uncouth, foul-mouthed, and lacking in gallantry, he was ridiculed and disliked. He held women in contempt and despised those men who treated them with respect, preferring instead to spend time with his handsome young favorites and to hunt, gamble, and drink to excess. No wonder the British people mourned the passing of the energetic Tudor rule.

The Stuart monarchy was weak in an age that was to witness social and economic progress with an ever-widening chasm between rich and poor. While the gentry prospered, the ordinary people, who formed the majority of the population, lived in abject poverty, often on the brink of starvation, as in the riot-torn years of 1629 and 1630 when the harvests failed. Wages were low and families worked as a unit, with wives helping out in the fields and gardens.

During the reigns of the Stuart kings James I and Charles I, the colonization of America was in its infancy. When Queen Anne ascended the throne in 1702, the opportunities open to a population of some 5.5 million people were far greater than they had been during Elizabethan times, and England was in control of a large empire in America, Asia, and Africa, becoming, by 1714, the greatest world power.

The Stuart economy was largely agrarian, the majority of people living in an agricultural society in a period of history traditionally regarded as the golden age of yeomanry. The yeoman's newfound affluence was reflected in his lifestyle—in his newly expanded house with its dairy and garden, in his household goods, and in his diet. And while the poor struggled to exist in wattle and plaster dwellings to which was attached a portion of land legally designated to be of four acres but in practice often much less, the nobility and gentry lived in great splendor, one family owning several houses serviced by numerous servants.

The years leading up to the Republic (1649-1653), when England was without a king, favored the landowning classes. Food prices were rising, wages were low, and the demand for wheat and timber rose steadily. Advantageous marriages were sought after, and many of the great noble families more than trebled their incomes from land. In the early part of the period, houses continued to be built of stone and timber in the E-shaped or T-shaped style popular with the Elizabethans. Later on, however, French and Dutch influences prevailed and brick started to become fashionable. Escalating foreign trade and travel brought new ideas, and gardens became an increasingly important part of the estates of the wealthy.

"A Strange New Feminine Brood"

During the seventeenth century, every young girl was trained to become a good wife and mother, in an age when a wife was required to "be of chaste thought, stout courage, patient, untired, watchful, diligent, witty, pleasant...."[1] Under English common law, women lost their financial independence completely upon their marriage. The early years of the century were still governed by feudal law, and a woman's husband stood as her feudal lord. Prior to marriage, her rights were those of her father, and he could dispose of her in marriage as he wished. Once married, she was completely subordinate to her husband, who demanded wifely subjection, deference, and humility, although it was his duty to honor her as a weaker vessel.

Francis Bacon considered wives to be "young men's mistresses; companions for middle age; and old men's nurses."[2] Wisdom and patience were expected of the seventeenth-century wife; she had to be her husband's serene companion, to minister to his wants and interests, and to give of her time and attention when it was demanded. Sexual liberation was all but impossible with frequent pregnancies fueled by inadequate contraception; sexual freedom continued, therefore, to be male-defined in what remained a male-defined society, with few women having any real desire for sexual equality.

A wife's "separate estate," introduced by the Court of Chancery during the Elizabethan era, whereby a wife could own property independent of her husband, was much in evidence by the time of the civil war (1642-1651). While a husband might dispose of his wife's consumable goods, her position, in what was termed a matrimonial partnership, precluded him from disposing of her estate without her consent. It was, moreover, possible for a wife to have a separate income under the terms of the marriage settlement, although this was a luxury enjoyed only by gentlewomen. And while some wives continued to participate in business, widows undertook the roles of money-lenders, landladies, and shopkeepers.

Some of the more privileged seventeenth-century ladies were almost as well educated as their male counterparts, often sharing a tutor with their brothers. They could speak several languages, read Latin, write in a legible hand, and grasp the elementary processes of arithmetic, the latter being of prime importance not only from the aspect of keeping their own domestic ledgers but because they were expected to take charge of the household and do much of the buying and selling when their husbands were absent from home. During the Civil War, these gentlewomen acted for their husbands "in their numerous and endless lawsuits....[T]hey leased their farms, they found a market for the crops, they kept the money hidden in strong chests concealed in mysterious hiding-places, and they wrote long and interesting letters to the absent ones, full of business and news."[3]

The Civil War also witnessed the emergence of several religious sects in which women were permitted to vote and debate and, with the abolition of censorship, to write and publish tracts. While women experienced a sense of freedom, patriarchal authority within the sects nevertheless prevailed, even though some sects maintained it was a woman's duty to obey her conscience only in spiritual matters: "The young women conversed without any circumspection or modesty, and frequently met at taverns and common eating houses; and they who were stricter and more severe in their comportment became the wives of the seditious preachers or of officers of the army. The daughters of noble and illustrious families bestowed themselves upon the *divines of the time* or other low and unequal matches."[4]

The war turned the world upside down, engendering new liberties and fostering a "strange new feminine brood" that gallantly defended the estates of their husbands, withstood sieges, and even dressed in men's clothing and fought alongside men in battle. Women's activism, however, was met with either ridicule or hostility, and when peace was once again restored, the idea of woman's timidity and subservience continued to be preached.

Few seventeenth-century wives were literate, although Puritan families ensured that their daughters could read the Bible. Girls married at an early age, suitable matches being arranged by parents for whom the property and rank of a prospective bridegroom were the main considerations. Gradually, however, women started to realize that their intellectual abilities, if properly exploited, matched those of men, and they began to complain about their lack of education. It was, they argued, a situation deliberately contrived by men so that they might continue to dominate and subjugate them, a theme that manifests itself in Hannah Woolley's *The Gentlewoman's Companion* (1675).

Feminist Mary Astell, in *A Serious Proposal to the Ladies* (1697), contended that if women were better educated, not only would they be more fitting companions for their husbands but they would also be better equipped for what was then their most important responsibility, the religious education of their children. In 1694, she wrote: "Were the men as much neglected and as little care taken to cultivate and improve them, perhaps they would be so far from surpassing those whom they now despise...." Astell's desire for women's intellectual advancement also prompted her to cite, as an example, Dutch women, who "keep the books, balance the accounts, and do all the business with as much dexterity and exactness as their own or our men can do."[5]

Feminism, however, was in its infancy, many middle-class women preferring instead to be idle and frivolous and to be treated by their husbands as mere decorative appendages. Feminine luxuries, gossip, and gambling suited them much better than striving to free themselves from the shackles of male domination.

Puritanism was no longer contained, and Oliver Cromwell became its champion when he abolished the Divine Right of Kings, causing doubts to be raised about the structure of mid-seventeenth-century society. As a result, the father, as head of the household, assumed a new, dictatorial authority; children, considered naturally sinful, received constant beatings; and the wife's duty was to uphold the family patriarch in all things. While in the eyes of the Puritans, woman's role was not diminished, her intellectual development was retarded and she remained her husband's unequal partner, repressed in spirit and regarded as inherently inferior, although she was no longer judged unclean and shameful and her soul was considered to be equal to that of a man in the sight of God. There was little evidence of repressed female spirit, however, in the women who journeyed to the New World, taking with them a wealth of multifarious household skills and continuing to shoulder the domestic responsibilities and the grinding burden of hardship and toil in the dangerous virgin terrain of North America.

Throughout the seventeenth century some eighty percent of the population of Great Britain were employed in agriculture at a time when fifty percent of the country was under cultivation or pasture and the remainder comprised of marshland, forest, and open heath. Working-class women labored alongside their husbands in isolated villages where the agricultural community was divided into three classes: yeoman farmers, husbandmen, and wage-earning laborers.

The yeoman's wife was in charge of the dairy, poultry, garden, and orchard and sold surplus produce at the local market. She was well versed in the use of the herbs that she grew and acted as the family physician, while on larger farms she organized and trained servants to perform the more menial household tasks. Of these women, Richard Surflet writes: "They have charge of the oven and cellar; and we leave the handling of hemp to them likewise; as also the care of making webs,…of ordering the kitchen garden; keeping of the fruits, herbs, roots and seeds; and moreover of watching and attending to the bees."[6] It was also their duty to assist their husbands with business matters, in addition to supporting the family, as can be seen from the proposal for colonists in Virginia offered by Merchant Taylors, a London livery company: "one hundred acres for every man's person that hath a trade, or a body able to endure day labour as much for his wief, as much for his child, that are of yeres to doe service to the Colony."[7]

The wives of husbandmen were often women who, as girls, had worked on farms. Their tasks included cultivating their gardens and tending the livestock. Their husbands usually worked on neighboring farms, and the family lived in a small holding at a fixed rent. At harvest time these housewives would help in the fields for wages fixed by the Quarter Sessions, which varied from county to county and corresponded to the price of corn in those counties. In the hay harvest they varied from "1d. [less than 1¢] and meat and drink, or 4d. without, to 6d. and meat and drink, or 1s. [7 1/2¢] without" and in the corn harvest from "2d. and meat and drink, or 6d. without, to 6d. and meat and drink, or 1s. without."[8]

In Yorkshire, women were employed to gather corn out of the furrows with wain-rakes, to pull peas for 6d. a day, to help with thatching for 3d. or 4d. a day, and for muck-spreading at 2d. or 3d. a day. Women were included in every kind of agricultural work from weeding corn for 2d. a day in Norfolk to shearing sheep for 6d. a day with food, 1s. without. Many of the poorer housewives spent time hand-spinning, both for financial gain and to clothe their ever-growing families. Flax or hemp was grown on allotments and spun and woven into linen to make shirts and household necessities, and from common land children collected pieces of sheeps' wool, which was also hand-spun into yarn.

For the wage-earning class, life was hard. Wages were low, and those of a wife would, on average, be 1s. a week with food. The frequency of a woman's labor depended on the number of children she had, and, generally speaking, the majority of lower class wives were unable to take work on a paid basis or at regular intervals. These women were usually worn down by poverty, malnutrition, and constant childbearing, broken in mind and body. At best they could earn 2d. a day and their food for working in the hay harvest; at worst, deserted by their husbands, they were forced to rely on the parish for support, having lost their economic position and been reduced to a state of pauperism.

The more fortunate of these laboring women were hired to perform seasonal tasks. Weeders and pickers were employed in Warwickshire during the woad harvest, female labor was used for hop and apple picking, and women workers were enlisted in the harvesting of tobacco and flax. Seasonal women workers were also employed to carry pottles of early strawberries in baskets on their heads to Covent Garden market, while others gathered wild herbs and watercress to sell. The citizens of East London at that time were supplied with the fruit and vegetables grown by local market gardeners and sold at Spitalfields, which was given a Royal Charter in 1682.

Elizabeth Pepys declared in her diary:

This day I did go a-strawberrying and such a pleasant pastime it be....Many a small reddish root did I gather to make up my medicine. 'Tis well known that without aid the strawberry does cool the liver and the blood, and the spleen, and the hot choleric stomach....'Tis the cordial from the roots though which is the most efficacious for the fastening of loose teeth and the hardening of the gums....[9]

The years following the Restoration of Charles II witnessed a rise in the position and talents of the nurserymen, many of whom were professional gardeners and had their nurseries either in Shoreditch or between Brompton and Fulham. In 1681, a large nursery was founded at Brompton Park on a site of one hundred acres which, two years later, employed twenty men and two women, the men earning 8s. a week and the women 4s. Over seventy years earlier, in 1606, the Gardener's Company of the City of London had received its Royal Charter, giving it the power to oversee all "plants, stocks, setts, trees, seedes, slippes, roots, hearbes and other things...in any market within the Cittie of London and six myles about." It could also burn produce that was "deceitfull or unprofitable," and no one could practice gardening without its permission.[10] By 1649, the Company had its own large market garden that employed 1,500 men, women, and children.

At the opposite end of the social scale, gentlewomen occupied themselves with domestic and horticultural affairs within the large estates of their country houses. Gardens were becoming more and more grandiose, with the flower garden rising in popularity and "ladies of quality" keeping herb gardens for medicinal and culinary purposes and picking fruit from vast orchards to make into pies and preserves.

Such ladies spent many hours in their stillrooms compounding simples and potions for the poor as well as decocting all the herbal preparations necessary to a large household. They would make herbal salves, lotions, ointments, and wound-drinks, possets, vinegars, and cordial electuaries. They would also prepare aromatic waters, perfumes, personal and household soaps, essential oils, and tooth-powders in addition to candied conceits, conserves, and syrups for the table. Estates such as these were self-sufficient, although luxuries were imported, and it was the duty of every Stuart housewife to oversee the growing of food, the brewing of drink, and the fashioning of garments.

Lady Anne Halkett, notable for the part she played in public affairs, led a simple home life and "was ever imployed either in doing or reaping good: in the summer season she vyed with the bee or ant, in gathering herbs, flowers, worms, snails, etc., for the still or limbeck, for the mortar or boyling pan, etc.,…making preparations of extracted waters, spirits, ointments, conserves, salves, powders, etc., which she ministred every Wednesday to a multitude of poor infirm persons, besides what she dayly sent abroad to persons of all ranks who consulted her in their maladies."[11]

The New World Settlers

The Pilgrim fathers took a variety of herbs with them to New England for use during the voyage and to plant in their newly made gardens. Both the culinary and medicinal virtues of these herbs were much appreciated by the passengers of the *Mayflower*, who numbered 102 people plus the captain and crew. Of the 102 colonists, 73 were male and 29 female, which included 20 boys and 8 girls as well as 19 male servants, 3 maidservants, and craftsmen hired on a temporary basis.

Once landed in the well-wooded area of the American coast at Cape Cod, the Pilgrims were befriended by the Indian Tisquantum, the only remaining member of the Patuxet tribe, which had once inhabited the area. From him they learned the rudiments of survival—how to plant Indian corn when "the young leaves on the oak tree were as big as the ears of a mouse" and how to place the fish known as ale-wives around the roots of the maize to ensure a successful harvest.[12]

It was decided that each family of the Plymouth Settlement should build its own house, which would have a plot of land three rods long and half a rod wide for each member of the family. The choice of position of the homesteads was determined by lot, and the houses were thereafter built to form a single street parallel with the stream.

Everyone worked with a will, sowing, planting, felling timber, building, hunting, and fishing in a land covered with oak trees, pines, juniper, sassafras, and other aromatic shrubs until illness struck and left just twenty-one men and six boys to do the work of the colony. Nevertheless, during that first season, twenty-one acres of corn were grown and six more acres sown with barley, wheat, and rye, while the gardens around the dwellings were brought under cultivation. Just six years later, the settlers were producing enough Indian corn not only to meet their own requirements but to sell the surplus at 6s. a bushel.

WOMEN OF THE COLONIES Colonial women, like their English sisters, worked hard and were confined to the realms of domesticity as, by law, they were subordinate to men. English common law decreed that a married woman's property and earnings belonged to her husband. A wife had no legal guardianship of her children, she could not enter into a contract, and she could not obtain a divorce except in New England. It wasn't until 1809, in Connecticut, that married women were granted the first legal concession allowing them to make wills. The colonial woman was an unequal member of a partnership, the *helpmeet* of her husband, and, living in a patriarchal society, if she found employment, she was paid considerably less than a man.

The establishment of marriage as a civil contract in New England during colonial times broke with the English ecclesiastical tradition and was an important feature of the period. Earlier colonial laws had dictated that marriages should take place before justices of the peace, and sometimes failure to comply resulted in the marriage being declared null and void.

In the middle states of the eastern seaboard there was a choice between civil and church weddings. This was the custom during the early years in the State of Maryland, for example, but later on the law dictated that all marriages had to be solemnized by the clergy. In the southern states of the eastern seaboard the English tradition prevailed, although, initially, only members of the established Church of England could perform the ceremony.

In New England there was a custom of formal public betrothal, as throughout the colonies certain procedures were adhered to: notice of marriage had to be given; evidence of parental consent had to be presented; the marriage had to be performed by authorized persons; and the marriage had to be registered in the public records. Throughout the colonies adults who remained unmarried were frowned upon, particularly if they chose to lead independent lives, and laws were passed taxing bachelors. Laws were also enacted to empower fathers to control the courtship of their children.

Land in New England was plentiful, and agriculture was intensive and served to hold the community together. A *plantation right* was granted to groups of applicants authorizing a settlement in an agreed area fractionally beyond the existing frontier line. If, after a couple of years, the settlement flourished, these people were then granted a *town right*, giving them the holding of the land and full representation in the general court. Holdings were afterwards assigned to individuals, varying from a small plot to thirty acres, which they could then cultivate, planting gardens and growing Indian corn and rye. The outlying pasture land and meadows, however, were designated as common land, regulated by town ordinances.

Large families were considered an economic advantage, and, in spite of the high mortality rate of children, there was a rapid population growth. Most women spent their childbearing years either in pregnancy or in childbirth, many of them bearing ten or more children. As in Great Britain, the vote was denied them;

there was no women's rights party and it was therefore considered unnecessary to actually debar them. In Virginia, though, it was enacted that "no woman, sole or covert" should be able to vote in the election of burgesses, even if she was a freeholder.[13] Women received the most basic of education, being encouraged in household skills rather than intellectual pursuits, although some of the daughters of well-to-do colonials attended female seminaries and others were taught in European schools.

The lives of these women were governed by the pattern of the seasons as they tended their gardens; preserved and cooked food; made candles, soap, butter, and cheese; and attended to the other numerous and mundane domestic chores such as laundering, spinning, and weaving. There was a division of labor by gender, but this was not strictly adhered to. Some women helped to plow and pitch hay, handled rifles for food and protection, and dug and harvested in the fields, in addition to caring for their oftimes large families. Rural family life was arduous and practical, and the New Englanders not only helped to add the American continent to the civilized world but also advanced the cause of liberty. C. W. Eliot said of Puritan women:

> Generations of them cooked, carried water, washed and made clothes, bore children in lonely peril...and sank at last into nameless graves, without any vision of the grateful days when millions of their descendants should rise up and call them blessed.[14]

The early settlers provided market places in their towns for the sale of meats and vegetables (all European towns of any importance had their own public markets at this time), and there was a market in Jamestown as early as 1617 and one in New Amsterdam in 1647. The sale of these comestibles was permitted only in the public market places; it was illegal to sell them elsewhere. This market system operated during both the colonial and the early national period in America, although, by the time of the Civil War, it was beginning to break up.

New England society during the seventeenth century was divided into several tiers: the aristocracy, which included clergymen and merchants as well as those of wealth and rank; the skilled artisans and freeholders, who were proud of their title

"Goodman" or "Goodwife"; the unskilled laborers, usually addressed only by their Christian names; the indentured servants; and the slaves, Indian and Negro. American colonial society was interwoven with ethnic culture: English, French, German, and Dutch, each culture bringing strong values of family unity to the community.

Native American women were part of the labor force long before colonization. Female servants and slaves imported by the colonists quickly joined this force, making colonial America a society in which virtually everyone worked, producing what food and household goods they could and bartering for what they were unable to supply themselves.

Imported Negro women slaves worked in the house and in the fields. Mixed marriages were banned, and the children of slave women automatically became slaves to their white planter owners. Attitudes at that time were such that slavery was an acceptable practice, a fact of life, with few white people stopping to consider either the moral issues or the religious abomination behind the concept. Added to which, native Indian slavery was extensive in the Carolinas, the general belief amongst the colonists being that the Indian religion was a form of devil worship and that the Indians who practiced it should be alienated and subjected. It was the Quakers in Pennsylvania who first questioned the morality of keeping slaves, whether Indian or Negro. Nevertheless, slavery continued to expand, with slaves supplementing white labor to some extent in all of the colonies.

Before the importation of African slaves, white female servants sometimes worked in the fields and, in families too poor to afford to keep bound labor, the wives tended the tobacco plants as well as carrying out their normal household duties. Wealthy women, on the other hand, used their servants and slaves to perform the necessary household tasks while they themselves supervised the dairy and the vegetable gardens and decided which crops should be planted, harvested, and sold.

From 1640 onwards, the women of the New Netherlands tended vegetable and flower gardens.

> Long ago, the care of plants, such as needed peculiar care or skill to rear them, was the female province....Into the garden no foot of man intruded after it was dug in the spring. I think I see yet what I have often beheld—a

respectable mistress of a family going out to her garden in
an April morning, with her great calash, her little painted
basket of seeds, and her rake over her shoulders to her gar-
den of labours.[15]

Around ninety percent of the colonists were engaged in agriculture and both women and children were employed on the
land. While the woman's geographical environment had
changed, the work she tackled daily had not. For rich and poor
alike, a woman's duty was that of running the household. For the
gentlewoman, her career continued to be that of wife and mother, although she would have had numerous servants to perform
the more menial tasks, while those of more humble degree continued to be "very ready to help and assist their Husbands in any
Servile work, as Planting when the Season of the Year requires
expedition: Pride seldom banishing housewifery."[16]

COLONIAL GARDENS Herb gardens were an important part of
everyday life. The housewife planted and tended them, cultivating
those used by the Indians as well as the ones with which she was
familiar. Soapwort was grown in abundance allegedly to relieve
the pain caused by poison ivy, and rue, clary, sage, tansy, and
camomile were also widely cultivated. The beds of the traditional
colonial herb gardens were divided by paths made of bricks that
met in the center where a beehive was positioned. The beds were
then edged with logs or boards to control invasive plants, and the
whole was surrounded by a picket fence. Colonial women, like
those left behind in the Old Country, concocted the salves, ointments, and lotions needed for the health of their families and dried
herbs for strewing and dyeing cloth and for culinary use.

When the settlers made the first gardens they naturally
copied the ideas they had used in England. The women planted
flowers such as marigolds, pinks, violets, double hollyhocks,
primroses, and columbines. They cultivated grape vines for making wine as well as apple, plum, and pear trees, in addition to
onions, parsnips, radishes, cucumbers, and turnips, surrounding
their gardens with hedges and ditches to keep out straying cattle.
But because in the early years the settlers' time was devoted to
growing the utilitarian plants necessary for the survival of the
colony, it was 1650 before colonial gardens were laid out in the
form of patterns.

By 1634, nearly four thousand Englishmen had gone over to the colonies, and around twenty villages had been formed on or near the shores of Massachusetts Bay. In these villages, houses and bridges were built and roads and fences made. By 1672, the gardens, planted with both English vegetables and herbs and indigenous American plants, were flourishing.

In the latter years of the seventeenth century the great plantations of Virginia began to appear, usually owned by wealthy Englishmen who were accustomed to well-kept parks and large expanses of land. Here, the vegetables and flowers were always grown near the house in gardens that were fenced, these early gardens taking as their inspiration the English Elizabethan knot gardens. The knots, which were edged with box, were often devoid of flowers so that the areas remained solely green. Any flowers that were cultivated, English roses, cotton lavender, gillyflowers, honesty, hollyhocks, sweet briar, feverfew, and comfrey, for example, were planted either in "open knots" or in borders.

Gardening in the Grand Manner

*O*n the opposite side of the Atlantic, gardening in the grand manner started to become more ambitious and diverse. As the century progressed, Italian, French, and Dutch influences became visible, and, by 1664, the knot garden was superseded by the *parterre*, made up of a variety of shapes woven into intricate patterns and designed to be viewed from the terrace or first-floor windows. The alleys between were filled with colored gravels or sands, and the beds themselves with low-growing flowers. Many of the parterres were designed by embroidery artists and, as a result, were known as "parterre de broderie."

Terraces lay in front of the grand country houses, from which the formally designed garden below could be viewed. The mount with its dominant summerhouse continued to be a feature, the fountain was still popular, and the sun-dial was coming into vogue. Bowling greens and lawns were de rigueur, as were the labyrinth, standing some two meters high and formed from pleached fruit trees, and the maze, with its clipped hyssop, marjoram, privet, thyme, savory, or lavender cotton.

Hedges of box, cypress, privet, rosemary, juniper, or pleached fruit trees separated the various garden areas, and high walls were commonplace, against which were grown peaches, nectarines, and figs. Clipped and trimmed greens were much in evidence as the passion for evergreens and topiary grew. Avenues were planted with a variety of wild trees, and roses, including the first American rose, *Rosa virginiana*, were widely grown. Alleys of firs, poplars, and pines embellished with cascades and statues abounded, and gazebos, built of stone or wood, became fashionable.

Vast orchards of fruit trees were planted: cherries, apples, pears, red and white plums, damsons, apricots, and quinces. Francis Bacon recommended that "for the main garden…there should be some fair alleys, ranged on both sides with fruit-trees; and some pretty tufts of fruit-trees, and arbours with seats, set in some decent order." He also suggested that "for gardens…the contents ought not well to be under thirty acres of ground, and can be divided into three parts: a green in the entrance; a heath or desert in the going forth; and the main garden in the midst…."[17]

The herb garden and kitchen garden were sited beyond the parterres, the herb garden being fashioned as a square or rectangle with beds of pot herbs, herbs for strewing, and an abundance of marigolds, gillyflowers, poppies, and peonies. In the kitchen garden could be found the newly introduced *scarlet runners*, French beans, globe artichokes, *runcivall peas*, cabbage, carrots (instituted by the Flemish immigrants), and, after the discovery of America, the Jerusalem artichoke, widely used by the Indians. Of vegetable growing, Samuel Hartlib wrote in 1659:

> *About fifty years ago this art of gardening began to creep into England, into Sandwich and Surrey, Fulham and other places. Some old men in Surrey, where it flourisheth very much at present, report that they knew the first gardeners that came into those parts to plant cabbages, colleflowers, and to sow turnips and carrets and parsnips, and raith-rape peas, all of which at that time were great rarities, we having few or none in England but what came from Holland and Flanders.*[18]

The labor-intensive gardens of the big estates were tended by a permanently employed gardener and an army of casual labor. Weeder women found work weeding the numerous paths and walks. Celia Fiennes, during a visit to Woburn, remarked upon "a Cherry garden, in the midst of which stands a figure of stone resembling an old Weeder woman used in the garden, and my Lord would have her Effigie which is done so like and her clothes so well that at first I tooke it to be a real living body...."[19]

During the years of the Commonwealth, the aristocracy introduced better farming methods as farms grew in size and arable land increased. Not many gardens were made, but soil and crops were greatly improved and more interest was shown in the cultivation of fruit and utilitarian plants.

The Huguenot refugees who came to England during the latter half of the sixteenth century from France and the Low Countries initiated the idea of floral societies, the first one of which is thought to have been established in Spitalfields. The most noteworthy ones prospered in Norwich, where a floral feast was held in 1637. By 1700, London and York were also promoting floral feasts, which were initially organized for the gentry but in which members of the working class were allowed to compete for prizes. Cottagers began to grow limited numbers of flower varieties, which they brought to a state of perfection. For example, Mistress Buggs of Battersea found fame with her particularly fine auricula.

Gardening Rules
for the Country Housewife

*O*ne important development of the seventeenth century was the appearance of relatively small urban gardens. While the gardens of the middle classes tended to be of medium size and quadrangular in type, the small gardens of the less affluent were formal in design, usually containing herbs and vegetables in rectangular beds surrounded by clipped box hedges and with a piece of topiary at each corner.

William Lawson's *The Country House-wife's Garden*, published in 1617, was a practical handbook that described the making of a small garden. The book was so popular that it went through numerous editions. Usually published with *A New Orchard and Garden*, it was the first book actually written for women gardeners. It drew upon Lawson's vast horticultural experience in "a plain and sure way of Planting, which I have found good by 48 Years (and more) experience in the North part of England."

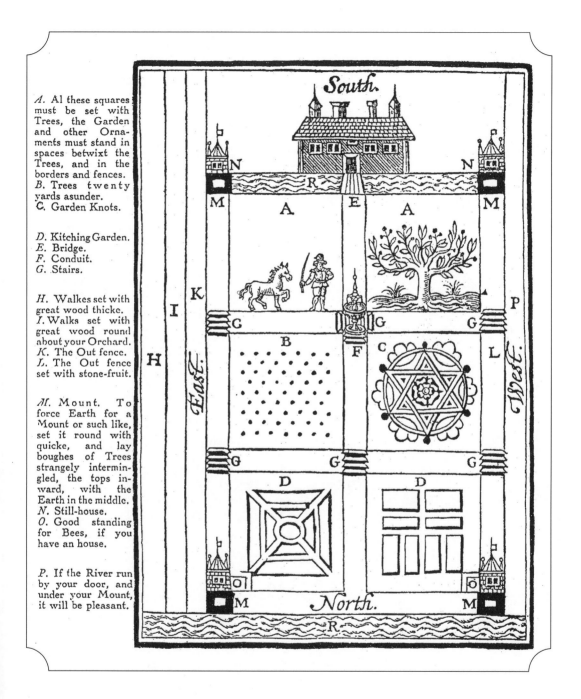

William Lawson's plan of an orchard (from William Lawson, A New Orchard and Garden, *1618).*

Knot garden designs for the country housewife (from William Lawson, The Country House-wife's Garden, *1617). Clockwise from top left: the ground plot for knots, Cinkfoil, Oval, Maze, Diamond, Cross-bow.*

The Country House-wife's Garden disclosed "secrets very nec-

essary for every HOUSEWIFE: As also divers new Knots for
GARDENS." The form that the garden took was left to the
housewife herself, but Lawson suggested a square with sufficient
room for walks and that the plot be bordered with such plants as
privet, raisins, fea-berries, roses, thorn, rosemary, bee-flowers,
hyssop, or sage. The housewife then had to decide upon the size
and design of the knot, with Lawson giving several plans to help
her in her choice, including a small shrub maze, so popular in the
seventeenth century, laid out in hyssop or rosemary.

Because herbs were of two kinds, it was necessary to have
two gardens: a flower garden and a kitchen or summer garden.
The soil needed to be fairly dry for the herbs to thrive, in addition to being plain and level and free from weeds. The best site
was, according to Lawson, on low ground to avoid the danger of
winds and, if possible, near a river. In the summer garden, rosemary, lavender, bee-flowers, hyssop, sage, thyme, cowslips,
peonies, daisies, clove-gilliflowers, pinks, southernwood, and
lilies were planted in raised beds at "Michael-tide" (the Feast of
St. Michael, 29 September) so that they would be well established before winter set in, although it was possible to sow them
in spring.

The kitchen garden was planted with pot herbs and had
"comely borders" of roses and lavender. Lawson did not consider
it necessary to raise these beds, as pot herbs required more water
and with the coming of summer the soil was necessarily drier.
The beds, however, had to be divided so that the housewife could
move easily between them to weed. Lawson also reminded her to
plant the tallest herbs such as fennel by the walls or in the borders and the lowest ones such as saffron, strawberries, and onions
in the middle.

He also laid down some general gardening rules for his country housewife to follow. All herbs in the flower garden, he told
her, had to be renewed every seven years, and she was advised to
have banks and seats of camomile, penny-royal, daisies, and violets as part of the garden because they "are seemly and comfortable." She was reminded that, when planting vegetables, artichokes, cabbages, turnips, parsnips, onions, and carrots required
whole plots, and she was encouraged to gather her own seeds
"dead, ripe and dry." She was also urged to harvest the leaves and

flowers of pot herbs and medicinal herbs in summer when the sap had risen, the roots being suitable for winter collection. "A good House-wife may, and will gather store of herbs for the pot, about Lammas (1 August) and dry them, and pound them, and in winter they will do good service." Lawson maintained that herbs did not require fertilizers and that seedlings should be afterwards thinned to not more than 1 foot (30 cm.) apart, with the larger-growing varieties at a greater distance. He finishes his treatise on a garden belonging to the mistress of the house by discussing the skill and pains of weeding, suggesting that this task be performed after a shower of rain and reminding the housewife "either to be present herself, or to teach her maids to know herbs from weeds."

Throughout the seventeenth century, the flower and kitchen gardens continued to be the country housewife's domain. The second half of the century witnessed a dramatic increase in the number of hardy and tender plants introduced into Great Britain, as a result of which gardens were improved, beautified, and enjoyed by the nobility and gentry. But the majority of the population worked long hours for low wages and had neither the time nor the money for such self-indulgence.

Subservience and Domesticity

By 1714, the yeoman class was disappearing, the wives of the peasantry were mere drudges, and the middle- and upper-class ladies led a life of relative ease, prompting the following stringent comment by Sir Matthew Hale, the celebrated Lord Chief Justice: "And now the world is altered; young gentlewomen learn to be bold, talk loud and more than comes to their share, think it disparagement for them to know what belongs to good housewifery or to practise it." Few ordinary seventeenth-century wives had the time to be idle, however, and of those even fewer had sufficient education to profitably fill any leisure time they had. Both custom and law favored male dominance and wifely subservience, duty, and respect.

Women, generally, were unaware of the wider life beyond domesticity, accepting their inferior position and having little ambition toward equality with men. The Stuart housewife reigned over her household, fulfilling the domestic role for which she had been trained from early childhood, if not with contentment then with a certain pride in the belief that she was "skilful in the worthy knowledges which do belong to her Vocation."[20] Her life was dull, devoid of culture and learning, and unhampered by the distractions of society. But the rumblings of intellectual discontent had been voiced and were set to grow louder during the years that followed as more and more women strove to secure the advancement of their sex.

THE GEORGIAN ERA

DURING THE YEARS 1714-1830, England, ruled by the Hanoverian dynasty, witnessed a period of transition, economic growth, and social divergence. It was an age of hedonistic extravagance for the rich and abject poverty for the poor, to whom more than twenty years of war with France brought the threat of famine and a deterioration in their beggarly existence. For those beyond the reach of pauperism, however, life was good. Working-class families were, for the first time, able to enjoy the ever-increasing world of leisure, and the middle and upper classes became even more affluent with the growth of commerce and industry, technological advancement, mass production, and new overseas trading agreements.

The four Georges were the linchpins of political life, each one supremely conscious of his consequential role in the fate of the nation. By 1830, Georgian England was both influential and wealthy. Its classical and Gothic architecture was impressive, and the country houses of the well-to-do, surrounded by opulent landscaped grounds, sprang up like so many mushrooms. Informed and cultured, the aristocracy and the gentry made up the polite society of the day in a pleasure-seeking age that was invigorated by the greater ease of travel, the diversity of literature, the lavish theatres, the pleasure gardens, and such diverting entertainments as were hitherto unknown.

Still Imprisoned in a Man's World

THE WOMEN OF ENGLAND The place of the eighteenth-century Englishman within this society was dependent not only upon birth, property, occupation, and rank, but also upon his personal connections with others and his ability to show deference and compliance on the one hand and condescension and patronage on the other. The position of the Englishwoman, however, depended, as always, upon that of her male protector, whether father, brother, or husband. Even though over fifty percent of the population was female, women continued to be molded into the roles of wives and mothers, spinsters and aunts, housekeepers and domestic servants. Intellectually, they were tightly constricted in a man's world, a world, incidentally, that was often coarse, aggressive, cruel, and lewd, where, as a direct antithesis to the elegant Georgian buildings, furnishings, fashions, and artistic culture, intemperance in all matters was freely indulged. Gluttony, promiscuity, and drunkenness dwelt cheek-by-jowl with style and luxury. Dirt was ever present, disease was rampant, behavior was gross, and manners alternated between formal correctness and abandoned lasciviousness.

Sexual purity was demanded of ladies before marriage, and divorce was rare, requiring a private act of Parliament. Gentlewomen, however, were often not as submissive as they seemed, many of them amusing themselves with innocent flirtations, others enjoying the forbidden fruit of clandestine affairs. Nevertheless, they belonged to their husbands, who had control over their fortune, taking no part in public affairs and being denied the vote. Custom dictated that a wife should obey her husband, defer to his whims and pleasures, and satiate his appetites. In the lower orders of society, men actually sold their wives as they would their sheep and cattle; wife beating was commonplace, and girls could be married when twelve years old.

Advantageous marriages were arranged by upper-class parents and were usually dictated by the gentleman's wealth, position in society, and family connections. Young girls often found themselves bound in wedlock to much older men, and any wife caught flaunting the chastity of marriage was quickly removed from her home and shunned thereafter by her husband. Lady Luxborough was one example. Banished to her husband's derelict estate at Barrels for her infidelities, she quickly set about putting the house in order and then, as a keen practical gardener, turned her talents toward redesigning the surrounding grounds with the help and advice of William Shenstone.

And yet, despite these obvious disadvantages, coupled with the burden of frequent childbearing, women generally considered it tragic to remain a spinster. "Old maids" were an embarrassment to their families, a laughing stock in the "polite world," and a butt for social satire. Women naturally wanted to marry well and entered into marriage contracts that took the form of business transactions.

As the century progressed, the English upper classes changed their attitude toward marriage; wives and mothers had a more positive role to fulfill, and young people were allowed to choose their own marriage partners. As the domestic situation changed with the advent of the paid housekeeper, ladies were free to spend more time shopping, paying and receiving calls, reading the latest novels and poetry from the circulating libraries, and squandering their pin money. It became fashionable for gentle-women to interest themselves in their children, to be motherly and domesticated, all of which brought a sense of purpose and fulfillment to their lives and a release from the tedium that surrounded them.

Women in the lower reaches of society had no such need for release; theirs was a working life, a life in which they toiled alongside their husbands, organizing the household and looking after the children and kitchen garden. It was traditional for these women, particularly in the early part of the century, to undertake heavy manual work both in industry and on the land. The coming of the factories brought new employment to younger women, although many continued to work in agriculture. Gradually, however, this changed with the surplus of male agricultural laborers, despite rural depopulation, and women were demoted to badly paid work such as weeding until they were eventually squeezed out of the labor market altogether. At that time there emerged a pattern of man as the breadwinner and woman staying at home.

In between the extremes of tremendous wealth and desperate poverty were the comfortably situated members of society: the country squires, the lesser gentry, those who had made their money from trade, and the professional classes. Living in stylish houses with grounds of up to twenty acres or in elegant town-houses in the newly built crescents, these *middling people* pursued the same pastimes and shared the same tastes as the upper-class gentry.

The parents of novelist Jane Austen enjoyed an easy competence at Steventon Rectory, and both were keen gardeners. While Mrs. Austen tended a productive vegetable garden and planted fruit bushes and strawberries with her husband, the Reverend Austen himself kept cows and pigs and grew wheat with the help of his bailiff, John Bond. Jane and her sister Cassandra were also dedicated gardeners, and references to gardens can be found in many of Jane Austen's works. Catherine Morland in *Northanger Abbey*, for instance, when discussing the merits of gardening with the General, remarked that "Mr Allen had only one small hot-house, which Mrs. Allen had the use of for her plants in winter, and there was a fire in it now and then."[1]

Georgian society also had its share of *bluestockings*, female intelligentsia who wished to develop their intellectual skills and artistic interests. By the middle of the century, London witnessed the arrival of the *salons*, an idea first introduced into the European capitals by aristocratic ladies primarily to further female intellectual pursuits but also to attract influential male guests who could bring power and prestige to their *soirees*.

The English *salonieres*, however, were largely wealthy middle-class females who encouraged, both spiritually and financially, talented but impoverished members of their sex to enter those areas of learning dominated by men. All women at this time, whatever their position in society, were actively discouraged from learning and from displaying any intellectual prowess. Accordingly, social intercourse between men and women that encouraged reasoning and a profound pleasure in the world around them became the lifeblood of the salons and of the gently nurtured Enlightment culture, the place where male and female could meet as cultural and intellectual equals. And, in spite of the fact that many of these so-called "enlightened" men, obsequiously deferred to and courted by the salonieres, continued to pursue the limited, traditional concepts of womanhood, those of subordination, inferiority, purity, and obedience, the salons succeeded in entering into and influencing those traditional bastions of male domination: politics and learning.

The first woman of the period to publish female literature was Sophia, "A Person of Quality," who in 1739 wrote "Woman not Inferior to Man." The unidentified writer condemned the fact that women's role was "only to breed and nurse children" and decried the universally accepted right of male privilege.

Mary Wollstonecraft, who, in 1790 published her *Vindication of the Rights of Men*, an incursion into the world of politics and an exposition of the injustice of a privileged landowning gentry, quickly turned her thoughts toward the vexed question of women's inequality. In 1792, she wrote her *Vindication of the Rights of Woman*, in which she challenged the notion of male superiority and addressed the injustices suffered by women and the pressing need for female education, the aim of which should be "to form citizens." Wollstonecraft passionately denounced marriage and woman's subjection to man, who attempted to confine her to the realms of domesticity and keep her in a state of ignorance. She likened a woman to a soldier, arguing that each had a form of power but without its attendant responsibilities and that each was often admired for entirely the wrong reasons.

She visualized a society in which man could carry out his duties as a citizen with a wife who could share those duties. Women, she maintained, were oppressed, and educating them, not necessarily to become intellectuals and not wholly for their own good but rather for the good of society, would make them into rational thinkers and free citizens. "Women, I allow, may have different duties to fulfil; but they are *human* duties, and the principles that should regulate the discharge of them I sturdily maintain, must be the same."[2]

Dubbed by Horace Walpole as a "hyena in petticoats," Mary Wollstonecraft affectively wanted women to become independent, to choose their own careers, to put an end to sexual double standards, and, as she herself had attempted to do, to discard the masculine ideals of the female role. But she was a product of the age in which she lived, an age that was not as liberal, liberated, or high-minded as Wollstonecraft herself, and she was unable to solve the contradictions because, in her eyes, many women continued to allow themselves to remain born victims and marriage continued to be "legalized prostitution."

Ladies in polite society enjoyed a leisured, though monotonous existence, their days consisting of sketching, embroidery, walking in the gardens, visiting their children in the nursery, drinking tea, and, of course, endless gossip. They might also ride, paint, press flowers, and take dancing lessons, many of them agreeing with the masculine conception of the female role. The minds of some of these ladies were as elegant as the clothes they wore, a phenomenon brought about by conversation and reading so that they could converse easily with their husbands and gentlemen of their acquaintance and adopt the role of sought-after companions rather than that of mere housekeepers. Gradually, these women began to gain confidence, to express opinions, albeit gleaned largely from their reading material, and to gradually spread their wings.

Some women, however, repeated the opinions voiced by their menfolk, while others spent their days languishing on sofas, weary and unwell, worn down by frequent pregnancies and repressed both in body and spirit. And yet, few women protested their fate; it was far easier to accept their lot than to find ways of changing it. They were inured to being dependent on men, as wives, daughters, and unmarried sisters, few of whom remained single by choice.

Marriages at the beginning of the eighteenth century were usually arranged, and, in law, wives had no rights concerning either their property or their children. Once married, the well-to-do lady was expected to obey her husband in all things, furnish him with heirs, supervise the household, make polite conversation, be well versed in feminine accomplishments, and be ladylike at all times. A married woman needed her husband's permission to make a will, and after her death he had the right to declare it null and void. Judged as the weaker sex, as inferior beings, throughout their lives all women were expected to conform to men's image of them and to live up to masculine expectations of obedience and virtue.

AMERICA'S CULT OF DOMESTICITY The daughters of the affluent American colonists, like their English sisters, were reared for marriage and taught domestic accomplishments from an early age. They, too, were married young and, unlike their brothers, were not apprenticed to any craft or expected to concern themselves with matters of business.

Behavior among eighteenth-century American gentlewomen was sadly lacking in decorum. Many of the women took snuff and smoked pipes in public. They were also accustomed to the coarse, sometimes obscene language used by their menfolk in their presence; indeed, many of them used profanities themselves. They seldom read books, instead spending their days taking care of their families and sewing.

The lower orders often placed their daughters as domestic servants or apprenticed them to a trade such as needlecraft, spinning, or weaving. Others became professional cooks, bakers, and pastry makers, while those of the poorest families were merely household servants. Girls served their apprenticeship until the age of sixteen or eighteen, or until they were married.

Large numbers of women became embroiled in political issues during the American War of Independence (1775-1783). They launched fund-raising events, undertook voluntary work for the troops, and protested against wartime atrocities, although always in private. Nevertheless, the leaders of the new republic refused to listen to their political outpourings, seeing their role as mothers and educators of sons who one day would be citizens of that new republic. To facilitate women's educational role, a number of female academies were founded at the end of the eighteenth and during the early years of the nineteenth century.

By the late eighteenth century, women were beginning to gain increasing legal rights. Their position in America was strengthened by the Declaration of Independence (1776) and the rights of the individual. Divorce, for instance, became easier to obtain, although in the colonial era divorces were comparatively rare and men obtained them far more easily than women. Wives began to have a personal identity, even though male attitudes toward women changed very little. In March 1776, when Abigail Adams wrote to her husband John, then a member of the Continental Congress but later to become the second president of the United States, she urged him to give consideration to women's status in society and to show more generosity toward them in the new code of laws. She warned him not to give husbands unlimited power, as this would result in women becoming rebellious. He ignored her plea, and the rebellion did eventually take place, although not until the 1830s when Negro slavery was denounced in public and work for the emancipation of both black slaves and women, who were shackled themselves, began in earnest.

On 23 April 1789, George Washington was inaugurated as the first president of the recently named United States of America. He himself was a farmer, as were the majority of the troops returning to their home on the eastern seaboard.

Meanwhile, farm life continued after the revolution in much the same way as it had done before. In New England, the settlers worked hard to grow crops on their small farms with the help of their wives and families, and they hired labor when necessary. Their output was usually sufficient to feed themselves and to have enough surplus produce to barter at the crossroads store for any items they were unable to produce. The women of New England worked in the fields only at harvest time. Generally their days were spent in an endless round of household toil, in addition to carding and spinning wool and mixing the wool with the linen from home-grown flax to produce linsey-woolsey. They made cloth by combining linen and cotton or cotton and wool, after which they bleached the cloth and dyed it with dyes made from wildflowers, hickory, and the sassafras tree.

The New England housewife also tended the vegetables in her kitchen garden, fed the chickens, and gathered the eggs. She cooked and baked, washed and cleaned, and made preserves, pickles, cheese, and candles. She also churned butter. Her daughters helped her by, among other tasks, weeding the garden and braiding and sewing straw hats for the menfolk. She also took part in quilting bees and apple-peeling parties, both of which were rare social events in her drab existence.

When the soil became overworked, impoverished, and exhausted, the family would look for a new home, packing their few possessions in an ox-cart and moving on. Many New Englanders went to Genesee, the war veterans went to claim the free land promised to them by the government, and the southerners went to the Cumberland Valley. The population of the country more than doubled to 9.6 million in the years between 1790 and 1820, and throughout the late eighteenth and nineteenth centuries, the frontier was pushed rapidly west as Americans moved in ever-increasing numbers.

The lifestyle of southern women differed from that of women in the north. The mistresses of southern plantations supervised large households as well as, in some cases, plantation business, particularly in the absence of their husbands. They oversaw vast numbers of household workers, directing them in tasks such as preparing food, caring for the children, and making cloth. They were also responsible for the training of female slaves as housekeepers, cooks, seamstresses, and gardeners.

It was during the early years of the nineteenth century that the wife started to be considered as a full-time mother and home-maker and the husband as the breadwinner. Motherhood and domesticity were revered, associated as motherhood was with purity and piety. Offspring were increasingly given the choice of a marriage partner, and marriage was seen as an emotional bond and not as a merging of property as had previously been the case. Husband and wife displayed their affection for each other and became more involved with their children, moving away from the belief that children were naturally sinful.

The cult of domesticity advocating separate spheres for men and women was given a tremendous boost by the influence of the middle class and of evangelical religion, which helped to rein-force social patterns. During this period an abundance of maga-zines, novels, poems, and sermons were produced concerning the state of women, their social position, maternal responsibilities, and appropriate behavior. Women's virtues were praised, their childrearing capabilities were elevated, and the home was desig-nated as their proper place in society. They were considered to be ineffective in the work place: domestic work, philanthropy, and teaching were ordained as their special havens.

Women were to be submissive, selflessly devoted to others, and pious. It was a suffocating atmosphere that stirred up rebel-lions and conflicting emotions in women.

The Agricultural Revolution in England

Agriculture continued to be the main form of employment for the working classes of eighteenth-century England, and what had been a controversial movement in the fifteenth and sixteenth centuries to enclose land was successfully employed by the Georgians. They converted arable open fields into arable enclosed fields and common grazing pasture into pastoral farms, aided after 1700 by an act of Parliament. Enclosure was not merely a question of molding the open field system into adjoin-ing fields and enclosing them with hedges and fences; rather it was a symptom of the new commercial farming economy. For many of the rural communities, enclosures meant pauperism as agrarian change gathered momentum and new husbandry tech-niques were introduced. Despite rural unrest, the agricultural

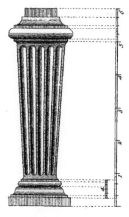

Tho.ˢ Langley Sculp.

*Pedestal for bustos
(taken from Batty
Langley,* The
City and Country
Builder's and
Workman's Treasury
of Designs, *London,
1750).*

revolution marched relentlessly on, and by the end of the century, England possessed a progressive agriculture that was in line with a rising population and a growing market for food.

Productivity increased dramatically, and while landlords and their tenants realized a new affluence, small farmers found themselves severely disadvantaged and the farm laborer's living declined with the removal of his traditional rights and a depreciation in his rate of pay. His wife suddenly found herself no longer able to augment his paltry wages from her cottage industry as the new industrial system began to bite. Food prices started to rise alarmingly, and reactionary food riots began to occur as the rural working class found itself regulated by the commercial market and not, as before, by tradition.

Farmers were urged to grow more cereal crops, which negated the need for year-round labor and led to the employment of farm workers on a casual basis, except at the peak seasons of harvest and sowing. Supply invariably exceeded demand. Among the growing casual labor force were large numbers of women in the north and west of the country who were willing to perform the heaviest of tasks in the harvest fields. Some of them undertook reaping for 10d. a day, as well as mowing, ploughing, threshing, muckspreading, and thatching, while women living in the southern and eastern counties performed the lighter tasks of raking and gathering.

Working-class women, young and old, spent their time sitting in their cottage doorways peeling osiers, a species of willow used in the making of baskets, while children gathered cowslips to make wine. Those living in Derbyshire and Kent could find employment in the fields during the camomile harvest. These cottage women would also plant flower seeds and do the weeding, tend the poultry, and collect peppermint for the still.

"Before I got into FOLKSTONE," observed William Cobbett, an ardent conservative, in 1823, "I saw no less than eighty-four men, women, and boys and girls gleaning, or leasing, in a field of about ten acres." Three years later, in September 1826, he was to comment with pleasure on the hiring out of land by farmers: "I saw a woman digging some potatoes, in a strip of ground, making part of a field, nearly an oblong square, and which field appeared to be laid out *in strips*. She told me that the field was part of *a farm*,…that it was, by the farmer, *let out in* strips to labouring people; that each strip contained *a rood* (or quarter of a statute acre); that each married labourer rented one strip; and that the annual rate was *a pound* for the strip."[3] Cobbett was extremely satisfied with the rent charged and delighted to see laboring families treated so fairly.

Traditionally, females have always been involved in seasonal farm work, and the introduction of more intensive and improved farming practices during the late eighteenth century created the need for laborers to carry out the tedious work of hoeing and weeding. Women were thought capable of performing these tasks and were employed by farmers as cheap labor. Unmarried women from Wales found horticultural employment in the Middlesex market gardens, where from April onwards they tended the crops and carried fruit and strawberries in baskets to London.

Cranberries, bilberries, and mushrooms were gathered by women and taken into the towns to sell, and during the strawberry season, groups of around one hundred women would leave the market gardens of Fulham for Covent Garden, carrying baskets filled with the fruit on their heads. These women were usually unmarried migrant workers from Ireland, Cardiganshire, and Shropshire. At the end of the season, they would return to their homes with their wages untouched. Watercress and herbs such as feverfew, red valerian, and hedge mustard were also supplied to Covent Garden market by herb women, who gathered them, along with dandelions and scurvy-grass, from the surrounding countryside.

London was surrounded by nursery gardens and orchards where women were employed to supply the citizens of London with fruit and vegetables. Asparagus, cucumbers, cauliflower, and lettuce, as well as strawberries, raspberries, currants, and gooseberries, were cultivated and harvested for the tables of the city along with melons and pineapples from the hothouses.

The Georgian era saw rapid agrarian changes, with agriculture emerging as a commercialized, economic activity that molded the rural landscape. Many of these changes were dictated and shaped by wealthy landowners, who used the profits from their fields and farms to finance the rebuilding of their country houses and the reshaping of their grounds and parks. As the tastes of polite society in literature and the arts changed, so did the style and designs of their gardens.

The first years of the century witnessed the emergence of the garden as a "picture" or series of "pictures," leading one from the other, of gentle curves replacing the straight lines favored by Le Nôtre, gardener to the French King Louis XIV. The artifice and formality of cut-work parterres, allees, topiaries, and elaborate flower beds were swept away to be replaced by meandering paths, lawns, terraces, and serpentine lakes. Trees were allowed to grow naturally, and the countryside around became part of the garden with the use of the *ha-ha*, a hidden ditch designed to keep cattle away and allow uninterrupted views. William Kent (1684-1748) advocated garden design as being essentially visual, composing "pictures" of idealized landscapes garnered from ideas that had fueled the latest architectural styles and the topographical paintings of seventeenth-century artists.

These new gardens were designed to mirror nature and liberty and became increasingly more relaxed and informal. Decorative herb beds were no longer considered to be suitable garden features and were quickly removed. Herbs, however, remained a vital part of everyday life and continued to be grown in simple beds, hidden from view within the walls of the kitchen garden, where they would be tended by the ladies of the house.

The aristocracy spent exhorbitant sums of money excavating lakes, moving hills, damming streams, digging out subterranean grottoes, building temples, and planting vast numbers of trees. Whole villages were disposed of if they interrupted the view, while distant features, such as a ruin or a church spire, were incorporated into the whole. By 1730, the landscape movement was firmly established.

During the second half of the eighteenth century, Lancelot "Capability" Brown became England's foremost landscape architect. His main addition to the landscape was the construction of lakes of every description that could be glimpsed not only from the house but also from several other vantage points. Having obliterated the outmoded formal gardens around the house, he proceeded to replace them with huge expanses of grass, and in place of the formal avenues of trees, he planted isolated groups that allowed vistas further into the landscape.

The lakes were bordered by serpentine walks, and artificial waterfalls, grottoes, hermits' huts, statues, obelisks, and Grecian urns were used to enrich the natural landscape. The urns were usually made from Coade stone, a mixture of ground glass, clays, and ground stone which, having been fired in a kiln, became frost resistant. Patented and manufactured by Mrs. Eleanour Coade, the material was widely used from 1770 onwards and apparently could not be distinguished from natural stone itself. Planting also became the rage, as tens of thousands of oaks, beech, elms, and firs were grown by nurserymen and plants flowed in from abroad. Camellias from Japan, hydrangeas from China, magnolias and rhododendrons, pelargoniums, and chrysanthemums were bought by wealthy plant collectors.

Grass was also considered to be a natural ornament, and in some aristocratic gardens, vast areas of lawn were weeded daily by weederwomen. The areas were scythed by teams of men, with women and children following behind to rake up the grass cuttings with wide, wooden-pronged rakes. The cuttings were then deposited in baskets and taken away in barrows. The women also pulled out the deeper lying moss and dead grass with metal rakes.

In 1809, the horse-drawn reaper was invented by the American Robert McCormick. Originally designed for the harvesting of cereals, it was used for cutting the grass around the house, although the scythe remained in fashion until 1830 when the English engineer Edwin Beard Budding, with his partner John Ferrabee, patented the first cylinder lawn mower.

Comfortably situated ladies often took an active interest in the garden, although they were reprimanded by John Laurence in his *New System—A Complete Body of Husbandry and Gardening* (1726):

> I flatter myself the Ladies would soon think that their
> vacant Hours in the Culture of the Flower-Garden would
> be more innocently spent and with greater Satisfaction than
> the common Talk over a Tea-Table where Envy and
> Detraction so commonly preside. Whereas when
> Opportunity and Weather invite them amongst their
> Flowers, there they may dress, and admire and cultivate
> Beauties like themselves without envying or being envied.[4]

It became fashionable during the Georgian period to take alpine holidays. The ladies, entranced by the abundant mountain flowers, many of them small and unusual, peeping out of

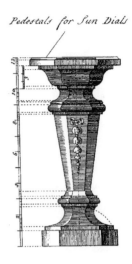

Pedestals for Sun Dials

Pedestal for sundial (taken from Batty Langley, The City and Country Builder's and Workman's Treasury of Designs, *London, 1750).*

crevices and growing on screes, would remove them to take back to England for their rock gardens. Mrs. Loudon, in her *Practical Instructions in Gardening for Ladies* (1840), mentions Lady Broughton, who in the 1820s constructed a large rock garden, the design of which was based on the mountains of Savoy. Taking several years to complete, the garden had alpine plants growing among rocks so big that visitors, when walking through them, felt as though they were actually walking in the Alps.

Grottoes were also a popular feature of the eighteenth-century romantic period, and well-to-do ladies spent many hours decorating them with vast amounts and varieties of seashells. Shells were avidly sought at auctions, brought in by the shipload, and even gathered from the seashores. Scallops, conches, Spanish purples, and ear (abalone) shells were lovingly placed by enthusiastic ladies on walls and ceilings, often in contrived patterns, where they mingled with felspar, quartz, coral, and fossils.

In 1756, Dr. Delany, with the help of his wife Mary, fashioned a large grotto from local minerals at Ballybeggan Castle in Ireland. Mrs. Delany, famous for her paper flower collages of botanical accuracy and tremendous charm, also designed and made a number of grottoes that could be approached by paths, although the usual mode of entry was by boat. Constructed for use on hot summer days, these damp, cool places had specially created platform areas where visitors could linger over light refreshments.

Many great ladies of aristocratic birth had a consuming passion for gardening. The Duchess of Beaufort cultivated exotics and species of foreign plants brought to England by the plant hunters of the day, and the Duchess of Portland spent fifty years developing the house, park, and gardens of Bulstrode in Buckinghamshire. A self-taught amateur naturalist (natural history was a popular pastime for eighteenth-century ladies), the Duchess was totally dedicated to the study of horticulture and used her considerable expertise to improve the estate. While choosing to retain the formal style of the garden within the vicinity of the house, she did, however, remove the kitchen garden to a less prominent position. She also planted trees, opened vistas, set up a managerie, erected garden buildings, and turfed new areas of lawn. Constantly acquiring new plants, she had many botanical and horticultural connections and was an extremely influential lady gardener.

American Gardeners: A Step Behind

On the other side of the Atlantic, eighteenth-century American gardens mirrored the formalism so recently rejected by Great Britain. Many wealthy Americans ordered their plants from London, Amsterdam, and Paris, even though numbers of them perished in transit. American gardeners tended to cling to the old garden flowers that were fast becoming unfashionable in England. Smaller manor houses and farms continued to adopt a formal garden design that was in direct contrast to the architectural styles based on the latest European designs. There was a mix of vegetables and flowers, an idea once popular in England and Scotland, although by the middle of the eighteenth century, herbs and vegetables were beginning to be grown separately from the flowers. In the farmhouses of New England, the flower garden was traditionally sited under the parlor windows in the front of the house, with paths dividing balanced beds.

South Carolina gardens were some of the earliest to be cultivated, and those in Charleston and the surrounding plantations brought particular joy to their owners. The first person to lay out a large-scale garden was Mrs. Lamboll, who, by 1750, was growing both flowers and "useful" vegetables. Mrs. Martha Logan and Mrs. Hopton were quick to follow her lead, and at the age of seventy, Mrs. Logan wrote a treatise on gardening, *The Gardener's Kalendar*. Published in 1770, after her death, it remained a sought-after gardening manual until 1808.

Flint's *Geography and History of the United States* refers to those first gardens of Charleston: "The houses of the suburbs are for the most part surrounded by gardens, in which orange trees with most splendid ripe fruit, monthly roses in full bloom and a variety of other flourishing plants display themselves. Upon the walls and columns are climbing vines and a great number of passion flowers."[5]

In 1750, Elinor Laurens, with the help of an English gardener, tended the Charleston garden created by her husband, in which she grew olives, capers, limes, ginger, alpine strawberries, raspberries, apples, pears, and plums. The grounds of the old plantations on the Cooper River had gardens specially designed for the ladies of the estate, one of them containing a vast water garden and a ruin of a Temple of Love.

After her marriage to Peyton Skipwith at the age of forty, Lady Skipwith moved with her husband into a new Virginia plantation house called "Prestwould," where she set about making a garden planted with native shrubs and flowers. A keen and meticulous plantswoman, she kept notes of her plantings, which included detailed lists of plants, methods of propagation, and the times when her plants were in bloom. In her garden, Lady Skipwith grew perennials and those plants indigenous to America, all of which would later appear in nineteenth-century cottage gardens. Her listings were many and varied and included honeysuckle, hollyhocks, hibiscus, wallflower, sweet William, snowdrop, candytuft, mignonette, mallow, celandine, columbine, grape hyacinth, Rose of Sharon, and marble and cabbage roses.

Ordinary American gardens of this period were purely utilitarian and usually were tended by women. The potato was not grown with any great success, tomatoes were raised for decoration because they were thought to be poisonous, and average garden flowers such as pinks, tulips, sunflowers, hollyhocks, and roses were the only form of embellishment. The estates of the wealthy landowners, on the other hand, were well laid out, often by foreign gardeners, and their owners took a keen interest in their design and management. It was not until the late eighteenth century that box, so vital to the American formal garden, was introduced, and that the first hothouse was built in New England for the cultivation of exotics such as pineapples.

American as well as English women botanists were extremely rare during the eighteenth century; Rachel Barret lived and worked in Wilmington, Delaware, and Queen Charlotte, although not generally regarded as a botanist, studied the subject with her husband George III at Windsor Castle. Generally speaking, though, the role of the American gentlewoman in the garden was similar to that of her English counterpart. She was largely confined to arranging flowers sent into the house by the gardeners, painting plant specimens, and collecting dried flowers for decoration, scrapbooks, and collage work. Meanwhile, the lower orders toiled on the land alongside their menfolk, few of them receiving any recognition for their labor.

In South Carolina, however, in the 1740s, Eliza Lucas, the daughter of a British naval officer, successfully cultivated crops of indigo on her father's plantation, from which blue dye was extracted and used in the dying of military uniforms. And in 1821, Miss Woodhouse, a farmer's daughter from Connecticut, sent a straw bonnet she had made from the smooth-stalked meadow grass *Poa Pratensis* to the Society of Arts in London. As a result of the Society's interest, several sowings of the seed were made in England by way of experimentation.

As in Great Britain, American horticultural societies were gradually springing up. By 1792 the Society for Promoting Horticulture was established in Massachusetts, which led to the creation of many beautiful gardens in Boston, and by 1828, the Domestic Horticultural Society had been started in Geneva, New York. The first of the weekly or monthly market fairs, for the sale of farm produce, took place in Berkshire County, Massachusetts in 1811, and flower shows, organized along the lines of the London Horticultural Society, established in 1804, were introduced, the first public display being held in Philadelphia in June 1829.

The Return of the Formal Garden

In Great Britain, floriculture displays were popular among the working classes, who formed florists' clubs where information on growing specialist plants could be exchanged. Floristry, the art of bringing individual flowers to as near perfect a state as possible, was a favorite pastime until the end of the nineteenth century. The main florists' flowers were tulips (although expensive), carnations, pinks, polyanthus, and auriculas, and the competition to perfect the blooms was fierce and mainly confined to those who worked at home. Both men and women raised varieties of flowers with an obsessive enthusiasm, the weavers of Paisley concentrating on perfecting pinks, the workers of Derbyshire preferring tulips. Floral feasts and shows were held in most towns, often three or four times a year; they usually took place in inns and beer-houses, with the winner carrying off a prize of a copper kettle or, later on, silver plate.

There were, surprisingly, beds of florists' flowers at Windsor, much to the annoyance of gardening authority and writer John Loudon. Also, George IV's gardener, John Gould, regularly exhibited at local florists' shows. But it was the Duchess of Clarence, later Queen Adelaide, who showed the greatest interest in floristry, regularly visiting local florists' gardens where she demonstrated her expertise in choosing the finest blooms.

The sectors of Georgian society who were forced to reside in or near a city because of their income or business often lived in the newly built villas with their smaller gardens. In the front were grass and flowerbeds, in the back, a lawn with a gravel walk and a small vegetable patch. Tradesmen's villas, with gardens of up to an acre, had magnificent flower beds at the front, while the late-Georgian villas, owned by the wealthy, had grounds of between ten and one hundred acres. There was not a set garden design, as such. Lady Grenville's house, for example, had elaborate parterres and beds of fuchsias, salvias, geraniums, and heliotropes scattered haphazardly throughout the grounds, an arrangement no doubt prompted by the lady's ardent horticultural enthusiasm.

Thomas Fairchild, in *The City Gardener* (1722), noted that in the courtyards of Georgian London, lilacs, jasmine, wallflowers, pinks, and daisies could be seen growing and that mulberries, figs, and cherries were also cultivated. The alleys around the Barbican were adorned with pear trees, apple trees thrived in large pots on balconies, and flowering currants brightened the yards of inns and tops of houses.

By 1818, however, gardening had begun to change in style and direction. The formal flower bed, set in an Italianate setting with clipped hedges, was re-designated as a central garden feature, and the garden itself was separated from the park, the large, enclosed area surrounding the country house. Straight gravel walks returned to favor, and statues and fountains were much in evidence. The naturalistic approach was on the decline, and an interest in the formal garden was once again awakening.

A LATE-GEORGIAN GARDEN

*I*n *The English Gardener* (1829), William Cobbett drew up a plan for the formal layout of a late-Georgian garden, 247 1/2 ft. (75.438 m.) by 165 ft. (50.292 m.), or 15 x 10 rods, with its borders, paths, and walks. By way of explanation and instruction, he advocated just one entrance into the garden at *a,* which he described as "a door-way in a hedge," and which led into a short path that was designed to reach a second doorway situated opposite in the wall at *b.*

The first part of the walled garden, *d,* measuring 58 1/2 ft. from east to west and 63 ft. from north to south, he called the hot-bed ground. Two doorways opened out of this area at *q* and *p* and were used to reach other parts of the garden. While walls bounded the north and west sides of the hot-bed ground, the east and south sides were enclosed by a hedge of yew, which was not to exceed 6 ft. in height to ensure that parts of the beds were not shaded by it. Cobbett maintained that it was necessary to have doors, as well as doorways, at *p* and *q* to prevent the wind from sweeping through. And, if the hot-bed area was too big for the gardener's use, he suggested that a compost heap be made on part of it, designating plots (or plats) *f, g, h, i, k* for the cultivation of garden plants in general, according to the season of the year. The borders *e* were 10 ft. wide and had to decline fractionally away from the wall.

Cobbett suggested that, if possible, all paths and walks be made of gravel to ensure that they remained dry in winter. Grass was considered to be totally unsuitable because not only was it frequently walked upon but heavily laden barrows were continually pushed along it, resulting in "a mass of dirt and ugliness."

The first task was to mark out the length and breadth of the garden with twine and stakes, after which the walks and paths were dug to the depth of the top soil, any excess earth being thrown to either side. The trenches were then leveled out, lined with stones, and about 6 in. (15 cm.) of clean gravel placed on top of them. Once this was done, the borders and plots were about 4 in. higher than the tops of the walks, and an edging of box was recommended to prevent the soil from falling onto the pathways.

Box, a compact, durable plant known to thrive in all kinds of soil, in sunshine and shade, and in wet and dry conditions, was planted perpendicularly in a very straight line close to the gravel as soon as the walks were laid out. Once in place, it was trimmed to a height of about 4 in., and the earth in the borders and plots was eased back and kept back for the first year to prevent the box plants from being washed back over the pathways. Once the box edging matured, it reached a height of about 7 in. on the gravel side and was about 3 in. higher than the soil in the borders. It was clipped on both sides and on the top in winter or very early spring and again in midsummer, a line or cord being used for the purpose of keeping it level.

Cobbett suggested construction of a shed, 40 ft. long and 7 ft. wide, in which to store tools and flowerpots and house the gardener in wet weather. It was to be sited at *r* in the outer garden, on the east side of the entrance at *a,* with the back placed toward the hedge. He also thought it necessary to have a water pump and cistern at the southeast corner of the hot-bed ground, from where water could be carried easily to all parts of the garden. The brickwork of the cistern was to be 9 in. thick and well cemented, and "the form should be circular, otherwise the sides might fall in."

Elegant, Stimulating, and Stifling

By the end of the Georgian era, the wheel had turned full circle. To a great extent, the naturalizing of estates and gardens had proved itself to be an activity for the educated, extended to just a small percentage of the population and requiring practical skills, philosophical inquiry, and vast amounts of money.

The age itself was, without doubt, both elegant and stimulating, and the economic, social, and cultural changes it witnessed were more deep-rooted than in any previous time. Although the latitude of the social order was imposing, it was still a man's world in which women were subordinate, different in nature and temperament, and therefore designed to play a passive, virtuous role.

Entry into the professions, public office, the universities, and the Church remained the prerogative of men, and there was no

William Cobbett's plan for the enclosure and formal layout of a late Georgian garden (from William Cobbett, The English Gardener, *1829).*

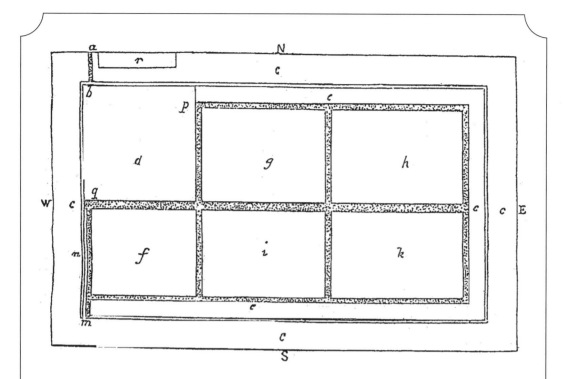

EXPLANATIONS OF THE PLAN.

1. The whole length, from outside to outside, from East to West, is 247½ feet, or 15 rod.

2. The whole width, from North to South, is 165 feet, or 10 rod.

3. The outside line represents the place for the hedge.

4. The double line represents the place for the wall.

5. The walks are described by dotting, and all, except the middle walk, are four feet wide.

6. The walk which goes all along the garden from East to West is six feet wide.

7. *a* A door-way through the hedge, 3 feet wide.

8. *b* a door-way in the wall, 3 feet wide, and 4 feet from the corner of the wall.

9. *c, c, c, c,* is the outer garden, a clear rod wide, between the wall and the hedge.

10. *d* is the Hot-bed ground, 58½ feet from East to West, and 63 feet from North to South.

11. *e e e* is a border, 10 feet wide, under the inside of the wall.

12. *f* is a plat of ground, 50½ feet from East to West, and 49 feet from North to South.

13. *g, h, i, k,* are plats of ground, each of which has 67 feet from East to West, and 49 feet from North to South.

14. *m* is a door-way in the wall, 3 feet wide, and 4 feet from the corner of the wall.

15 *n* is a border, 4 feet under the inside of the West wall.

16. *p* is a door-way in the Western hedge of the Hot-bed ground.

17. *q* is a door-way in the Southern hedge of the Hot-bed ground.

18. *r* The tool-house.

19. The letter N points out the *North side* of the garden ; the letter E the *East side*, and the other letters the South and the West sides.

organized feminist movement to challenge it and to campaign for women's rights. The rumblings of female discontent had manifested themselves in just a handful of brave rebels such as Mary Wollstonecraft and were by no means taken seriously. The only way a woman could rise in the world was by marriage. It was a bleak existence, filled with fashionable fribbles, petty accomplishments, and suffocating boredom, an existence from which both gender and society prohibited escape.

CHAPTER FIVE

THE VICTORIAN AGE

Prosperity, Progress, and Peace

THE REIGN OF QUEEN VICTORIA witnessed economic and social changes
hitherto undreamed of. It was a period of prosperity, of accelerating industrial and commercial advancement, a time of progress and peace, an energetic age of reform and material achievement. Gradually, the discontent of the
1830s became a thing of the past as a new code of behavior, breathing morality and
respectability into the life of the nation, replaced the coarseness and lasciviousness
of the Georgian era. Rigid ideas of social order and individual behavior became an
accepted way of life to the newly created industrial society.

This was a time of opportunity, an age of vigor and youth; the 1871 census
placed the mean average age at 26.4 years. It was also a period of resourcefulness and
innovation, with the coming of the railways; the construction of bridges, hospitals,
and civic buildings; and the advent of new technology. It was an authoritarian age
that saw the rapid rise of an urban population, which took the place of the country's
historically agricultural society.

Such vast and far-reaching change heralded a rise in the standard of living, particularly for those manufacturers who fed the increasing demands of industry—the
self-made men who formed the backbone of Victorian England, members of the
highly moral, respectable middle class whose star was in the ascendancy. Proud of
their success and new-found wealth, they ensured for themselves and their families
a solid, comfortable lifestyle that manifested itself in the building of large villas and
mansions and the employment of servants.

The middle classes were the most rapidly rising social group, the families of
which, as in all spheres of Victorian society, were dominated by the *paterfamilias*,

who aped the aristocracy and patronized those whom he considered his social inferiors. His word was law and he demanded, and got, unquestioning obedience from his wife, children, and servants, all of whom were totally dependent upon him.

The Ladies Begin To Rebel

Confined to the home, Victorian women were expected to be passive, submissive, gentle, and, above all, pure. Totally separated from the oftimes brutal and material masculine world, their existence revolved around domesticity as they managed the house, supervised the children and servants, and provided comfort and companionship for their husbands. Generally speaking, they accepted their lot in an era governed by strict moral conventions, when intellectual pursuits were frowned upon and employment outside the home was virtually unheard of. Family life was formal and repressive. Many Victorian wives spent their days confined to a sofa, either recovering from a pregnancy or preparing for the next.

At the close of the eighteenth century, women were deemed incapable of making judgements and having views of their own. "Marriage was the great aim and end of life of the English girl," vouchsafed Lady Violet Greville in the Victorian journal *Womanhood*:

> *For this desirable consummation she was trained, modelled, and designed. The long weary hours of needlework, the dull domestic duties, the short constitutional undertaken in thin shoes and white stockings, the narrowness of outlook, the stifling and subjection of all natural and youthful activity to the demands of the lady-like, served as a mere probation for the greater freedom of wedlock.[1]*

By the end of the nineteenth century, however, a catalogue of campaigns had been fought and won and women began to break free from the shackles of male dominance. At the beginning of Victoria's reign, women were totally devoid of any rights of their own; upon marriage their property became that of their husband, and divorce was denied them, as were custodial rights over their children.

The Victorian era provided little opportunity for strong-minded, independent women. Instead, women were encouraged to involve themselves in humanitarian efforts to help those in less fortunate circumstances. Many upper- and middle-class ladies showed little interest in the cause of feminism. Some opposed it, and others vehemently condemned parliamentary franchise. Nevertheless, the battle for female enfranchisement was set to rage fiercely as a growing number of women began to call for the right to vote in both municipal and parliamentary elections.

Working-class women, meanwhile, continued struggling to cope on small incomes, hiring themselves out to employers eager to secure cheap labor, working long hours, and living in appalling poverty. They were preyed upon by industrialists who found their passivity and submissiveness exactly suited to the abominable conditions prevalent in their factories and mills. In some ways, however, working-class women were better off than their wealthier sisters in that they could choose their own husbands, handle their own paltry wages, and manage their own affairs.

But change was coming both to the lower orders and to the middle and upper classes. In 1867 in Edinburgh, London, and Manchester, the first women's suffrage societies came into being. One of the founders of the Manchester Society was Dr. Richard Pankhurst, husband of the future Mrs. Emmeline Pankhurst. The Representation of the People Bill of that year had given the franchise to rate-paying male householders (those who pay a property tax) and to "better-off" men lodging in towns, further highlighting the discrimination against females. As a result, in April 1868 at the Free Trade Hall in Manchester, the first British women's suffrage meeting was held, at which it was decided to seek the vote for women on the same terms that it had been, or would be, granted to men. The federation was spearheaded by Lydia Becker, an ardent suffragist until her death in 1890.

The Custody of Infants Acts of 1839 and 1873 gave custody to mothers of children under seven and sixteen years, respectively; divorce became slightly easier with the divorce law reform of 1857, and in 1870, women were permitted to keep any monies they earned. Further emboldened by the women's property acts of 1870 and 1882, the latter allowing wives to control their own property, women began to rebel against their subservient position in society.

Under the provisions of the 1869 Municipal Franchise Act, unmarried women ratepayers were empowered to vote in council elections, while the 1870 Elementary Education Act allowed them not only to vote in school board elections but to stand for election to the local school boards. In 1884, however, the women's movement suffered a crushing blow when another Representation of the People Act enfranchised agricultural laborers but refused to recognize women. It was the 1894 Local Government Act that finally opened up the much coveted political arena to both married and single women.

The 1894 Act resulted in the election of Emmeline Pankhurst to the Chorlton Board of Poor Law Guardians. Prompted by soaring unemployment in the winter of 1894-95, Mrs. Pankhurst organized food kitchens and campaigned for the reform of the Poor Law. In 1898, Richard Pankhurst died, leaving his family in reduced circumstances. His widow was forced to accept a registrarship of births, deaths, and marriages in Manchester to generate an income. But it was Christabel Pankhurst who became politically embroiled in the suffrage cause after her meeting with feminists Eva and Constance Gore-Booth and Eva's friend Esther Roper, a meeting that led to her becoming a member of the North of England Society for Women's Suffrage (NESWS) and the Women's Trade Union Council.

In 1897, the National Union of Women's Suffrage Societies (NUWSS), a federation of sixteen women's groups, was formed. It had as its leader Mrs. Henry Fawcett, who, as Lydia Becker's successor, had drawn the suffrage societies together under the umbrella of the NUWSS. Because of its gentle, ladylike approach, the organization was largely ignored by both the government and the public, and it was to be the militant stand of the suffragettes in the years following that was to finally draw attention to the vexed question of female enfranchisement.

The Education Act of 1870 had brought improved secondary education for the daughters of middle-class families, and universities gradually began to accept female students. London University began awarding degrees to women in 1878. Among the rising professions for women was that of horticulture, and, by

the end of the nineteenth century, colleges were being established for their training of women in this field. Arthur Harper
Bond founded Swanley Horticultural College in 1889, to which
women were later admitted, and the Lady Warwick Hostel was
inaugurated in 1898 by the Countess of Warwick for the daughters of impoverished landowners, offering courses in horticulture,
dairying, beekeeping, poultry farming, and fruit-growing.

Writing in *The Lady's Realm* in 1897, Wilhelmina Wimble
noted that "a little more than five years ago the women's branch
of the Horticultural College at Swanley was started [Swanley had
opened its doors to women in 1891); and the experiment has fulfilled the most sanguine expectations of its promoters."[2] The fee
for women students was seventy pounds a year, to include all
charges apart from "medical attendance, laundress, books and
separate rooms." The students resided in a house near the college, and the two-year course covered "every branch of the art
and science of horticulture," in addition to beekeeping, dairying,
and poultry rearing. Successful students were awarded a diploma,
and in 1896, a Swanley student, Miss Gulvin, won the coveted
Royal Horticultural Society medal in the annual examinations.

Early in that same year, three "girl-gardeners" were appointed to the gardening staff of Kew Gardens. The Gardens caused a
near riot by employing women dressed in thick brown bloomers,
which incited the young blades of the day to ogle them from the
upper decks of London omnibuses. One London newspaper published a verse describing the scene:

> *They gardened in bloomers, the newspapers said;*
> *So to Kew without waiting all Londoners sped;*
> *From the tops of the buses they had a fine view*
> *Of the ladies in bloomers who gardened at Kew.*

The phenomenon came to an abrupt end, however, when these
young ladies were ordered by Kew's director, Sir William
Thistleton-Dyer, to wear long coats to disguise the bloomers.

The Duke of Westminster also employed three Swanley-
trained women, and other aristocratic landowners chose female
head gardeners with similar backgrounds. One school in the
north of England appointed a lady holding a Swanley diploma as
gardener and lecturer in chemistry and botany. Such was the
growing interest, in fact, that "the only difficulty, at present, that

the College has to meet, is that the demand for the trained women gardeners exceeds the supply."[3]

Gardening for the Masses

The Victorian Age witnessed a dramatic upward trend in gardening for the masses. Scientific knowledge increased, and exotic plants were sent back from every corner of the world by intrepid plant hunters. By the middle of the century, a deluge of magazines and books offering advice on every aspect of horticulture were published to meet the enthusiastic demand. Some were written by women specifically for women.

Gardening writers John and Jane Loudon saw women as potential gardeners, Mrs. Loudon recommending that "all persons fond of gardening, and especially ladies, who have sufficient leisure,…manage their gardens themselves, with the assistance of a man to perform the more laborious operations."[4]

As a large percentage of the population drifted from the countryside into the towns, gardening became a recreational activity, particularly among the affluent middle classes, whose suburban villas, with their surrounding gardens, allowed them to indulge their horticultural fantasies. Gardening held a certain novelty as a pastime for bored middle-class wives, who found it a remarkable way of filling the time, inspired, no doubt, by Jane Loudon's vigorous, no-nonsense approach to the subject:

> A lady with a small light spade may…succeed in doing, with her own hands, all the digging that can be required in a small garden…and she will not only have the satisfaction of seeing the garden created, as it were, by the labour of her own hands, but she will find her health and spirits wonderfully improved by the exercise, and by the reviving smell of the fresh earth.[5]

CREATING A VICTORIAN FLOWER GARDEN

To create a Victorian flower garden, the design had first to be drawn on squared paper to a scale of 1 sq. in. to 1 sq. ft., with paths between the beds not less than 2 ft. wide to allow for ease of walking and mowing, colored green or red depending on

APPENDIX.

———

Since publishing the last Edition of this Work, it has been suggested to me that it might be very greatly improved by the addition of some plans of flower-gardens, accompanied by lists of plants of various kinds. Acting upon this suggestion, I have added to my Work this Appendix, in which I shall give four plans of flower-gardens, designed by Mr. Loudon himself, and published by him in the "Gardener's Magazine" in the course of the year 1843, with lists of plants for each, arranged by practical gardeners. I shall then give a few examples of rock-work, with lists of rock-plants, and plants for an Aquarium; and I shall add to these a few other lists of plants adapted for different purposes.

———

FLOWER GARDENS.

Fig. 61 is the working plan of a geometrical flower-garden, which is intended to have gravel-walks between the beds. The beds themselves are all numbered, for the convenience of planting, and they are drawn to a scale which is given below the plan. The following list, which was sent to Mr. Loudon by Mr. Ayres, of Blackheath, will keep the beds full of flowers from June till October:—

1. *Verbèna* Hendersònii, purple.
2. *Lobèlia* lùtea, yellow.
3. *Sálvia* pàtens, with *S.* chamædryoìdes, dark blue, round the sides; and Sanvitàlia procúmbens, a dwarf annual with yellow flowers, in the bottom, to cover the ground.
4. Bouvárdia triphýlla, red scarlet.
5. Tournefórtia heliotropioìdes, pale blue.
6. *Verbèna* teucrioìdes, the queen, white.
7. Campánula carpática, dark blue.
8. Verbèna amœ'na, pale lilac.
9. Same as No. 3.
10. Pentstèmon *gentianoìdes* coccíneus, scarlet.
11. *Verbèna* purpùrea, purple.
12. *Lòtus* jacobæ'us lùteus, yellow.
13. Díplacus glutinòsus, orange yellow, in the vase, with Lobèlia *Erìnus*, blue, to droop over the sides; and *Œnothèra*

macrocárpa, pale yellow, in the bed.
14. *Petùnia* purpùrea, purple.
15. *Verbèna* Drummóndii, pinkish lilac.
16. *Heliotròpium* peruviànum, violet.
17. Pelargònium compáctum, rose scarlet.
18. Pelargònium, the Basilisk, brilliant scarlet.
19. Calceolària rugòsa, yellow.
20. Lobèlia ramòsa, dark blue.
21. Nierembérgia filicaúlis, French white.
22. *Verbèna* Tweedieàna supérba, dark crimson.
23. *Verbèna* Neíllii, violet.
24. *Verbèna* Buístii, pale rose.
25. Pelargònium Manglèsii, variegated white.
26. Pelargònium zonàle, Frogmore scarlet.
27. Calceolària bícolor, yellow and whitish.

A plan of a flower garden on gravel (from Mrs. Loudon's The Ladies Companion to the Flower Garden, *1849, 5th edition).*

28. *Anagállis cærùlea grandiflòra*, dark blue.
29. *Nicrembérgia calycìna*, white.
30. *Verbèna Tweedicàna latifòlia*, crimson.
31. *Petùnia* crubéscens, blush.
32. *Verbèna odoràta ròsea*, pale pink.
23. Pelargònium, variegated ivy-leaved, white.
34. *Agératum mexicànum*, pale blue, to be pegged down.
35. *Petùnia* hýbrida, purple.
36. *Anagállis Monélli màjor*, dark blue.
37. *Lobèlia bícolor*, pale blue.
38. Pelargònium, Smith's emperor, scarlet.
39. *Agératum grandiflòrum*, pale blue.
40. *Petùnia* purpùrea, purple.
41. *Anagállis Phillípsii*, dark blue.
42. *Lobèlia grácilis*, pale blue.
43. Pelargònium, the Shrubland, scarlet.
44. Pelargònium compáctum, rose scarlet.
45. *Heliotròpium corymbòsum*, violet.
46. *Verbèna teucrioìdcs*, white.
47. *Petùnia* hýbrida, purple.
48. *Nicrembérgia* intermèdia, purple.
49. *Sanvitàlia* procúmbens, yellow.
50. *Sálvia pàtens*, &c., the same as No. 3.
51. Campánula Barrelièri, pale blue.
52. *Verbèna* multífida, pale pink.
53. Pentstèmon frutéscens, scarlet.
54. *Verbèna Hendersònii*, purple.
55. Calccolària integrifòlia, yellow.
56. Same as No. 3.
57. Campánula gargánica, blue.
58. *Verbèna teucrioìdcs*, white and pink.
59. Bouvárdia spléndens, scarlet.
60. Same as No. 13.

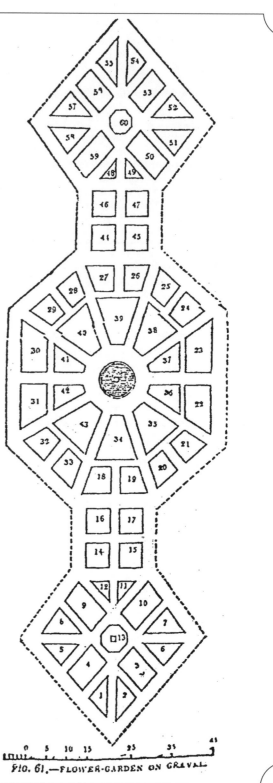

FIG. 61.—FLOWER-GARDEN ON GRAVEL.

whether grass or gravel was to be used. The beds were then tinted in accordance with the colors of the flowers to be planted in them, or strips of color were placed on the beds and moved around until the desired effect was achieved. Once the colors for the various beds had been decided, plants of the same color were then selected and placed in a reserve garden until they were needed.

To lay the flower bed, the ground was first dug and raked over. Then the paper plan was transferred by covering the ground with squares made by placing wooden pegs at regular distances and fastening string around them. The string was then covered with white chalk and pulled tightly with a sudden jerk so that the chalk was transferred to the ground, leaving a pattern of white lines forming regular squares, each with an area of 1 sq. ft. The lines were then traced with a pointed stick, and the proportion of each square to be used was copied from the paper plan.

Circular beds were outlined by taking a piece of string the length of the radius and tying a stick to each end. One stick was then placed in the ground to mark the center of the circle, the string pulled taut, and the perimeter traced in the soil using the second stick. An oval was made by tracing two circles, the outer line of one touching the center of the other, after which short lines were drawn at the top and bottom and the central lines rubbed out. Square beds were created by using just four pegs, one at each corner, with chalked string tied from peg to peg and, similarly, an oblong by joining two squares and taking off the corners if desired.

Once the beds had been traced out, the walks were laid with turf or gravel, care being taken to keep them exactly within their own boundaries. The beds were also kept precisely in their correct forms, as any irregularity produced a bad effect. The plants, once sited, needed to be well tended: "Every lady should have two or three hand-glasses, of different sizes, always at her disposal, even during summer, for the convenience of sheltering newly transplanted plants."[6] And the plants had to cover the whole of the bed but could not project beyond the outer edges, which would give "the idea of carelessness and neglect."

The splendor of the Victorian garden depended largely upon the wealth of its owner. The Neo-Italianate style with its fountains, vases, sculpture, and terraces was popular with the aristocracy, a more modest version being later employed in the villa gardens. However, there was no one style of Victorian garden as such, but rather a mix of features from a number of movements, the Gardenesque style, advocated by John Loudon, providing the commonality. Ribbon borders and geometric beds were much in vogue, as existing lawns, important garden features since medieval days, were cut up into circles, squares, and diamonds and filled with dense patterns of showy, gaudy annuals: zinnias, pelargoniums, petunias, salvias, and fuchsias. "Bedding-out" became an obsession, making a spectacular display during the summer months but leaving the beds empty during the winter, a practice much frowned upon by William Robinson, author of *The Wild Garden* and *The English Flower Garden*.

Gardening became an ever-increasing cult, with just about every sector of society participating—from the landed gentry and wealthy industrialists who competed with each other to build magnificent conservatories, vast terraces, and extravagant parterres crammed with rare and expensive flowers to the humble florist with his pots of dahlias and chrysanthemums. Rustic work, a legacy of the Georgian Era, rose in popularity as pergolas, tables, chairs, sofas, and even hermits' huts were built from tree trunks, branches, and twigs, and flower boxes were covered with bark. Rose gardens, arboreta, water gardens, and ferneries abounded.

During Victorian times, there was a craze for hunting out ferns and collecting them to take home and plant in a garden fernery, plant case, or conservatory. Organized fern hunts became the vogue. It is possible that the craze was inspired by George William Francis in his book *An Analysis of the British Ferns and Their Allies*. First published in 1837, the book provided details of where in England various ferns could be found.

In the nineteenth century, rock gardens or "rockworks" became an important feature of the garden, some of the more elaborate representing mountain ranges modeled from crushed marble and spar and filled with the newly introduced alpine plants. The herbaceous border also came into fashion, popularized first by William Robinson and then by Gertrude Jekyll. Jekyll's design work, begun in the late 1870s, lent itself to the use of flowers in a diversity of landscapes, particularly the woodland garden and the water garden, although Jekyll is probably best known for her work with the herbaceous border, or Jekyll border as it came to be called, which in part had its origins in the aesthetic theories of the arts and crafts movement under the leadership of William Morris.

Abandoning the brightly colored bedding schemes, Gertrude Jeykll, who was trained as an artist, sought to replace them with graduated, color-coordinated plants based on color harmony and contrast, blending both the texture and color of flower and leaf. Her garden at Munstead Wood, with its main flower border 200 ft. (61 1/2 m.) long and 14 ft. (4 1/3 m.) wide, was the embodiment of her flair for graded colors. In 1889, Jekyll met the young architect Edwin Lutyens, and in partnership they built and designed one hundred houses and gardens in the period leading up to the First World War.

THE KITCHEN GARDEN The walled kitchen gardens of the great country houses were one of the glories of the nineteenth century. Labor intensive, they were tended by an army of staff, overseen by a head gardener. Elderly women found casual employment hand-picking caterpillars from the cabbages or hoeing, and weeder-women were paid 10d. (6¢) a day to clear paths and terraces. The poet, novelist, and market gardener R. D. Blackmore is known to have employed "besides the men, half a dozen women young and old, as labourers in his gardens; some English some Irish; and he says that every season the two sets of women have a pitched battle on the ground."[7]

The kitchen garden was also de rigueur for the newly constructed villas. Kept out of sight of the house, it was planned to supply year-round vegetables, fruit, and herbs for the family, in addition to flowers for cutting. The kitchen garden was designed on a cruciform plan with two paths splitting the plot into quadrants and meeting in the center. Each quarter was then planted with fruit, vegetables, and herbs, and the pathways edged with apple, plum, and pear trees with herbaceous borders planted at their base. Mrs. Beeton suggests that "the main part of the kitchen garden, divided as it is into several small plots, might have the edges of each plot devoted to espalier apples and pears, or trees of these kinds trained on the cordon system, with pyramid trees at the angles, the central portions being devoted to vegetables."[8]

Ladies forced vegetables and raised cuttings and early seedlings in deep hotbeds made by forking substantial amounts of stable manure into the bottom of brick or wooden frames and covering them with thick layers of soil. Here, produce would be planted and protected by the sloping glass roofs of the frames, the more sophisticated of which had removable panels at the bottom so that fresh manure could be added when the original supply cooled down.

Throughout the century, the importance of the kitchen garden increased with the growing demand for vegetables and the massive rise in the varieties of fruit available, a fact largely due to the dedication of nurserymen such as Laxton and Rivers and to the acceptance of Mendel's genetic laws of inheritance, the result of which was the furtherance of international cross-breeding.

INDOOR GARDENING The invention of the Wardian case by Dr. Nathaniel Bagshaw Ward, surgeon and amateur botanist, revolutionized the transportation of exotic plants, shrubs, and cuttings from countries such as China, India, Africa, and South America, ensuring, for the most part, their survival and thus adding to the Victorian desire for grandeur and ostentation. These cases were also used to grow plants indoors, particularly ferns, as they created a stable, clean environment that excluded fumes from coal fires and gas lighting. As the craze for Wardian cases spread, they became more and more fantastic in design, some resembling miniature palaces, others boasting fountains, aquariums, and ornamental centerpieces.

Greenhouses and conservatories were considered part of the ladies' domain, stimulating their horticultural interest and allowing them to cultivate the flowers to which they were likened. In 1845, the tax on glass, levied at the end of the seventeenth century, was abolished, giving rise to "glass palaces" and luxurious "winter gardens" as extensions of the drawing room. There were dome-shaped, octagonal, and hexagonal conservatories, some with fountains, others lit by gas or Chinese lanterns. Furnished in style and comfort, they were often used for festive gatherings. The heated ones displayed maidenhair ferns, rubber plants, camellias, arum lilies, and azaleas; the ones without heat contained yuccas, harts-tongue ferns, roses, and hydrangeas.

Ladies near city centers exerted their skills toward other forms of indoor gardening. Wooden troughs lined with zinc or lead were placed in window recesses and planted with passion flowers, trained to hang down to make a screen for sunny windows. The winter cherry, with its scarlet berries and bright green foliage, also provided an effective window decoration. Hyacinths, carnations, picotees, pansies, violets, fuchsias, mignonette, and tulips were planted in profusion in window boxes and miniature greenhouses, both inside and outside the window. And, with the latest *a la Russe* dining fashion came the vogue for floral table decorations, usually as centerpieces. Balconies were laden with greenery, colorful annuals in summer, evergreens in winter, and draped with ornamental climbers. Conservatory gardens filled with ferns and foliage plants were popular, as were hanging baskets containing canary-bird flowers, convolvulus, petunias, and varieties of roses.

Flower-stand gardens with clematis-covered trellises could be found in corners of the drawing room, and etagere gardens, made up of shelves for potted plants, graced the walls. Victorian ladies also interested themselves in mantelpiece gardening, which began in the autumn when coal fires were lit and bulbs could be planted to take advantage of the warmth. Plant cabinets constructed across bow window recesses with fitted glass doors were also much in vogue and housed balsams, Japanese lilies, and achimenes. Portable screens covered with ivy were placed over sofas, and large pots of campanula stood in drafty corridors.

The craze for gardening was taken one stage further with posies depicting the *language of flowers*, which could be discreetly sent by admirers to the objects of their affection. Camellias, orchids, and lilies of the valley were made into sprays for the hair, and gentlemen wore fashionable *coat-flowers*. Ladies spent their leisure hours drying leaves, flowers, and grasses to decorate firescreens and grew everlastings to place in vases on mantlepieces. They skeletonized leaves for decoration and arranged grasses and dried seed pods in baskets under glass domes to prevent the dust from settling on them. Arranging cut flowers was another important occupation that became increasingly more popular as all sorts of contrivances were designed to contain them and keep them fresh.

The Victorian Poor

*T*he lower orders of Victorian society, particularly in urban areas, however, had no gardens to cultivate. Many lived in poverty and squalor in overcrowded conditions where cholera epidemics were commonplace and raw sewage flowed along unpaved streets. These conditions were of great concern to the wealthier classes, and the provision of public parks in the new cities became a priority. Sometimes allotment gardens were available on the outskirts of towns, but the rents were high and it was usually the tradespeople who benefited from them.

The idea of allotments was also popular in the country, where many cottages were without gardens because of the Enclosure Acts, and the movement grew as allotment societies began to spring up, although much depended upon the generosity of landowners and farmers to set aside land for the purpose. And, while the principle was applauded by the gentry, most farmers were known to be hostile, fearing that their laborers would become too independent and that the granting of land would lead to thefts of seeds and a slackening-off of the amount of work done on their farms. Nevertheless, in 1887, an Allotments Act was passed authorizing local authorities to buy up land for allotments for farmworkers.

The Smallholdings Act of 1892 empowered county councils to borrow monies from the Public Works Loan Commission to set up smallholdings that would then be sold to any agricultural worker able to pay twenty percent of the cost and the remainder in installments over a period of time. It was designed to ensure that laborers remained on the land by allowing them to grow vegetables and fruit and to keep poultry to supplement their meager wages. County councils, however, were reluctant to become involved, and even when land was selected, it invariably proved unsuitable. Also, many farm laborers were unable to come up with the required initial capital so few took advantage of the scheme.

A number of the clergy involved themselves in providing cottagers with allotments in the belief that the produce cultivated on the small plots of land would not only improve the families' diet but help to reduce the poor rate (money paid to the needy by the local parish). Some of the allotment schemes did in fact stipulate that any allotment holder claiming parish relief forfeited his right to that allotment.

The productivity and multiformity of the cottage garden were part of the charm of the Victorian countryside. Straight, neat rows of carefully planted vegetables co-existed with a glorious abundance of sunflowers and foxgloves, roses and sweet peas, hollyhocks, mignonette, sweet Williams, and lavender. Paths were edged with shells, and handsome cherry trees took pride of place. Cottage garden societies were founded, and cottagers exhibited their produce in local flower shows where prizes were awarded for the best onions, turnips, and cauliflower, the best gooseberries, pears, and plums, and the best pot plants and flower arrangements.

Still, the lot of the farm laborer in his "tied" cottage, which could be occupied only as long as he worked for the owner, was far from idyllic, although agriculture remained the largest source of employment, reaching its peak in 1851 with nearly 1.25 million male and around 143,000 female workers. To a large extent, farmers relied on the cheap labor provided by women and children working in "gangs," a system that continued into the 1850s and 1860s despite the 1843 report condemning it. Women and children were hired and paid by gang masters, who contracted their labor to farmers. Victorian reformers were appalled at the moral dangers involved in men and women working in close proximity for lengthy periods of time. Their concern led to the 1867 Gangs Act, after which, gang masters had to be licensed by justices of the peace, women were no longer permitted to work in gangs with men, and children under the age of eight could not be employed.

Harvest time was busy and women worked in the fields from dawn until nightfall, earning 2s. (15¢) a day in Lincolnshire for reaping and gleaning and helping to rake, bind, and stook. Flora Thompson writes of gleaning or "leazing," of women and children picking up ears of wheat that the horse-rake had missed: "Up and down and over and over the stubble they hurried, backs bent, eyes on the ground, one hand outstretched to pick up the ears, the other resting on the small of the back with the 'handful.' When this had been completed, it was bound round with a wisp of straw and erected with others in a double rank...beside the leazer's water-can and dinner basket."[9]

Women were also employed in the fields to hoe and weed the corn, to sow seed, gather potatoes, and pick fruit and vegetables. They pulled turnips by grubbing up the lower half of the root with a hooked fork called a hacker. Female labor was used in manure spreading and for pea picking and hop picking, for which the women were paid 1s. 4d. to 2s. (10-15¢) a day. A. J. Munby, a barrister and poet, noted in his diary on 25 June 1870 that at Isleworth near Twickenham he encountered the "figures of women and girls, rough-clad and picturesque," who told him they were pit workers from the Black Country, and that they worked in the market gardens "for nine weeks or so" and then went "back home when the fruit is over, in August."[10]

Although in some parts of the country gangs of women were still being hired out to farmers in 1894, the number of female agricultural laborers was beginning to decline as the women themselves became more reluctant to work in the fields. Many of the cottagers' daughters were going into service at a time when the demand for domestic servants was at its peak. Wages in industrial towns and cities were higher than those in agricultural districts, and despite the terrible living conditions, there was general drift by agricultural workers toward the urban areas, causing widespread rural depopulation.

With the repeal of the corn laws in 1846 came the shift toward free trade, stimulating overseas commerce. World trade was subsequently accelerated by the gold rush in California in 1849 and in Australia in 1851, which increased the world's gold reserves. Railways were extended, transportation became easier, and great strides in industrial and commercial development were made. Exports boomed, as did imports, especially imported foodstuffs brought in by steamships that could carry a vast tonnage of grain.

During the final decades of the century, however, Britain experienced economic difficulties, largely because of her dependency on foreign trade, which resulted in factories closing and unemployment rising, particularly in agriculture. The British farmer was forced to produce items that were not imported, with the result that mixed farming (both crops and livestock) increased. The Board of Agriculture was set up in 1889 to advise and instruct and to undertake programs of research, but by that time the "Golden Age of British Agriculture" was already over.

American Bloomers

*T*he changes in the lives of American women were also far-reaching during the nineteenth century, and suffragism, as in Great Britain, played a major part in those changes. Throughout America, women fought alongside men for safer working conditions, shorter hours, and enfranchisement. More and more women joined organizations with a view to changing their country's laws, which would give them basic civil and political rights. The Women's Rights Convention at Seneca Falls in 1848 issued the Declaration of Sentiments, which enumerated those rights to which, as women, they were excluded.

Margaret Fuller, a committed American feminist, advocated that woman's basic need was for freedom and equality, with special reference to her right to own property on an equal basis with men and to enter any profession she chose. Mrs. Elizabeth Cady, meanwhile, published a feminist version of the Bible from which she excluded all "immoral" extracts.

By the middle of the nineteenth century, American feminists were beginning to promote the idea that women were neither weak nor delicate and well able to enjoy the exercise and physical health experienced by men. With the invention of the bicycle came a new sense of freedom and liberation for women, not to mention exercise. They now had the freedom to travel, prompting the American suffragist Amelia Bloomer to design a costume to be worn by women when riding a bicycle, to which she gave her name. She was concerned, however, that the attention her "bloomers" received would detract from her feminist activities, and she later abandoned the garment. To the feminists, however, the "bloomer" was a symbol of women's emancipation. And, although the women who sported bloomers were met with derision, they continued to wear them until, ultimately, they became the standard item of apparel for ladies participating in gymnastics or athletics.

The American Civil War (1861-1865) gave women in the north many new employment opportunities in addition to extra work on the farms. Women also took up jobs in factories, arsenals, and sewing rooms, jobs usually done by men, to meet the demands for vital war equipment. Women also entered government departments and were employed as teachers, although they

were rarely paid as much as men and had to endure male prejudice in the workplace. And when the war was over, they were
dismissed to make way for the returning veterans.

The war catapulted both northern and southern women
from their domestic domains into the workplace, accelerating
the women's cause and the desire to continue in paid employment. And, although women made many gains during these
years, few were made in the political and legal arenas. The
Emancipation Proclamation of 1863 placed the abolition of slavery as a Union war goal, and in that same year the Women's
Loyal League was organized to coerce Congress to enact the
Thirteenth Amendment, eventually passed in February 1865,
abolishing slavery throughout the United States. The League
also hoped to persuade the government to grant suffrage for
women, a hope that was to lead to disappointment.

In 1861 at the start of the war, all army nurses were male, but
the needs of the war and female determination made possible the
entrance of women nurses to both the front line and established
hospitals. Elizabeth Blackwell, the first U.S. woman doctor of
medicine, helped to establish the United States Sanitary
Commission, which undertook to improve sanitary conditions at
army camps and to raise money for medical supplies. There were
seven thousand societies of the Sanitary Commission, which, by
1865, had raised some $50 million (£33.3 million) by means of
donations, lotteries, and "sanitary fairs." As a result of the vast
amounts of money raised, the soldiers were provided with extra
nurses and surgeons as well as fruit and vegetables to supplement
their diet and other items that the U.S. government failed to
supply.

Most southern women supported the Confederacy. A few of
them actually disguised themselves as men and joined the
Confederate Army. And while others sent items of ladies' under-
wear to any man who was unpatriotic as a symbol of their disapproval, some became spies in their patriotic zeal to serve the
Cause, bringing military intelligence through the Union lines.
Not all southern women behaved heroically, however.
Prostitution began to flourish, although often as a last resort and
out of hunger and desperation.

A few of the plantations along the Mississippi held more
than one hundred slaves, while some estates had between ten

and fifty. Most slave owners, however, had from one to ten slaves, who were generally used as an extension to family labor. Many southern women disliked slavery and developed an empathy with the slaves on their husbands' plantations, while others considered slaves to be a burden to their owners. There were, of course, women who were jealous of the sexual relationships between their husbands and female slaves, which happened all too frequently, and there were also a number of women who viewed themselves as being on the same level as their slaves, as they, too, were subordinated and subjected to the will of the master.

The war years saw farms and fields without male labor, which prompted the anxious, war-weary women to take over, many of them driving teams and performing heavy tasks on the land. In the South, women and children tried to protect their livestock and homesteads as the war crept closer and closer, but the devastation was crippling and by the end of the war the South had become impoverished, its economy totally destroyed.

Charlotte Perkins Gilman, who published *Women and Economics* in 1898, was a U.S. non-Marxist socialist feminist whose ideas had their foundation in the social Darwinist theory, popular at the end of the nineteenth century. Social Darwinism was the application of Darwin's theory of the evolution of species to the understanding of human society: man was the product of the reciprocal action between heredity and environment. Gilman viewed individuals as products of their environment, the economic conditions within their social environment being the most important factor. Within this belief she deduced her theory of female subordination and the nature of women's character. She maintained that the dependence of the female on the male for food occurs only in the human race, that monogamous marriage was a social development only, and that women *could* be economically independent. Wives who did housework did not have economic independence; they did not get paid for looking after the home or for being mothers, and they could not take their services elsewhere for payment. As a natural result, they were dependent, whatever their formal rights. Gilman regarded this dependence of the female on the male as the enslavement of the woman by the man.

After the Civil War, women's clubs were established for women of the middle and upper classes wishing to expend their energy outside the home. Many of these clubs were political, moral, and educational in purpose. Generally speaking, though, the women's club movement was focused on reform and philanthropy, examples of which were The Philadelphia Female Anti-Slavery Society founded in 1833 and The Daughters of Temperance in 1840. Later on, however, cultural clubs such as Sorosis, founded in New York in 1868, began to appear, and at the end of the Civil War, these clubs were organized at a national level. In 1889, the cultural clubs joined forces to become the General Federation of Women's Clubs, and in 1890 the patriotic clubs the Daughters of the American Revolution and the Colonial Dames of America were founded.

The Woman's Christian Temperance Union (WCTU) originated in the Woman's Temperance Crusade of 1873 to 1874, when the women of Hillsboro, Ohio began a crusade of prayer against the saloons. Hymns were sung and prayers were offered both inside and outside the buildings, and, as a result of their action, the traffic in liquor disappeared from some two hundred towns in around twenty states in less than two months.

The WCTU itself was founded at meetings held in Cleveland, Ohio between 18 and 20 November 1874, which were organized by leading church women from Chautauqua, New York. The growth of the Union was rapid, and it soon made itself felt in public affairs as its members worked tirelessly to persuade U.S. citizens that drinking was morally wrong. During the latter part of the nineteenth century, the WCTU had as its president Frances Willard, a lady of tremendous energy and vitality, who led the Union from strength to strength as it strove to obtain a variety of reforms including social purity, votes for women, and free kindergartens. By 1900 every state had scientific temperance instruction in all of its public schools.

American Women Gardeners
As Professionals

Mrs. Loudon, in her widely read book *Gardening for Ladies* (1840), encouraged women to garden for the health-giving properties involved. She told her readers that any lady, using a small, light spade, could do all of the digging necessary in a small garden completely by herself. Ladies on both sides of the

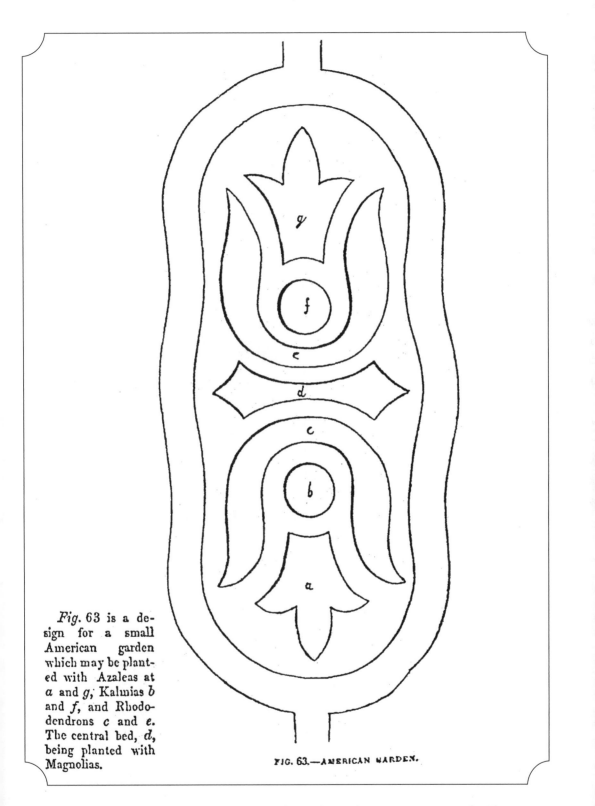

Fig. 63 is a design for a small American garden which may be planted with Azaleas at *a* and *g*; Kalmias *b* and *f*, and Rhododendrons *c* and *e*. The central bed, *d*, being planted with Magnolias.

FIG. 63.—AMERICAN GARDEN.

A plan of an American garden (from Mrs. Loudon, The Ladies Companion to the Flower Garden, *1849, 5th edition).*

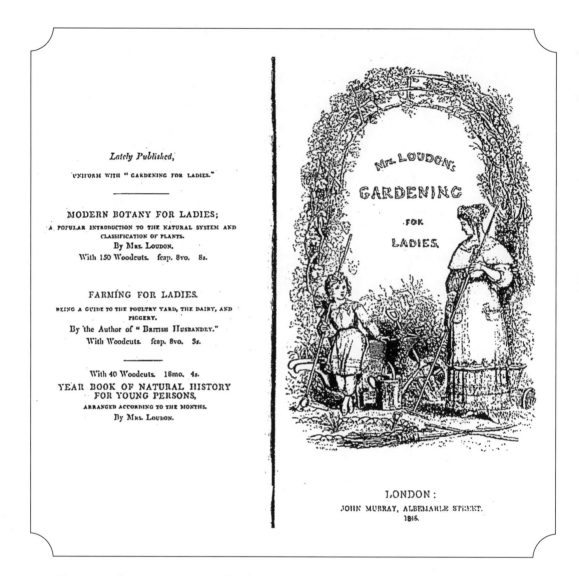

Lately Published,

UNIFORM WITH " GARDENING FOR LADIES."

MODERN BOTANY FOR LADIES;
A POPULAR INTRODUCTION TO THE NATURAL SYSTEM AND
CLASSIFICATION OF PLANTS.
By MRS. LOUDON.
With 150 Woodcuts. fcap. 8vo. 8s.

FARMING FOR LADIES.
BEING A GUIDE TO THE POULTRY YARD, THE DAIRY, AND
PIGGERY.
By the Author of " BRITISH HUSBANDRY."
With Woodcuts. fcap. 8vo. 3s.

With 40 Woodcuts. 18mo. 4s.
YEAR BOOK OF NATURAL HISTORY
FOR YOUNG PERSONS,
ARRANGED ACCORDING TO THE MONTHS.
By MRS. LOUDON.

MRS. LOUDON'S
GARDENING
.FOR
LADIES.

LONDON :
JOHN MURRAY, ALBEMARLE STREET.
1846.

Illustration from Mrs. Loudon's book Gardening for Ladies, *1846 (7th edition).*

Atlantic were very interested in gardening at this time, particularly when the new mass-produced greenhouses were introduced, which allowed them to grow all the tender plants with a great degree of success. The American novelist Harriet Beecher Stowe was also a great advocate of ladies' gardening. She believed that stirring the soil and breathing the fresh morning air were of great benefit to them and would give them a fresh and beautiful complexion, bright eyes, a cheerful temper, a vigorous mind, and a pure heart.

American gardens at this time were intimate, individual, and personal to their creators, in direct contrast to the more formal gardens of the previous centuries. Moreover, women began to study botany seriously, which resulted in the role of nature studies changing from the religious sentimentalism of the first half of the century to the more scientific studies of the latter half. Some lady gardeners were especially enterprising; a Miss Clara Lippincott, for example, who lived in Minnesota, set herself up as a seedswoman, sending her seeds all over the world. The idea was a novel one, and one that resulted in Miss Lippincott netting several thousand dollars a year from her enterprise.

American gentlewomen began to design gardens for family and friends, and landscaping gradually became acceptable as a profession for women. Magazines of the time, *Garden and Forest*, for example, actively encouraged the participation of women in landscape architecture, and in 1899, the American Society of Landscape Architects was founded by nine men and one woman.

Beatrix Farrand, a leading landscape architect, designed gardens for the Yale and Princeton campuses and for Dumbarton Oaks in Washington D.C., while the Cornish Art Colony in New Hampshire influenced Rose Nichols and Ellen Shipman in their decision to pursue landscape architecture as a career. Contributions to American gardens were not limited to professional women, however. Amateur horticulturists cultivated plants and wrote books about their experiences and their acquired knowledge.

Anna Warner published *Gardening by Myself* in 1872. In her book, Warner, who gardened with her sister Susan on a small semi-island in the Hudson River across from West Point, provided a general description of both her own garden and the horticultural knowledge she had gained while creating it. She recommended old-fashioned hardy flowers informally planted, her own garden having mixed beds of perennials and hardy annuals arranged in clumps and drifts of colors for a successive display of blooms. Most of the flowers she used—larkspur, scabious, and cornflowers, for example—were grown from seeds or cuttings, or they were transplanted from the wild. *Gardening by Myself* was written to encourage women to do their own gardening.

In *Island Garden*, written in 1894, Celia Thaxter, a poet and essayist, described in detail her garden on Appledore, one of the Isles of Shoals off Portsmouth, New Hampshire. Beautifully and poetically written, Thaxter's book describes how she single-handedly succeeded in making a garden on windswept Appledore without help. She described the flowers she grew and where she planted them.

Returning every summer to Appledore from the family home in Boston, Thaxter made her garden on a small piece of land in front of her cottage, filling it with foxgloves, poppies, larkspur, lavender, sunflowers, cornflowers, peonies, and hollyhocks, all the old-fashioned cottage flowers. Hers was a naturalist's garden, and Thaxter was an advocate of dense planting, planting that would ensure continuous color. She planted *phlox drummondii* amidst the tall perennials, pansies and verbenas, asters, and pop-pies, her favorite flower, so that every piece of ground was covered in a stunning display of color. She covered every inch of space in successive plantings that would form a continuous bloom, festooning the porch which overlooked the garden with vines, honeysuckle, white clematis, wisteria, and hops.

Thaxter held an informal summer salon in her parlor during the 1880s and early 1890s to which came the aesthetes of the day: the artists, the poets, and the musicians. Her garden was also the subject of many paintings by the American impressionist Childe Hassam, who was a regular visitor to Appledore from the mid-1880s to 1913.

The books by Anna Warner and Celia Thaxter contain information about the plants themselves. Both authors take an aesthetic approach to flower gardening, using perennials in unre-strained groups and long curves of color, a scheme that led to the introduction of a themed approach of tones of single colors, usu-ally white or blue, into American gardens.

In 1901, Mrs. Edward Gilchrist Low founded the Lowthorpe School of Landscape Architecture, Gardening, and Horticulture for women in Groton, Massachusetts. The school was patterned after Swanley College in England, where she herself had trained, and affiliated with Boston's Simmons College. Its three-year course emphasized design, construction, history, and fine arts. Part of the horticultural syllabus was devoted to tending the colonial house and garden on which the college was sited as well as its commercial nursery. The continuing demand for horticultural education for women was thwarted in 1900 by Harvard University when it allowed only men through its doors, forcing the Massachusetts Institute of Technology to phase out its coeducational courses in landscape architecture. Women wishing to enter the profession had to be strong-willed and tough. Not only was it extremely difficult for women to find work in this male-dominated sphere, if and when they qualified, but it was now becoming virtually impossible to find a school or university at which they could train.

American Farming

Northern farmers grew wheat, corn, and flax, and the whole family helped on the land, assisted by mechanized products of the Industrial Revolution. Southern farmers, or planters, on the other hand, living in a much kinder sub-tropical climate, grew tobacco, sugar, rice, and cotton, using slave labor as the most efficient means of producing it.

Families often joined forces for tasks such as barn-building, field-clearing, and corn-husking, the women working alongside their menfolk. Scutching flax was a social event in which both men and women participated, hanging bunches of flax on posts and then beating them with pieces of wood to clean and straighten the tangled fibers. New farming techniques and marketing methods, however, were quickly adopted, and these, coupled with the relaxed method of land ownership and readily available capital, made nineteenth-century American farming commercially viable and totally different from the British system of closed communities, limited ambition, and the practice of farming the same piece of land from one generation to the next.

During the nineteenth century, many New England farmers left the land to go west. Farms were put up for sale, and the countryside became neglected and abandoned. Farmhouses were often sold to businessmen, lawyers, and the like who used them as country homes, and of the farmers who remained, many soon realized that if they were to survive, they would have to specialize. Instead of growing grain, they turned to producing lettuces, potatoes, cucumbers, cabbages, and onions, and they did very well financially. Orchards also proved profitable, as a high percentage of apples were turned into applejack, the local drink.

The American frontier continued to be pushed west by the pioneers. From 1750 to 1850, it had moved to just beyond the Mississippi, after which the rush of settlers across the prairies and plains stretched from Chicago to Denver and from the western slopes of the Rockies to the Pacific. After long, hazardous journeys by wagon, usually undertaken in large groups, the settlers were met with forest land that had to be cleared and tamed. Many of them had no experience in cultivating virgin country as they set out from the coastal cities of the East, bringing with them the railways and the telegraph, which were vital to successful and profitable farming.

"The Glories of the Empire"

The magnificence of Victorian England was symbolized by the Great Exhibition of 1851, where the enormous strides being made in British industry and trade were on show. The Victorians were proud of their country and of their success, reveling in the glories of an empire that embraced a quarter of the world's population, all of whom pledged allegiance to the Crown. The Industrial Revolution generated wealth and prosperity; it witnessed the rise of the middle classes and played a major role in the advancement of feminism, changing the lives of so many Victorian women. Opportunity and economic advances gave these women independence, freedom, and equality with men in as much as they had the right to work for a living. Marriage was no longer the only outlet for a woman's energies.

In 1896, the honors list of London University was "very creditable to women." Miss Hull gained first-class honors in the Bachelor of Surgery examination, and Miss Aldrich became the first lady "Master in Surgery," while the second-class honors of women were "too numerous to name."[11] The "New Woman" was no longer malleable and docile, and despite Queen Victoria's open hostility toward the "mad, wicked folly of Women's Rights,"[12] the scene was already set for the long and bitter struggle that was yet to come.

CHAPTER SIX

THE GOLDEN YEARS

A Time of Promise

THE BRIEF REIGN OF EDWARD VII (1901-1910) had far-reaching effects that were to remain unchallenged until the onset of World War I. The huge disparity between rich and poor was generally accepted in a hierarchical class structure that seemed to generate little envy or hatred. These years were a time of promise, a time of progress when the worst aspects of Victorianism were laid to rest. And, most importantly, they were years that witnessed the continuance of Great Britain as an affluent, influential world power in a golden age of peace and tranquility.

Dignified and affable, with a commanding personality although relatively bourgeois in his tastes, Edward VII inspired a set of social values that placed wealth rather than birth as one of the main criteria for entry into polite society. He nursed the monarchy through a difficult period of transition in an ever-changing world that was no longer prepared to adhere to the rigid code of Victorian morality but was eager instead to adopt the *laissez faire* philosophy and the permissive, though discreet, standards of a new century. These standards were dictated by an extravagant, pleasure-loving king with a zest for life and a genuine concern for the welfare of his subjects.

For the British people, life was better than it had been during the reign of Queen Victoria. In the towns and cities, working hours were shortened, bringing an increase of leisure. Employers were starting to show consideration toward those they employed, and safety regulations and improved working conditions were introduced by legislation that enforced a strict control over the hours worked by young people and placed an upper limit of a sixty-hour working week for women, who made up almost one-third of the workforce. Of these women, 1.5 million, a number that was to rise to over 2 million by 1911, were employed in domestic service, an occupation that was widely viewed as good training for marriage. Many working-class women also found employment in factories, for which they were paid the derisory sum of 11s. 7d. (87¢) a week, while others toiled in shops and offices and in "sweated" trades such as boxmaking, dressmaking, and millinery.

At the beginning of the century, the English countryside was in a state of decay, economic necessity forcing many of the rural population into the towns and cities. The national economy was slowing down, and the aristocracy and gentry were no longer financing their privileged existence from land, choosing instead, like their Victorian forebears, to be shareholders in industry, despite the fact that Great Britain was no longer the leading industrial nation.

Dairy farming produced the best income at a time when only seven percent of the country's workforce was engaged in agriculture and state subsidies were non-existent. Corn was imported from America, where mechanical harvesters and multi-furrow ploughs were in widespread use and railways and steamships carried produce with ease and rapidity, effectively undercutting the British farmers. As a result, the acreage of arable farming declined, as did agricultural employment. The depression of the 1870s had greatly damaged farming, and while cheap female labor continued to be used at harvest time, young women tended to gravitate away from rural isolation toward urbanization, usually finding employment as domestic servants in middle-class homes.

For those who remained in the country, wages plummeted below the poverty level, male laborers in 1907 earning an average wage of 17s. 6d. ($1.30) a week. The standard of housing, already appalling, was worsened by the fact that landlords no longer received rents high enough to enable them to undertake repairs and improvements. In 1908, a Smallholdings Act was passed to encourage farm laborers to have a stake in the land they worked. The rural poor were further helped by the provision of allotments, at a rent of 5s. a year in the County of Wiltshire, for example, on which they could grow fresh vegetables for their families. This Smallholdings and Allotments Act of 1908 reiterated that it was the duty of allotments authorities to make provision for allotments for rural laborers where there was a need

and where the demand was high enough. Under the terms of the
Allotments Acts of 1908-1925, allotments were to be provided
by the borough, urban district, or parish councils. In 1909, there
were 58,548 allotments, a number that more than doubled to
130,526 by 1914.

The British Feminists Revolt

*I*n 1897, the first women's institute had been formed in the
small community of Stoney Creek in Canada. Its purpose was
to broaden the outlook of farm women, to educate them, to allow
them to meet socially, to work together, to be involved in the
social lives of their communities, and generally to improve their
own quality of life. The institute's founder, Adelaide Hoodless, a
farmer's daughter whose fourth child had died at the age of eighteen months as a result of drinking contaminated milk, was
determined to educate mothers and to save them from a similar
loss. She was equally determined that these women should
receive lectures and demonstrations in domestic science and
homecrafts, which would give them a greater understanding of
food economy and hygiene and how to scientifically take better
care of their children and raise their families' standard of living.

After speaking at the Agricultural College of Guelph in
1896, Hoodless had been invited by a young farmer, Mr. Erland
Lee, to address the all-male Young Farmer's Institute in nearby
Saltfleet. In view of the many women present at the venue, it
was afterwards decided to arrange another meeting, and on 19
February 1897, the first women's institute was inaugurated. At
Mr. Lee's suggestion, the government of Ontario sent a female
dairy farming instructor to speak to the women, and it was she
who established the second women's institute and gave it its
motto, "For Home and Country," which has endured throughout
the years. By 1915, there were more than 800 women's institutes
in Canada, with the first one in Great Britain appearing during
the same year.

For the upper classes of Great Britain, life was very different.
The main occupation of frivolous, well-heeled young females was
that of enjoying life to the full and of eventually making a brilliant match. No paid work was thought suitable for these "dar-
lings" of Edwardian society in an age that encouraged feminine

leisure and stifled freedom and independence. Once married, however, although a wife no longer forfeited her property, she was still expected to defer to her husband in all matters; any children of the marriage belonged to him by law, and should the couple separate, the husband had first claim to them. The tradition that all single ladies should be maintained by their families continued to prevail, and despite opportunities for entry into universities, few paid employments were open to women. The professions continued to remain largely the prerogative of men, although the barriers of masculine prejudice were gradually being eroded in areas such as medicine and teaching.

During the first decade of the twentieth century, sexual radicalism was gathering momentum in the arena of feminism, although it was the least supported cause. On both sides of the Atlantic, female suffrage took center stage. Both in America and in Great Britain, middle-class women dominated female organizations. American women considered themselves more radical and less class conscious than their English sisters, tending to join multi-issue organizations—clubs, settlement houses, and consumers' leagues—that British feminists chose largely to avoid. These multifarious groups were far more energetic in America, but it was the British activists who led the way in political involvement, social purity, and militant suffrage tactics. Nevertheless, the feminists of both countries were united in their desire to improve the position of women and to seek justice for them at the hands of men, in both the private and public sectors.

The birth rate started to fall as the well-to-do began to practice birth control, which resulted in upper- and middle-class ladies having more time on their hands. At the same time, the idea that the only career for women was marriage was fast disappearing as the younger element of society began to rebel against traditional conventions and to pursue their own ideas of independence. Impoverished aristocratic gentlemen began to seek rich American wives, and by the end of Edward VII's reign, American heiresses had enriched the British peerage by some £40 million.

The newly emerging self-image and position of women accelerated the push toward emancipation by the feminist faction as it clamored for female enfranchisement. In October 1903, the Women's Social and Political Union (WSPU) was formed, destined to become the suffragist platform for new and untried

Women Gardeners:
A HISTORY

IRON AGE AGRICULTURE.
Figuier L'Homme Primitif.
Reprinted with permission
of the Mary Evans Picture
Library, London.

PEC 4903 Ms 65/1284 f.6v.
JUNE: HAYMAKING by the Limbourg
brothers, Les Tres Riches Heures du
Duc de Berry (early 15th century).
Musee Conde, Chantilly,
France/Giraudon/Bridgeman
Art Library, London/New York.

A WALLED TOWN GARDEN, also known as "Le Rustican du Cultivement des Terres" compiled by Pierre Croissens of Bolougne, translated into French by the dictate of Charles V of France, 15th century, Livre des Prouffits Champetres et Ruraulx (15th century). British Library, London/ Bridgeman Art Library, London/ New York.

"THE HARVEST HOME" (ca. 1815). Rowlandson. Dr. Syntax. Reprinted with permission of the Mary Evans Picture Library, London.

A Busy Family Do the Gardening Together (1864). Unnamed artist in the *Illustrated Times*.
Reprinted with permission of the Mary Evans Picture Library, London.

"The Apple Gatherers" by Frederick Morgan (1856-1927).
Roy Miles Gallery, 29 Bruton Street, London W1/Bridgeman Art Library, London/New York.

PICKING VEGETABLES IN AN
ENGLISH VEGETABLE GARDEN
(ca. 1900). Helen Allingham.
Reprinted with permission of the
Mary Evans Picture Library,
London.

GIRL IN A GREENHOUSE (1906).
Rudolf Eichstädt. Reprinted with
permission of the Mary Evans
Picture Library, London.

THE FIRST LADY GARDENERS AT KEW (photograph ca. 1895).
Reprinted with permission of the Royal Botanic Gardens, Kew, Richmond, Surrey, UK.

A FLAXPULLER near Yeovil, Somerset during World War I. Reprinted with permission of the Imperial War Museum, London.

PLOUGHING WITH TRACTORS during World War I. Reprinted with permission of the Imperial War Museum, London.

HEDGING AND DITCHING during
World War I. Reprinted with
permission of the Imperial
War Museum, London.

GIRLS OF THE GTC (Girls Training
Corps) clearing and digging a
garden at 145 Piccadilly, London.
Reprinted with permission of the
Imperial War Museum, London.

acts of militancy. On 13 October 1905, Annie Kenney and
Christabel Pankhurst interrupted a liberal meeting in
Manchester by demanding that women's suffrage be addressed.
They were arrested, and when they refused to pay their fines of
5s. and 10s., respectively, Christabel was subsequently sentenced
to seven days' imprisonment and Annie Kenney to three days. It
was the first time that women in Great Britain had been jailed
for their political beliefs, and a mass demonstration was held in
Manchester's Free Trade Hall to welcome them back to liberty.

Under the leadership of Mrs. Pankhurst, female suffrage
gained impetus. The WSPU opened an office in Clement's Inn
in 1906 with the equally formidable Mrs. Emmeline Pethick-
Lawrence as its treasurer. Once established, the Union continued with its aggressive harassment of the liberal government,
and, while the "autocracy" of Emmeline Pankhurst caused a rift
in the membership in 1907 that led to the formation of the
Women's Freedom League in 1908, the suffragettes remained
firmly united in their political stance. As a result, the government was under constant attack, as women chained themselves
to railings and hurled bricks through windows in a bid to persuade the House of Commons to put through a suffrage bill.

In 1907, the Qualification of Women Act was passed,
enabling women, married or single, to become councillors or
aldermen, mayors, or chairmen on county or borough councils. It
was not enough. On 29 June 1909, the highly publicized March
on Parliament took place; 108 women were arrested, and 3,000
policemen turned out in force. At 9 o'clock, stones were hurled
through windows at the Privy Council, Treasury, and home
offices. The window breakers were also arrested and given the
choice of a £5 ($7.50) fine or a term of imprisonment of between
four and six weeks, depending on the size of window broken; all
of the women chose imprisonment. Having refused to wear
prison dress, they were forcibly stripped and placed in solitary
confinement, whereupon they decided to reject all offers of food.
Six days later they were released, and by August 1909, hunger
strikes became the Union's adopted policy.

By going on hunger strikes, the suffragettes served only a few
days of their prison sentences, a situation that compelled the
home secretary to order them to be force fed. This heinous experience was immediately condemned not only by the WSPU but
by a number of eminent medical practitioners.

In the Queen's Hall on 31 January 1910, Mrs. Pankhurst announced that all militancy would cease until further notice. But harassment of the government continued in a non-militant way. Actually, militant activities remained suspended until 21 November 1911 apart from one week in November 1910. On 18 November 1910, when the WSPU discovered that the Conciliation Bill had not been mentioned by British Prime Minister Asquith when Parliament reconvened, 300 women, organized into groups of twelve, headed for the House of Commons, where they met, for the first time, with police brutality. Although 115 of them were arrested, the home secretary decided not to press charges.

The day was thereafter known by the suffragettes as "Black Friday," and it was followed on 22 November by a march on Downing Street, where the windows of Asquith's car were broken along with those at the colonial and home offices. The violence erupted after the prime minister stated that facilities would be given in the next Parliament for proceeding with a bill the suffragettes knew would have little chance of getting through the Commons. Although all charges against them were afterwards withdrawn, 159 women were arrested.

From November 1911, civil disobedience continued. Amidst the battle cry of "Votes for Women," shop windows were smashed, fires engulfed churches, golf course greens were cut up, and post boxes destroyed. On Friday, 12 March 1912, windows in Downing Street and eleven other London thoroughfares were shattered with stones, weights, and small hammers by bands of suffragettes who marauded through the city leaving a trail of destruction behind them. In two hours, they caused thousands of pounds worth of damage, and 120 women were taken into custody. Three days later, a warrant was issued for the arrest of Christabel Pankhurst, who was in France at that time. Those suffragettes who did go to prison as a result of the orgy of vandalism found themselves serving sentences with hard labor.

On 8 June 1913, suffragette Emily Davison died from the injuries she received when she threw herself under King George V's racehorse at the Derby at Epsom, and in the summer of 1914 Mrs. Pankhurst herself was arrested during an attack on Buckingham Palace by members of the WSPU. On the eve of World War I, eleven suffragettes were still in prison, and others continued to walk in fear of the Cat and Mouse Act (1912), which empowered the government to release from jail those suffragettes who were near to death from hunger-striking, and to re-arrest them once their health had been restored.

In a Class of Their Own: Edwardian Women Gardeners

Not all Edwardian women were ardent feminists. There were many who were of the opinion that "men are not those selfish, jealous, ungenerous brutes which they are said to be by the present-day female apostles of woman's emancipation."[1] But there were others strong-willed enough to pursue both their independence and their chosen vocation. One such lady was Frances, Viscountess Wolseley, who founded the Glynde School for Lady Gardeners in Sussex in 1902-1903 as an educational and commercial establishment. In the face of parental disapproval (dutiful daughters of wealthy Edwardian families were not expected to be independent), Frances set herself the task of learning all she could about farming and gardening. With unflagging energy, she traveled throughout the British Isles, on the Continent, and in America to gain more detailed and commercial knowledge and read all available literature on the subjects.

Her school was a huge success, and as the number of students grew, it became necessary for her to expand and to rent an extra 5 1/2 acres of land to make into a garden, which she called "Ragged Lands." During the two-year course, the students learned about vegetable, fruit, and flower growing, in addition to the history of garden design and how to run a business on a commercial basis. The school soon acquired a considerable reputation and its fame spread. In 1913, Viscountess Wolseley was awarded the title "Citizen and Gardener of London" for her services to horticulture, and the school itself gained a bronze medal for an exhibit in the Chelsea Flower Show.

The Glynde School, with Gertrude Jekyll, Ellen Willmott, and Mrs. Theresa Earle as its patrons, went from strength to strength, and Lady Wolseley saw her students as future head gardeners on large, private estates, as teachers of botany, and even as owners of their own market gardens. Other training establishments began to follow her example, and by 1907 University

College at Reading was permitting both men and women to take R.H.S. (Royal Horticultural Society) examinations, in addition to awarding diplomas to all of its students, irrespective of gender. Swanley students continued to receive their diplomas, and in 1911 the National Political League was formed to help ladies find employment on the land. The Royal Botanic Society in London's Regent's Park and the Edinburgh School for Women Gardeners catered solely to women students, while the London County Council started to offer horticultural training at both day and evening classes.

In April 1901, the Countess of Warwick stated that "although a considerable number of women students at her hostel had been established in careers both remunerative and useful, yet the scheme had outgrown the limits of one woman's responsibilities and means."[2] Accordingly, in 1903, the Lady Warwick Hostel, initiated in 1898, moved to Studley Castle in Warwickshire and by 1904 had given training to 146 full-time students. While Lady Warwick's dream of placing females who had no intention of marrying on agricultural settlements both in this country and in the colonies failed to transpire, the three-year training program itself met with success. It is interesting to note, however, that the majority of women horticultural students at this time came from the professional classes and not from the upper classes, which this establishment had initially tried to target.

Edwardian gentlewomen had an extensive knowledge of the poets of nature. They also studied and painted wildflowers and read books on botany, some of which were written by women. They keenly observed plants and their habits and the animals for which they provided food and shelter. These leisure pursuits and educational activities were considered "proper" and fitting to their station in life.

Edith Holden, however, unlike most of these young women, had real artistic talent. From the age of thirteen she was a pupil at the Birmingham School of Art, and, when she was twenty, her tutors suggested that she study with Joseph Denovan Adam, a well-known animal painter of the time. The Holden family moved from rural Warwickshire to Olton, near Birmingham, and Holden's *Nature Notes for 1906* were written over the first year she spent in her new home. In them she recorded all the birds and flowers she had observed in this new and unfamiliar area.

There were, of course, those eminent lady gardeners who had not received any formal training as such for their chosen vocation. Ellen Willmott, who inherited Warley Place in Essex after the death of her parents, was a very wealthy young woman who was able to spend vast sums of money on her garden and is reputed to have employed more than eighty gardeners to tend it. A friend of Gertrude Jekyll, who described her as "the greatest of living women gardeners," Willmott also acquired properties and gardens in the south of France and in Italy.[3] She made a serious study of botany and in 1904 became the first female Fellow of the Linnaean Society. Her love of flowers, particularly roses, is evident in her writing, and she was closely associated with the National Rose Society. Willmott's *The Genus Rosa* was published in parts between 1910 and 1914.

Her garden at Warley, with its collection of rare plants, gained international repute and was used to illustrate her book *Warley Garden in Spring and Summer* (1909). Willmott knew many of the famous horticulturists of the day, was a life member of the Royal Horticultural Society and a trustee of the RHS Gardens at Wisley, and was awarded the Victoria Medal of Honour in Horticulture. She was greatly influenced by the ideas of gardener and writer William Robinson, an advocate of a natural style of gardening, creating the Warley alpine and wild gardens so much admired. Many plants were named after her or her garden, which sadly turned into a wilderness when she lost most of her fortune in German investments during World War I. She was forced to spend the rest of her days in virtual pauperism.

Mrs. Theresa Earle, a contemporary of Ellen Willmott, came to gardening late in life after the death of her husband. Talented, artistic, and well read, Mrs. Earle broadened her horizons by travel, writing *Pot-pourri from a Surrey Garden* in 1897 when in her sixties, followed by *More Pot-Pourri* and *Pot-Pourri Mixed by Two.* She wrote in a practical way, responding to various horticultural questions and problems with practical answers and suggestions, and regularly attended shows of the Royal Horticultural Society in Westminster, from which much of her knowledge came. Earle was also greatly influenced by William Robinson's *The English Flower Garden* (1883), frequently quoted in her books, which soon proved indispensable to country house society.

There were many similarities between Mrs. Earle and Miss Gertrude Jekyll; both ladies were artistic and educated, and both enjoyed cooking and foreign travel. Gertrude Jekyll also came late to gardening when extreme myopia ended her career as an artist. Jekyll, too, was extremely practical, encapsulating her considerable artistic knowledge and tastes within her gardening. Ever enthusiastic and interested in everything around her, she bought a fifteen-acre plot of land in Munstead Heath, south of Godalming, in the 1880s, which she called Munstead Wood. The garden that she made there, influenced as it was by the arts and crafts movement, the ecological ideas of William Robinson, and her own mastery of the use of color and knowledge of the great gardens of England and Europe, was breathtakingly beautiful.

The triangular plot, which was divided into three areas, included a kitchen garden and nursery ground, a flower garden, and a woodland garden. Six years after she had begun her garden at Munstead, Jekyll met the talented architect Edwin Lutyens, with whom she formed a partnership that was to endure until the outbreak of the First World War. Together they designed and completed eighty houses and gardens before 1913 and collaborated on the planting of the war grave cemeteries when hostilities ceased.

Lutyens designed both the cottage that Jekyll so lovingly called "The Hut" and the Munstead Wood house, an embodiment of all the finest techniques of the arts and crafts movement. The Munstead Wood house was completed in 1897, after which time Jekyll was able to finish her garden while undertaking the many design commissions that were offered to her. Motivated by her firm belief in the unity of house and garden, she sought perfection, inspiring a new generation of gardeners and using Munstead Wood as the basis for her prolific writings, *Wood and Garden* (1899), *Home and Garden* (1900), *Wall and Water Garden* (1901), *Flower Decoration in the Home* (1907), and *Colour Schemes for the Flower Garden* (1908) being some of her best known works.

THE MUNSTEAD WOOD MAIN FLOWER BORDER

Jekyll planted her Munstead herbaceous border with a painter's eye, using controlled colors, combined with order, to create a picture. The "main hardy flower border," as she called it, was 61 1/2 m. (200 ft.) long and 4 1/3 m. (14 ft.) wide. It was sheltered from the north by a sandstone wall 3 1/3 m. (11 ft.) high and covered with bay and laurustinus, choisya, cistus, and loquat planted in a 90 cm. (3 ft.) wide border, in front of which was an alley, invisible from the front of the border but convenient for working at the back. These shrubs, Jekyll maintained, "show as a handsome background to the flowering plants."[4]

Gertrude Jekyll was of the opinion that the border itself should be at its best in late summer and that no attempt should be made to have it in full flower in June, the time when the later-blooming perennials were beginning to cover the ground. Clumps of *Iris Pallida dalmatica*, however, could already be glimpsed earlier in June among the grey foliage and the blue-purple blooms of *Geranium ibericum platyphyllum*, and the white, slow-growing *Dictamnus fraxinella* was to be spotted together with white and pink meadowsweets, foxgloves, and Canterbury bells. Long-established *Iberis sempervirens* were to be found growing onto the path at the front of the bed, and *Yucca gloriosa* and *Y. recurva* were beginning to throw up spikes as bushes of ornamental *Euphorbia wulfenii* turned greener and *Choisya ternata* and *Clematis montana* continued to bloom in the middle of the wall.

Vibrant color was added by brilliant displays of Oriental poppies, intermingled with gypsophila and dark orange *Lilium croceum*. While dahlias and hollyhocks had already been planted out, any bare spaces in the border were filled with half-hardy annuals—African marigolds, pure white single petunias, ageratum, tall striped maize, white cosmos, sulphur sunflowers, *phlox drummondii*, nasturtiums, and *Trachelium caeruleum*—and with bedding plants such as geraniums, salvias, begonias, gazanias, calceolarias, and verbena.

Before planting, the border was dug and cleared of weeds, and a mulch of half-rotted leaves and old hotbed material applied. At each end of the border, for which Miss Jekyll used a specific color scheme, stachys, santolina, *Cineraria maritima*, sea-kale, and lyme grass formed the groundwork of grey foliage, together with rue, yucca, and *Clematis recta*. At the western end, flowers of blue, grey-blue, white, palest yellow, and palest pink were partially intergrouped and partially planted in masses. The coloring then went through stronger yellows to orange and red, with the strongest colors in the middle of the border. The strength of the color then receded through orange and deep yellow to pale yellow, white, and palest pink against a blue-grey foliage, until purples and lilacs were reached at the eastern end.

When viewed in front and from a distance, the whole border could be seen as one picture, "the cool colouring at the ends

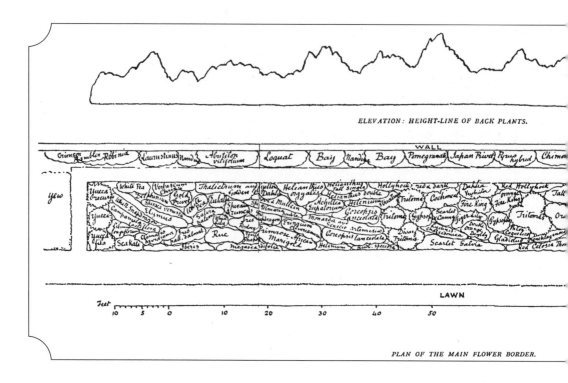

ELEVATION: HEIGHT-LINE OF BACK PLANTS.

PLAN OF THE MAIN FLOWER BORDER.

enhancing the brilliant warmth of the middle." But, when viewed from the wide path next to the border, each portion became a picture in itself, every one of which was "of such a colouring that it best prepares the eye, in accordance with natural law, for what is to follow."

Trailing nasturtiums were grown at the base of the poppies and trained to cover a large part of the brown seed heads of the gypsophila in autumn, while the white everlasting pea was planted behind the delphiniums, the seed pods of which were removed to allow the white peas to trail over them. When the peas had finished flowering, they were replaced by clematis, and tall plants such as *Helianthus orgyalis* were trained down at the back of the yellow part of the border. Other plants treated in this way were the tall rudbeckia "Golden Glow," dahlias, and michaelmas daisies, as well as antirrhinums, the leaf axils of which would throw up flower stalks that would cover the whole area with blooms. Thus, by the end of July, the whole border was beginning to reflect Miss Jekyll's scheme, although it was really at its best during the second week of August.

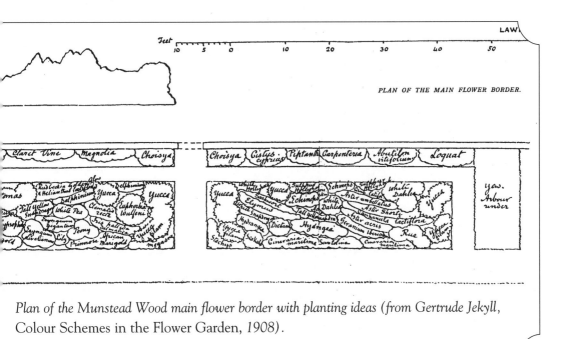

Feet
10 5 0 10 20 30 40 50

PLAN OF THE MAIN FLOWER BORDER.

Claret Vine Magnolia Choisya   Choisya Cistus Piptanth Carpenteria Abutilon Loquat
                                           cyprius   vitifolium

Yew.
Arbour
under

Plan of the Munstead Wood main flower border with planting ideas (from Gertrude Jekyll, Colour Schemes in the Flower Garden, 1908).

British Cottage Gardens

While well-heeled Americans were experimenting with fresh planting ideas from Great Britain, the British upper and middle classes were using cottage planting as a basis for their herbaceous borders. Dating back to the Middle Ages, the cottage garden itself was simple in layout, with straight paths, a jumble of old-fashioned flowers, and rose arches over the doorway. Vegetables were grown in rows, along with gooseberry and currant bushes, raspberry canes, and strawberries, while herbs, mixed with other plants, flourished near the kitchen door.

In *Lark Rise*, Flora Thompson writes that cottage women cultivated a flower garden in which "they grew all the sweet old-fashioned cottage garden flowers, pinks and sweet williams and love-in-a-mist, wallflowers and forget-me-nots in spring and hollyhocks and Michaelmas daisies in autumn. Then there were lavender and sweetbriar bushes, and southernwood, sometimes called "lad's love." It is interesting to note, though, that "the women never worked in the vegetable gardens or on the allotments, even when they had their children off hand and had plenty of spare time, for there was a strict division of labour and that was 'men's work'.... Any work outside the home was considered unwomanly."[5]

Because money was in short supply, cottage women collected their own seeds, often exchanging them with their neighbors. Plants would also be taken from the wild, and genera that could be propagated easily were widely grown, with the odd, unusual specimen arriving from the estates of the gentry if one of the village men happened to be employed there as a gardener. The women also grew plants in pots both inside and outside their cottages. Terracotta urns stood in shady corners and by doors, and pots of geraniums, begonias, and calceolarias filled windowsills and obscured the light.

Bright, scented flowers were cultivated in abundance, many self-seeding from year to year within borders so full of plants that there was virtually no soil to be seen between them. Most cottage women had little spare time to spend on their gardens, so the plants were, of necessity, hardy, not prone to disease, easy to increase, and strong-growing. Gertrude Jekyll observes in *Old West Surrey* that "the old double white rose, brother of the pretty pink Maiden's Blush, never seems so happy or looks so well as in a cottage garden,"[6] while in small greenhouses hydrangeas, fuchsias, lilies, begonias, and geraniums were grown, with half-hardy annuals in pots and a clematis over the door.

Apple trees abounded, and rhubarb was forced in old buckets and terracotta pots. Because meat was a luxury for the cottager, vegetable production took priority. Peas, beans, potatoes, and root crops were widely cultivated, and any spare produce was sold off at the local market to generate extra income. There was no garden design or "scheme," as such, but rather a hodgepodge of color and perfume as larkspurs, cornflowers, hollyhocks, sunflowers, and red-hot pokers jostled for position, with polyanthus, laced pinks, and auriculas, originally florists' flowers, surviving in later years only in the gardens of the cottagers.

Women participated in local shows where cottagers could exhibit their prize vegetables. "The fact is not a little remarkable, and certainly gratifying, that in country districts where women make a complete 'hobby' of raising vegetables and flowers, they succeed remarkably well, as the awards at horticultural shows where they exhibit will prove." One old lady in the south of England had a large garden "in which she raised such remarkably good specimens as to carry all before her, except to beat one rival competitor, and he was the village policeman."[7]

Flowers for cutting were often grown by cottage women, both to display indoors and to decorate the local church on Sundays. As the century progressed, the decorative use of cut flowers became very popular with all classes of society. Cut flowers also provided an attractive business proposition for any lady who was "well-equipped with a love of the work, with a desire to learn, and with capital enough to tide her over the first year."[8]

Flowers were worn in abundance by Edwardian ladies, and the gentlemen sported fresh flowers in buttonholes. In London, cockney flower women with large wicker baskets cried their wares outside the entrances to city theatres. Floral decorations at the dinner table would often match the gown of the hostess, and *epergnes*, ornate tiered centerpieces, were still popular, although they were longer and lower than in Victorian times for ease of conversation. More open flower arrangements were introduced at this time. For example, in *Flower Decoration in the House* (1907), Gertrude Jekyll suggested an arrangement whereby a central bowl of flowers was linked to individual bowls by means of sprays of foliage laying on the table. It was also a time when "large fortunes" were being made from carnation culture and when many lady gardeners specialized "in Parma violets, and Russians grown in frames" and who made "very useful incomes from the art."

Gertrude Jekyll writes:

I have learnt much from the little cottage gardens that help to make our English waysides the prettiest in the temperate world. One can hardly go into the smallest cottage garden without learning or observing something new. It may be some two plants growing beautifully together by some happy chance, or a pretty mixed tangle of creepers, or something that one has always thought must have a south wall doing better on an east one.[9]

Miss Jekyll exploited the informality of the cottage garden in her planting schemes, as, for the first time, cottage garden plants began to appear in the gardens of the wealthy, often in the herbaceous borders she planted, making these gardens ever more stylish and sophisticated in those last lazy days before the clouds of war began to gather.

Technology and Consumerism in America

By 1900, virtually every industrial nation had become aware of an upsurge in consumer spending brought about by an overwhelming desire at all levels of society for a materialistic display of wealth which manufacturers were quick to recognize and act upon. Advertising was expanded, as were ploys to promote sales and to develop new retail outlets. Department stores, such as Macy's in New York City, had been established during the second half of the nineteenth century. These stores used visual means to appeal to potential customers, such as large windows of temptingly packaged products and expert window dressing to entice prospective purchasers inside. The wealthy, of course, needed little encouragement. They had always enjoyed spending money, as in 1905, for example, at a ball given by Mrs. Astor, when 3,000 roses were used to decorate a table.

This was also a time when, because of the expanse of rural areas between major towns, the mail-order catalog became popular, allowing country dwellers to buy goods which normally they would not have had the opportunity to acquire. As new items such as sewing machines, typewriters, and domestic appliances began to flood the market, it became obvious that new methods of selling them would be needed. Accordingly, credit buying was made available, and sales programs were developed involving traveling salesmen visiting the homes of potential customers to demonstrate these new and very desirable luxury items.

The dawn of the new century brought many changes. Manners became less formal as middle- and working-class women took employment in shops and offices and walked the streets without a chaperone. Better-heeled women, who now had more time on their hands partly brought about by the new advances in technology, wandered leisurely around the department stores, some of which boasted refreshment rooms where unaccompanied women could sit and drink coffee without fear of being thought "fast."

The early 1900s saw the emergence of the "S-bend" figure as the mass production of fashionable clothing gained momentum. It was a time when manner of dress proclaimed an individual's station in life. The "New Woman" wanted her clothes to be a statement of her independence while still retaining her femininity. This was achieved by stiff corsets to nip in the waist and by wearing severe, almost masculine, outer garments that added a deceptive air of fragility and delicacy to the wearer. Tight lacing was frowned upon, and clothes became more fluid as the century progressed, with the coat and skirt becoming extremely popular as street wear in both Europe and the United States. Severely cut blouses and sober hued skirts were also high fashion. By way of contrast, though, in May 1913, ladies wore frilly paper dresses trimmed with daisies and roses to May Day parties.

At the turn of the century, it was thought that women should indulge in only moderate exercise and that anything too vigorous might result in them being unable to bear healthy children. Male sports were definitely not permitted, although, as the century wore on, women did take part in skating, golf, and badminton. Both tennis and gymnastics were considered ideal exercise for women, but cycling was frowned upon.

The Women's Organizations

Employment for women outside the home was frowned upon by the majority of American men at this time. They considered women to be both physically and mentally incapable of coping with paid employment, and they were outraged at the idea of a married woman neglecting her domestic duties to take up a job outside the confines of the home. Industrial expansion, however, increased the demand for labor, and more and more women began to take up paid employment even though they were receiving only half the wages of a man in the same job.

With the advent of the twentieth century, new women's organizations started to embroil themselves in women's concerns. Women in factories, for instance, strove to improve their working conditions, and the Women's Trade Union League linked the improvement of industrial conditions to women's suffrage. The National Federation of Business and Professional Women's Organizations was founded by businesswomen and mothers, while teachers and nurses created groups of their own. The Young Women's Christian Association came into being at this time, as did the Girl Scouts and clubs for working women.

Many of the women's groups concerned themselves with politics. The National Woman Suffrage Association and its rival, the American Woman Suffrage Association, both founded in the 1860s, worked to secure the franchise for women under their new, amalgamated name—The National American Woman Suffrage Association (NAWSA)—after the two organizations merged in 1890. Conditions for a more widespread protest started to emerge as women's role began to be questioned in earnest.

In 1890 the General Federation of Women's Clubs had been created, and the state federations in 1894. By 1912, the Federation had more than 1 million members, and club aims were laid out in the "Federation Bulletin and Club Woman." Consumer and conservation issues were seen as important, as were settlement projects and the protection of women and children by law. Wealthy women were encouraged to help those of lesser means so that there would be no class discrimination amongst members, allowing the Federation to operate in a democratic way. The Federation, incidentally, was proud of the strong position of U.S. women, although it did tend to focus not upon women's rights but upon the services women could perform, as it continually ignored the pressure to endorse suffragist views.

During the years leading up to World War I, suffrage and prohibition were the dual causes of the women's movements. Protests of American activitists were no less vociferous than those of their British sisters. American women resorted to acts of violence and individual state campaigns, with militant female temperance supporters setting fire to saloons in Kansas, Missouri, and Massachusetts. The American Equal Rights Association demanded the vote not only for women but also for Negroes. The New England Suffrage Association, however, confined itself to the single issue of female enfranchisement.

On 8 March 1907, a march of war widows and women garment workers took place in New York. These women were demanding equal rights and better working conditions. The police intervened, and many of the women were arrested. The following year, again on 8 March, women in the needle trade marched in the Lower East Side of New York to commemorate the anniversary of the previous protest. As before, the police were there to meet them as they protested against child labor and sweatshops and demanded that women be given the vote.

As a result of these two marches, it was proposed at the Second International Conference of Socialist Women, held in Copenhagan in 1910, that the protests be remembered annually and that 8 March be designated as International Women's Day. This proposal was sanctioned, but, by the end of the 1930s, the day was no longer recognized. It was re-instated, however, in the early 1970s, and the United Nations gave the day official recognition in 1978.

American Gardening As Recreation and Vocation

While Gertrude Jekyll was planting her English gardens, on the other side of the Atlantic horticulture was becoming more and more popular, in spite of the fact that the prejudice against physical contact with the soil by women was still prevalent. The advent of the automobile brought with it a growth in suburban life, and millions of U.S. citizens began to take up gardening as a recreational pursuit. The variety of available plants increased with hybridization, and the market was flooded with horticultural books and magazines, with garden clubs, nurseries, and plant societies springing up like so many mushrooms.

In the early 1900s, Mrs. Francis (Louisa) King moved with her husband to their new home, Orchard House, in Alma, Michigan. Influenced by her mother-in-law's interest in herbs, and by the ideas of William Robinson and Gertrude Jekyll, Mrs. King set about planting the Orchard House garden, which she was to immortalize in her books.

In 1910, her first gardening article was published in *The Garden*, in which she wrote about flowers and how they could enhance each other and a succession of blooms be achieved. Throughout her writings ran the theme of the perennial garden, its design, color scheme, and plants. To gardeners of affluent means she recommended the services of a landscape architect, but to those in impecunious circumstances she gave help, advice, and ideas, suggesting, for example, that a "trial" garden, hidden from view, might be cultivated where plants could be grown before being placed in the main display area.

In 1912, Mrs. King helped to establish the Garden Club of Michigan, of which she was the first president, becoming founder and vice president of the Garden Club of America the following year. At a time when women were largely excluded from the professions and higher education, Mrs. King influenced women's thoughts toward horticulture as a force for democracy through both her writings and the organizations she helped to establish.

In the nineteenth century, hobby gardening became very popular in America. Those who had the time, opportunity, and money went into the country to develop gardens purely for aesthetic purposes. The Cornish Colony of New Hampshire started its life in 1885 when the sculptor Augustus Saint-Gaudens began spending his summers there and his friends started to turn the farmhouses into summer residences and pasture land into gardens.

Known as the home of good architecture and good gardening, the Cornish art colony was dense with art and with gardens, some of them small, all of them simple but beautiful. The gardens at Cornish showed deference to site and prospect. Every garden was individual and personal to its creator. The emphasis was placed on work rather than leisure, and hired labor, except when absolutely necessary, was frowned upon, as each garden was kept within the care of its owner. Interestingly, the Cornish Colony vigorously supported women's rights, founding the Cornish Equal Suffrage League in 1911.

It was to Cornish that Rose Nichols came with her parents in 1889 and Ellen Shipman visited with her husband in 1893. During her early years at the Colony, Ellen Shipman became an extremely competent gardener under the encouragement and guidance of Charles Platt, a master of formal landscape design. Eventually, she was able to establish her own practice as a landscape architect, opening an office in Cornish in 1912 and working with Platt on some of his garden design commissions.

Rose Nichols took drawing and architecture lessons from Platt while studying horticulture at the Bussey Institute. She pursued her architectural studies at the Massachusetts Institute of Technology and the Beaux Arts School of Architecture in Paris and apprenticed herself to a New York architect. Nichols augmented her knowledge by traveling widely and by visiting gardens on the Continent. Consequently, by 1903 she was able to list herself as a landscape architect, receiving her first commission for a private estate in Newport, Rhode Island in 1904.

American writer Frances Duncan gained most of her horticultural expertise working in a tree nursery in New York and eventually became the assistant editor of *Country Calendar*. After seeing Cornish for the first time, she was so impressed with the Colony's gardens that she bought a cottage close by so she could write about them from first-hand experience. During her long career she wrote many articles and books, including *Mary's Garden and How It Grew* (1904), *The Joyous Art of Gardening* (1917), and *Home Vegetables and Small Fruits* (1918).

Many American women who were practicing landscape architects at this time wrote books on the subject, in which they usually placed great emphasis on design, composition, organization, and the use of color in the flower garden, the areas with which they were most involved. The books produced by these landscape architects were written in a style that would interest and influence their mainly female readership and encourage readers to respond to newfound opportunities in landscaping. Intelligent, educated amateur gardeners also wrote books, often about their own gardens. Helena Rutherfurd Ely, for instance, wrote *Woman's Hardy Garden* in 1903, and Bostonian Mabel Cabot Sedgwick published *The Garden Month by Month* in 1907, which contains many lists of herbaceous plants arranged both by color and by the month in which they flower.

For the working and middle classes, gardens at this time were generally laid out in the style of the cottage garden, tastefully designed and beautifully kept. Enclosed by vine-covered fences or by hedges, these gardens were planted with shrubs (in 1913, white lilac, forsythia, pink japonica, and rose bushes could be purchased for 25¢) and with hardy perennials that were often placed in rectangular shaped beds, bisected by gravel or grass paths. Hollyhocks, sweet Williams, foxgloves, phlox, larkspur, and dahlias all grew in profusion. Old gardens and their flowers witnessed an upsurge in popularity, and continuous bloom brought about by a succession of flowers was very important. Carefully chosen hardy perennials, annuals, and bulbs gave a sequence of flowers from April to November.

In Virginia, old gardens were filled with shrubs and perennials. Here, flower beds bordered with box could be found, the focal point of the garden being a sundial that added a touch of formality. Intersecting paths radiated from the sundial, and the whole garden was enclosed by flowering shrubs. Meanwhile, the old, traditional, family gardens continued much as before, with any new ones being planted in the old style.

The 1890s onward witnessed the return to Great Britain of wealthy Americans, people who had either made or inherited vast amounts of money in the States and who had decided to migrate back to the "Old Country." In 1893, William Waldorf Astor bought Cliveden, in Taplow, Buckinghamshire, and in 1907, Mrs. Gertrude Winthrop bought The Manor, Hidcote Bartrim, in the Cotswolds, Somerset, for her son Lawrence Johnston. Not surprisingly, the arrival of Americans such as these resulted in a blend of the New World, the classical, and the English cottage-garden styles of gardening, peppered as they were with a French sophistication.

Impending War

The people of the Edwardian Era had witnessed the birth of the welfare state, the continuing double standards of a society in which men upheld their social dominance over women, and the tireless struggle of the suffragettes to win the right to vote and to divide the all-male ruling class. But life for the majority of the British people had been tranquil and uncomplicated. Now, at the end of the "Golden Age," the peaceful years were giving way to the inevitability of the German might. Fears of war were ever present. The nation was on the brink of the greatest war the world had ever known, in which millions would be killed and families torn apart. Life as the British people then knew it was about to disappear, and nothing would ever be the same again.

CHAPTER SEVEN

WORLD WAR I

Of Patriotism and Women's Suffrage

THE OUTBREAK OF THE FIRST WORLD WAR on 4 August 1914 was greeted by the British public with a surge of patriotic enthusiasm. On that glorious August bank holiday weekend, no one doubted the outcome of the war or that it would be over by Christmas. For those who enjoyed the summer sunshine, life was exhilarating and the prospect of war an exciting one. Few people realized that the feverish euphoria gripping the country would soon burn itself out and that national pride would eventually be overtaken by tragedy and loss as the grim and bloody conflict wore on.

"Your Country Needs You," proclaimed posters showing the face and pointing finger of Lord Kitchener, Secretary of State for War, in a dramatic appeal for the "first hundred thousand" volunteers to enlist. The response was impressive: 750,000 men took the colors in August and September, the number rising to 1 million by the end of the year as working-class men followed the patriotic lead of the government and the upper and middle classes.

In the early months of the war, rumors of spies and saboteurs were rife. Germans, or those with German-sounding names, came under attack, and emotions ran high as war fever mounted. Strikes were called in factories employing foreign labor, and pacifist meetings ended in violence.

For those left at home, the biggest disruption to civilian life, apart from increasing food prices and Zeppelin raids, was the government's intrusion into their day-to-day activities. Under the terms of the Defence of the Realm Act (DORA) of 8 August 1914, the government was empowered to secure "the public safety and defence of the realm." The Act was revised throughout the four years of conflict, enabling the government to take over factories, control food supplies and distribution, determine air-raid precautions, and instigate press censorship.

As women began to replace men in a wide range of jobs, their role and status changed dramatically. For the first time, working-class girls were able to choose employment other than the traditional domestic service. The number of women employed in July 1914 was 3,224,600, rising to 4,814,600 in January 1918, with many of them doing work never before done by women.

Women still labored under the "double standards" of Edwardian times, however, in what was basically a man's world, filled with chauvinistic attitudes and prejudice. Nevertheless, the war accelerated the process of emancipation, bringing with it a certain laxity in sexual morality and an increase in economic and personal freedom, which were visible in the confident behavior and changing appearance of women in general. Newspapers were filled with complaints about their short skirts and cropped hair, as morals declined, class barriers were lifted, and emotions heightened by the carnage on the battlefields of France.

Women Join the War Effort

With the declaration of war, suffragette militancy was suspended, all imprisoned suffragettes released, and the WSPU placed at the disposal of the government. Christabel Pankhurst, newly returned from exile, toured the country with her mother, who explained to the country's women at packed meetings the "right is might" German policy while Christabel called for national food rationing and for married women to have an income of their own.

On 17 July 1915, at the suggestion of Lloyd George, then Minister for Munitions, and anxious for women to enter the factories, Mrs. Pankhurst organized a mass march of some 20,000 women demanding the "Right to Serve." And in that same summer, amidst protests from Members of Parliament that women were non-voters and should not be included, the National Registration Bill came into force, officially recognizing women as a necessary part of the war effort. On 15 August, under the terms of the bill, all men and women between the ages of 15 and 65 had to register their ages and occupations.

The vexed question of how far the feminist movement should go in supporting the war effort, rather than pursuing its pre-war aims, was answered by Mrs. Pankhurst, who attested that suffragism should be abandoned in favor of patriotism. Many suffragettes handed out white feathers to young men in civilian clothes, and non-suffragettes, fired by the rhetoric of Christabel and her mother, joined them.

Both Emmeline Pankhurst and her daughter made national propaganda and recruitment their prime targets, although Mrs. Pankhurst gravitated more and more toward employing women in the interests of the nation. Christabel, aware of the government's anxiety about securing the military involvement of the United States, went on two occasions, 24 October 1914 and 30 January 1915, to address largely pacifist women's suffrage audiences in New York's Carnegie Hall. By October 1915, the feminist newspaper *The Suffragette* had been patriotically renamed *Britannia*, its pages reinforcing the necessity for military conscription, the war of attrition, and the internment of aliens. The Pankhursts worked tirelessly to convince the female population that the "Women of Britain Say—Go!"

The membership of the National Union of Women's Suffrage Societies (NUWSS) fell to 33,000 in 1916, partly because its middle-class members occupied themselves with voluntary organizations and partly because of its opposition to the war. A new Women's Service Bureau was set up by the NUWSS to assist women faced with unemployment and to provide information about helping the war effort. This was followed by a Women's Interests Committee, the aims of which were to demonstrate that women were capable of undertaking men's work and to prevent the exploitation of cheap female labor.

The laudable approach of the suffrage movement allowed women to utilize the opportunities afforded by the war. The movement's cause was helped by the establishment of a Ministry of Munitions, which actively encouraged women into the munitions factories, by the First Military Service Bill of 5 January 1916, conscripting single men between the ages of 19 and 30, and by the Universal Conscription Bill, at the beginning of May, which conscripted all men, single or married, within this same age group. While women themselves were not "called up," as such, they were required, under the terms of the various government and voluntary schemes (the Women's Land Army, for example), to sign a contract that committed them to either six or twelve months' national service.

WOMEN AGRICULTURAL WORKERS As industrial production came to a halt, the immediate economic effect of the outbreak of war was to create unemployment, particularly among women. It was a situation that was soon reversed, however, as the requirements of the armed forces produced a new demand for labor. In addition to employment in munitions factories, there was also a need for female agricultural labor at a time when British farmers were producing just twenty percent of the country's wheat and £5.5 million ($8.25 million) of vegetables were imported from abroad. Food imports were high, fifty percent in 1914, and the government never questioned the Royal Navy's ability to keep them at this level, despite the menace of German U-boat attacks.

At first, no priority was given to growing food. Farmers themselves had little idea of how the country's food production stood because, like the majority of the population, they believed the war would be over in a matter of months. Their main concern at that time, in addition to the requisitioning of some 9,000 draught horses by the army, was the recruitment of skilled farmworkers into the armed services, leaving a dearth of male labor. The government's proposed plan to replace these workers with volunteer women, some of whom had been activists in the women's suffrage movement, was met with rage and dissension on the part of the farmers.

The government had also decided not to give farmers any financial incentives to increase their acreage of cereals, a decision based on the peacetime "Report of the Royal Commission on Agriculture of 1903." The Report had stated that there was little risk of the supply of imported food ceasing and therefore no real reason for the government "to protect domestic agriculture."

By the spring of 1915, the situation worsened as the U-boat blockade intensified. Food prices soared, and the government's enlistment campaign beggared the agricultural industry of its male workforce. And yet, many women who volunteered for agricultural work failed to find employment because farmers baulked at the idea of putting women to work on the land, preferring instead to employ schoolboys and elderly men. The harvest of that year, however, saw a twenty percent increase in wheat planted by those farmers shrewd enough to realize that prices would rise, with or without government intervention.

In response to the crisis, a committee headed by Lord Milner was established to look into the country's food production and formulate ways of increasing it, should the war continue after the harvest of 1916. Its recommendations were that farmers should be given financial incentives to plough up grassland and a guaranteed minimum price for wheat, in return for changing crop rotations and discarding outmoded farming methods.

Lord Selborne, president of the Board of Agriculture from May 1915 until June 1916, recommended that War Agricultural Executive Committees (WAECs) be appointed, although these were not to prove effective until December 1916, when the newly formed coalition government, under the leadership of Lloyd George, came into power. And it wasn't until January 1917 that the much-needed Food Production Department within the Board of Agriculture was established, after which the 1917 Corn Production Act came into force and matters finally improved.

With the abatement of the U-boat threat in the summer of 1915, the government failed to respond. The harvest of 1915 was good, in spite of the haphazard assortment of labor, mostly military, made available by the government; and continuing supplies of imported grain from Argentina and America helped to diffuse the situation. Lord Selborne appealed to farmers to increase their food production, but his plea for patriotism went largely unheeded. Farmers continued to plough their usual acreage, although this, in fact, dropped below the pre-war average, mainly because no guaranteed minimum prices were forthcoming and the ever-present threat of the recruitment of more skilled male workers remained.

One of the tasks of the WAECs was the organization of female labor, and in February 1916, Women's Farm Labour Committees were set up with their own district committees and village registrars. Any woman registering for work was given a certificate and a green armband with a red crown after 30 days' service. The wages were low, the estimated rate for 1918 being

2s.10d. (21¢) a day, and the work heavy and dirty. Yet the spring and summer of 1916 saw 140,000 volunteer village women variously employed in gardening, weeding, and fruit and hop picking. Fifty percent of these women were given certificates and almost all received green armbands.

While the government encouraged village women to return to the land, it was also eager to attract middle-class women from urban areas. Accordingly, a mobile unit, the Women's National Land Service Corps (WNLSC), was formed in January 1914, with a strength of 2,000 workers by the end of the first year. After six weeks' initial training, these women were then put to work on farms as ploughwomen, milkers, and carters (drivers of two-wheeled horse-drawn carts).

With true patrician grace, upper-class ladies made their presence felt in many areas of the war effort. Lady Londonderry recruited women land workers through the agricultural section of the Women's Legion, formerly the Women's Emergency Corps and Women's Volunteer Reserve, bullying the Board of Agriculture into giving her a grant of two hundred pounds. The venture failed, however, and eventually was closed down. Meanwhile, competitions in agricultural skills were held exclusively for women throughout the spring and summer of 1916, but they did little to change the attitude of the farmers regarding female employment, most of them continuing to opt for a man, skilled or unskilled, in preference to a woman.

That autumn, Asquith's government was urged to impose state control on the war effort, in all its forms, and to dispense with the mixture of voluntary and government-controlled schemes, the former usually organized by strong-willed, upper-class ladies bent on having their own way. The harvest of that year was poor; wheat stood at 58s.5d. ($4.38) per quarter, and the weather was cold and wet. Storms and flooding in the early part of the year had retarded crop growth, with the result that winter wheat was below average and hay was storm-damaged.

German U-boat activity was at its height in the spring of 1917; passenger and merchant ships were torpedoed, and corn supplies were low. The government rather belatedly ordered farmers to plough up an extra 2.5 million acres of land to ensure the success of the 1918 harvest. Wastelands, parklands, and ornamental gardens went under the plough in the autumn of 1917, with farmers requesting 50,000 soldiers to help. By

Christmas, in view of the heavy casualties at Passchendale, the farmers had received just 35,000. They were, however, offered the services of the newly formed Women's Land Army (WLA) and had little choice but to accept.

THE WOMEN'S LAND ARMY The Women's Land Army had started as the Women's National Land Service Corps (WNLSC), founded in 1914 under the sponsorship of the Women's Farm and Garden Union, which was formed in 1910. The WNLSC strove to create a favorable impression among rural communities regarding the employment of female labor; in 1916, it had placed 870 women on the land. Taken over by the government in 1917 to become the Women's Land Army, the organization continued to operate its Land Service Corps, recruiting part-time labor for harvesting and fruit-picking, some of its members later becoming instructors and forewomen to the new WLA recruits. It provided sterling service in recruiting 4,000 volunteers to bring in several thousand acres of flax in the summer of 1918 at a time when the crop was in great demand for aircraft wing fabric and military tents and equipment.

With the formation of the WLA, under the direction of Dame Meriel Talbot, the total number of women employed on the land in July 1918 was 113,000, a rise of 33,000 over the summer of 1914. The first appeal for volunteers, which went out in March 1917, was met with a response of 30,000 women, most of whom left non-manual occupations to enlist.

The WLA was divided into three different sections: agricultural, forage, and timber cutting. The agricultural and timber-cutting sections required women to enroll for a minimum of either six or twelve months, while the minimum service time for the more specialized forage section was a year.

All new recruits were issued a WLA handbook, which contained the following directive:

> *You are doing a man's work and so you are dressed rather like a man; but remember that just because you wear a smock and breeches you should take care to behave like an English girl who expects chivalry and respect from everyone she meets. Noisy or ugly behaviour brings discredit, not only upon yourself but upon the uniform, and the whole Women's Land Army.*[1]

Land girls were not permitted to be seen without an overall after working hours, to smoke in public, to wear jewelry, to frequent public houses, or to put their hands in their pockets. They were often expected to be in bed by 9:00 P.M. in the winter and 9:30 P.M. in the summer, a rule that was invariably ignored. Land girls worked six days a week, with Sunday a free day, and were often billeted in poor accommodations. They earned a minimum weekly wage of 18s. ($1.35) in 1916, rising to 20s. or 22s. in 1918, depending on whether or not they had gained a certificate of training. Out of this meager wage, incidentally, a deduction was taken for board and lodging.

The registration and selection of new recruits was a long, drawn-out procedure. Candidates, having first decided on their length of service time, then had to appear before a selection board. The two main requirements were morality and mobility; girls could be sent anywhere in the country where their services were needed. For this, they received a free uniform, a weekly wage, and free travel on taking up or changing employment.

The selection board was required to take up references, a slow and laborious task that was often abandoned. Consequently, many able girls were turned down, while others, not prepared to wait, found employment through the Labour Exchanges or enlisted with one of the other recruiting agencies.

The Board of Agriculture questioned whether it was worth the expense of training women when the war might soon be over. County authorities, agricultural colleges, and farm institutes, which had always provided courses for men, were reluctant to adapt them or to supply new ones for women. Some colleges mounted training courses of several weeks' duration, for which a fee was charged, but, eventually, members of the WLA got them free. Because these courses were so short, "trained" women were offered to farmers without any real knowledge of what was expected of them, enraging farmers even further and prompting some to send them home.

The free uniform entitlement offered to WLA recruits by the Board of Agriculture & Fisheries' West Kent Women's Agricultural Committee consisted of: two overalls, one hat, one pair of breeches, one jersey, one pair of leggings, one pair of boots, one pair of clogs, and one mackintosh. After initial training and one month's satisfactory work on the land, the land girl was then issued a second outfit of: one overall, one hat, one pair of breeches, one pair of boots, and one pair of leather leggings.

Each volunteer was instructed to "remember always what a uniform stands for: discipline, obedience, loyalty, be always very proud of it, and never do anything to disgrace it."[2] After the completion of one year's service, the land girl was then issued a third outfit that had to last "a full twelve months," namely: three overalls, one pair of leather leggings, two hats, two pairs of boots, one pair of clogs, and one pair of canvas and leather leggings.

Recruits who chose to join the agriculture section of the WLA had to deal with two types of crops: one for human consumption and the other for animal fodder. Root crops were of great importance, and land girls were expected to grow and harvest potatoes, turnips, mangolds, and fodder beet. Most of the work was done by hand. Once pulled, mangolds and turnips were placed in piles, which were then forked into carts, taken back to the farm, unloaded, and finally sorted. Potato planting and stone-picking were two of the more strenuous tasks performed by the land girls, along with flax-pulling and hoeing.

Forage workers, who provided forage for army horses, were more closely involved with army camps, many of them guarding forage dumps against spies and saboteurs. Some of the land girls in the forage section were sent to France, where, under the watchful eye of the Army Service Corps, they cared for and broke mules and horses.

Perhaps the most arduous of WLA tasks were those performed by the members of the timber-cutting section, who stacked and carted trees they had felled and sawed into lengths. For this heavy, back-breaking work, they were eventually rewarded with the grudging respect of their fellow male employees.

At the time of the 1918 harvest, 16,000 WLA recruits were working on the land, and in the summer of that year, Lloyd George made an impassioned plea to the women of the country to help save the harvest. Restrictions on the use of German prisoners were lifted, agricultural camps established, and gangs of POWs sent to where the need was greatest. Throughout 1917 and 1918, tractors began to take the place of horses. Organized by the county committees, the Fordsons supplied by the United

States were the most popular, although British caterpillars and three-wheeled "Ivel" models were also much in evidence. By 1918, there were 23,000 tractors in use throughout the English countryside.

One of the largest grain harvests ever known was sown in the spring of 1918, with 7 million acres of grain planted in England and Wales. Despite wind, rain, and a shortage of labor, coupled with the onset of an influenza epidemic in October, a splendid harvest was brought home, with an increase of more than fifty percent in pre-war wheat levels.

KEW GARDENS In order to counter the belligerence of farmers, Lord Selborne decided that more women should receive some form of agricultural training, as farmers would take a trained woman in preference to a raw shop girl or typist. The length of wartime training courses varied from two weeks to two months. Women were admitted to Studley College and Swanley Horticultural College, which had catered solely to female students since 1902; the Board of Agriculture was sending girls on three-week courses, although the usual course length was two years.

From June 1915 onwards, Kew Gardens employed women, some of whom had trained at Swanley and were "keen and fond of their work."[3] Employment was found for them in the herbaceous ground, where they trimmed hedges and helped push round a heavy mower. Most of them found amusement in the reaction of the British public upon discovering women taking the place of men.

As more men enlisted, women were employed "under glass," working in the decorative pits (the special decorative department at Kew Gardens) and in orchids and ferneries. At one time, the decorative department was staffed almost entirely by women, earning for itself the title "Coutts' harem" (Mr. Coutts was one of the male gardeners employed at that time). Women gardeners were at first viewed with suspicion by their male colleagues, but once they had proved themselves equal to any task, they were accepted and there was "real comradeship" between the sexes.

The number of women working at Kew varied; in 1917, there were twenty-seven female gardeners and four sub-forewomen. Although there was as yet no women's guild, the group was united, particularly in its patriotic decision to grow vegetables, afterwards pressing for land on which to cultivate them. They approached the curator, Mr. W. Watson, "but he had no suggestion to make," so they approached Sir David Prain (director of Kew), who agreed to allow them to use the land off Mortlake Road next to the newly formed Ministry of Pensions.

A committee, consisting of four men and one woman, was elected, and each allotment-holder given an entitlement of five rods of land; the foremen received ten. All had to agree to put half of their plot down to potatoes and to allow them to be sprayed as part of Mr. Cotton's spraying experiments. That first year, the potato "seed" was bought locally and proved unsuccessful. The next year it was decided to try the Scottish "seed" that had been planted in front of Kew Palace, this time with great success.

A good yield was obtained from the crops grown in the allotments, and with the introduction in 1916 of British Summer Time (one hour in advance of Greenwich Mean Time), the plots were worked during weekday evenings and on Saturdays. Anyone found wasting produce, however, had it confiscated by the Committee, who sent it to Richmond Hospital.

VEGETABLE GARDENING On 4 August 1914, the Royal Horticultural Society sent a letter to the press stating that anyone with land not under cultivation should grow vegetables so that the winter's food supply might be increased. The Society then distributed 50,000 free leaflets throughout the country advising the public of the types of vegetables that could be sown as late as August, with the result that "very many persons who acted upon the suggestion had supplies of young and tender vegetables all through the autumn and early winter."[4]

At one of the Society's fortnightly meetings on 17 November 1914, vegetables grown from seed planted in August at Wisley were on display. In the spring of 1915, the Society issued a pamphlet, costing 3d., postage free, on vegetable growing for small gardens and allotments.

Shortly after the outbreak of war, the Board of Agriculture had asked householders to keep spare vegetable seedlings so that they might be given to allotment holders, although steps were not taken until late in the war to increase the number of allotments under cultivation. In December 1916, local authorities were empowered to seize all unoccupied land without the consent of the owners. In February 1917, U-boat warfare began in earnest in an effort to starve the British people into submission. Accordingly, any wasteland and playing fields were quickly subdivided into allotment plots, dug, and planted.

Under the provisions of Section 23 of the 1908 Allotments Act, every allotments authority had to provide plots for residents in their areas if there was sufficient demand, and in 1917, campaign inspectors were appointed by the government to find more vacant land, requisitioning ground from landowners under the Defence of the Realm Act. In 1914, there were 130,526 allotments under cultivation, rising to 1,330,000 in 1920, as the war introduced a whole new section of society, including many women, to the classless occupation of vegetable gardening.

The Royal Horticultural Society produced a variety of pamphlets to help the novice gardener, and it also awarded "Certificates for Diligent Interest in Plants." In 1915, Hilda Howe came in first in the Waterloo Wesleyan Girls' School competition for the best kept garden plot, and Ivy Scott, from the same school, came in first for the best collection of wildflowers. Interestingly, in the St. Mark's, Birmingham, Amateur Gardening Society, of the eleven members awarded certificates for window-box gardening, only two were women. But for the good upkeep of back and front gardens (which usually had a small lawn with flower beds in the front of the house and a larger strip of garden at the back, including a vegetable plot), of the eighteen members from the same society who received certificates, five were women.

"The growing of flowers on an allotment at the present crisis would probably be regarded as pleasure-gardening at the expense of the community for the sole benefit of the individual," stated W. H. Morter, Fellow of the Royal Horticultural Society, in his lecture "The Future of Allotments" at the RHS on 14 August 1918.[5] The escalation of the war had made the growing of vegetables an even greater priority, prompting the RHS to publish a pamphlet, "The Cultivation and Manuring of the Kitchen Garden," in 1917, providing instructions for the amateur horticulturist.

*T*he pamphlet "The Cultivation and Manuring of the Kitchen Garden" recommended double-digging or trenching in autumn or winter. To double dig a plot up to 10 yds wide, a 2-ft-wide strip was marked out along one end (as in **diagram A**), using a garden line (a piece of string with a sharpened peg of wood attached to each end used to measure dimensions). The top spit (a spade's depth) of **Section 1** was removed and piled in heaps on **Section E.** A trench was then made in **Section 1** by removing the soil, and the underlying second spit broken up. This trench was then filled with the top spit from **Section 2** and the process repeated through **Section 3,** the trenches being of the same width. Finally, the piles of earth at **E** were used to fill the last trench.

It was suggested that a wider plot be divided lengthways into strips about 6 yds wide, as in **diagram B, I & II,** and a trench taken out as before along one end of **Section 1,** throwing the top spit alongside the same end of **Section II (at E).** The sections were then worked as before, with trench **X** filled with the top spit from **Y.** The gardener then worked back on **plot II** until the last trench was made and filled with the pile of soil heaped at **E.**

Double-digging was ideal because the broken-up soil would hold more air and water, providing the crop roots with plenty of nourishment. The weather would break down the surface lumps into a fine tilth, which could then be hoed before sowing. Ordinary digging was recommended if cultivation was not begun until the spring.

The pamphlet advised hoeing to keep weeds down and to retain moisture in the soil. It also recommended that manure be applied to improve the general condition of the plot. To "sweeten" the soil, a dressing of slaked lime was used on heavy soils and chalk on light, the ground having first been tested with litmus paper to determine acidity. Various types of lime were used: quick-lime (caustic and dangerous), spread at the rate of 28 lb to a square rod, if the soil was full of pests; fresh slaked lime, applied in heaps at the rate of 28 lb per square rod, for stiff clay soils; and powdered chalk or limestone, spread at the rate of 28 to 56 lb to the square rod, for light soils. Finely broken seashells were also used, and gas lime (lime used to purify gas), obtainable from local gas works, was applied in autumn to destroy soil pests.

Decaying vegetable matter, leaf mold, and stable and farmyard manures were also commended, the latter dug in during the

A World War I plan showing how to cultivate and manure a kitchen garden (from "The Cultivation and Manuring of the Kitchen Garden," 1917).

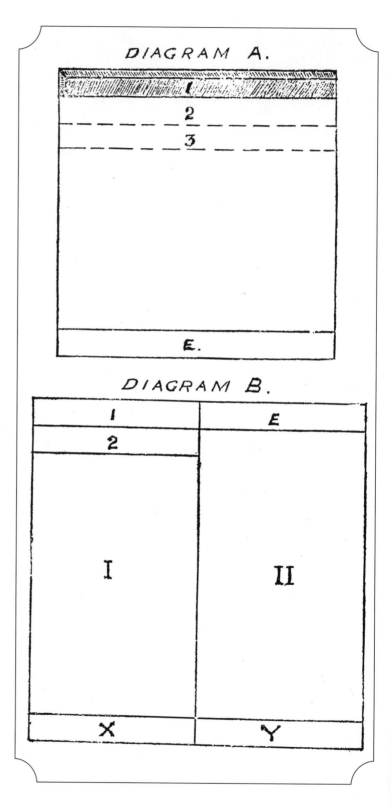

autumn or early spring with two to four barrow loads to the square rod. Also recommended was green manuring—done by sowing a catch crop (a secondary crop), allowing it to grow until the ground was needed for planting the main crop or other crops, and then digging it in—as well as general manures such as Peruvian guano, dried blood, bone meal, and leather dust. People were also reminded that "house sewage is valuable and should be used wherever it is available."

Artificial manures also had their place in wartime gardens, as they contained either nitrogen, potash, or phosphorous. A dressing of an artificial, phosphorus-rich manure was suggested for use on ground already treated with farmyard manure. Nitrogenous manures were also widely used, as they were active in assisting leaf growth, and it was considered advisable to apply them as spring dressings.

HERB GROWING During the war years, it was necessary to cultivate medicinal herbs in larger quantities than before. Herbs had previously been imported from Austria and Germany, and the patriotic owners of large country houses, anxious to make up the shortfall, turned for help and advice to the RHS, which observed that "many ladies take a great interest in the history and uses of medicinal plants, but have probably paid no attention to improving the strains by cultivation. This is a subject well worthy of attention, and could easily be studied by the aid of an intelligent gardener."[6]

Many "educated women with small incomes" joined the Women's Herb-growing Association, formed at the outbreak of the war. These ladies collected and dried medicinal herbs and delivered them to central depots in parcels of seven, fourteen, twenty-eight, or fifty-six lbs. in an effort to augment their slender purses. There was also a demand for dried culinary herbs, such as mint, angelica, thyme, basil, and sage, and spaghum moss was harvested in large quantities for use as bandages.

Members of the National Herb Growing Association collected the leaves of Atropa belladonna, henbane, *Datura stramonium* (thorn apple), and comfrey, in addition to dried marigold (*Calendula officinalis*) petals, "an ideal crop for village children to collect," at 2s. per lb. The Association noted that only small quantities of "good Foxglove leaves" were forthcoming and urged all its members to continue gathering them, as "every pound is wanted." It also mentioned that it had not received as much Colchicum corm (meadow saffron or autumn crocus), at 6d. per lb., as it had hoped for.

Dandelion roots were being purchased by the National Herb Growing Industry at 15s. per cwt (hundredweight, 112 lbs) for large roots, 12s. 6d. per cwt for mixed sizes, and 10s. 6d. per cwt for small roots, consignments of less than 14 lbs being paid for at the rate of 1d. per lb. Coltsfoot root was bought for 12s. 6d. per cwt and 1s. 6d. for 14 lbs, and woody night shade leaves, stripped from the stem, at 9s. per cwt. Both women and children collected many of these herbs, and a lot of women also cultivated them in their gardens and allotments.

THE FOUNDING OF THE FIRST WOMEN'S INSTITUTE In September 1915, the first Women's Institute (WI) was founded in Anglesey, North Wales, introduced into Great Britain from Canada by Mrs. Alfred Watt, one-time secretary of the Advisory Board of WIs of the Columbia, Canada Department of Agriculture. Mr. Nugent Harris, general secretary of the British Agricultural Organisation Society (AOS), gave his full approval because he realized that the WIs could provide a way of organizing food production and preservation in rural areas. In October 1916, Lady Gertrude Denman became chairman of the AOS subcommittee, and by 1917, the Board of Agriculture had taken it over, setting up a WI section within the Women's Branch of the Board's food production department, under the direction of Dame Meriel Talbot.

On 5 September 1917, the first County Federation of WIs was formed in Sussex, and in October, the first annual general meeting of WI delegates was held and the National Federation of Women's Institutes was formed. The aim of the WIs, then as now, was "to improve and develop conditions of rural life" and to give "all countrywomen the opportunity of working together through the Women's Institute organisation, and of putting into practice those ideals for which it stands."[7]

The WIs improved the lives of many village women, enabling them, for the first time, to meet regularly and carry out useful war work. The Institutes also encouraged women to plant vegetables and herbs to help the national effort. By 1919, there were more than 1,200 branches of WIs throughout the country.

The American "Army at Home"

In the United States, President Woodrow Wilson sanctioned a huge propaganda drive designed to make the American people hate the enemy and, contrary to their traditional isolationism, love the war. An avalanche of printed material was produced to add greater impetus to the "hate the hun" campaign, as historians published pamphlets supposedly "proving" that Germans were a degenerate race. The teaching of German in schools and colleges was forbidden, German books were removed from libraries, and German and Austrian music was banned. Added to which, German patents and properties were taken over for American use by the Alien Property Custodian.

The suffrage movement in America was largely pacifist, although it was instrumental in organizing a meeting at the Hague, where the Women's International League for Peace and Freedom (WIL) was established. When the League's proposal for a negotiated peace failed, U.S. women embroiled themselves in the war effort, replacing men in factories, education, public service, and on the land, patriotically regarding themselves as "the army at home."

At the outbreak of war, the Women's Land Army of America was organized in New York City by the Women's National Farm and Garden Union and the Garden Club of America. By the end of the war, 15,000 "farmerettes" had been placed on farms throughout the country. As in Great Britain, U.S. farmers were hostile toward female workers, but the increasing shortage of male labor quickly changed their attitude, and women were, to a large extent, accepted as part of the workforce.

The University of Georgia established a department of home economics for women within the College of Agriculture under the direction of Miss Mary Creswell, formerly of the United States Department of Agriculture. Mrs. Samuel Inman, chairman of the Georgia division of the Women's Committee Council of National Defence, upon reviewing the patriotic work of Georgia women in May 1918, stated: "We are beginning a new era in our agricultural prosperity and we need trained women as teachers and workers, and it is a happy condition that now our girls can be trained in their own state to develop what is theirs."[8]

In 1913, both the Women's National Agricultural and Horticultural Association and the Garden Club of America were

WILL YOU

use a hoe?
mend fences?
follow a plow?
drive a tractor?
help with the milking?
work in the orchards?
help in the hay fields?
pick in the berry patch?
harvest the small vegetables?

Imitation is the American impulse. The United States will not need the example of England to prove that women can till the soil, or the courage of the French or Canadians to prove that they can endure it.

This Spring and Summer, more than last year, girls and women in units organized for this important war work—those of extreme wealth with those in moderate circumstances—girls from college, business, offices, city homes—will go to the country for as many weeks and months as they can. Will you help carry through?

This outfit, designed expressly by *Best & Co.,* for women farm workers, is sold *complete* for 15.00. The garments may be purchased separately also.

BREECHES of khaki-colored "tough stuff." $3.25

COAT BLOUSE—of khaki "tough stuff" also, made to wear over a shirt waist or without one; with low neck as pictured, or converted to high. $5.75

For warmer days, the blouse comes in blue jean. $3.95

PUTTIES—are canvas with spiral lacing. $1.25
SHOES—made on our Famous Orpic Last Patented; sturdy, but absolutely flexible. $5.75

HAT—a soft sport shape capable of many modifications, cut from khaki-colored "tough stuff" and offering ample protection from wind and sun. $.95

Camp and College Sellers, Paula A. Matzner, in Charge

Best & Co.

An outfit for American women farm workers offered by Best & Co. during World War I (reprinted with permission of the Schlesinger Library, Radcliffe College, Cambridge, MA).

founded, an indication of the professionalism entering into the area of women in the garden. The former, whose membership included both amateur and professional, did much to build up women's interest in horticulture, and the Garden Club's influence helped to preserve historic gardens and ensure the protection of indigenous plants. The founders of the Garden Club of America were some of the most influential women of the day: the Biddles of Philadelphia, the Ridgeleys of Baltimore, and the McCormicks of Chicago.

The general feeling among professional American men at this time, however, was that the employment of women qualified in horticulture and landscape architecture "would do little less than undermine the entire American way of life."[9] Nevertheless, women did find employment, despite a resistance that sometimes verged on violence, graduating from such faculties as The Cambridge School of Architectural and Landscape Design for Women in Cambridge, Massachusetts, and The Lowthorpe School of Landscape Architecture, Gardening, and Horticulture in Groton, Massachusetts.

Herbert C. Hoover was put in control of food production and distribution, and, among other measures, he fixed the price of wheat at $2.20 a bushel and introduced a grain corporation to buy and sell it. After the Lever Act of August 1917, Hoover considered it unnecessary to impose food rationing, choosing instead to promote a campaign that would persuade all patriotic citizens to limit their consumption of food and to cut out all waste. This, in turn, led to "wheatless Mondays" and "meatless Tuesdays," with chefs and citizens alike experimenting with such delicacies as whale meat, horse steak, and vegetable lamb. Children were encouraged by patriotic mothers to "hooverize" their plates, and, as a result of "hooverization," America was able in 1918 to export three times its normal amounts of sugar, meats, and breadstuffs. Interestingly, there were more than 12 million workers in agricultural employment in the States during World War I.

For the first time in the country's history, women became members of the armed forces. The marine corps recruited around 300 and the navy over 10,000; the army employed several thousand but in a civilian capacity. The number of women engaged in war industries, however, was small, around 1 million women replacing the men on active service. These women were not paid as much as men. They hoped that, by supporting the war effort, women would be rewarded with national enfranchisement as well as higher wages. This did not transpire, however, and at the end of hostilities most of them left their wartime employment.

Generally speaking, the U.S. government did little to encourage women to support the war effort, expecting them merely to take part in traditional female activities such as food conservation programs, knitting warm clothing for soldiers, preparing bandages for the injured, and encouraging the sale of war bonds. Possibly as a token gesture, a Women in Industry Service in the Department of Labor and a Woman's Committee of the Council of National Defense were established.

The Committee on Public Information, set up by President Wilson on 14 April 1917, had, as one of its many tasks, to devise a selection of war propaganda activities designed to appeal to women. One such activity was to persuade women to sell Liberty Bonds to help finance the war. For the less well-off, savings certificates were on sale, each one holding twenty war-savings stamps with a monetary value of $5. Also on sale were twenty-five-cent thrift stamps, sixteen of which could be exchanged for a war-savings stamp. In addition to the final Victory Loan drive, there were four other drives, producing together approximately $20.5 billion.

As in Great Britain, many Americans believed that the war would soon be over. Nevertheless, its effects were quickly felt by the U.S. public as stock markets crashed, exchanges closed, and foreign markets were disrupted, making the winter of 1914-1915 one of hardships for many Americans.

On 4 August 1914, Wilson issued a proclamation warning U.S. citizens not only to refuse to participate in hostilities but also to observe wartime regulations. Meanwhile, allied propaganda was at work. The British, in September 1914, established a propaganda bureau in London. American public opinion was closely monitored by one of its divisions, which reported weekly to the British Cabinet and kept in close contact with U.S. newspaper correspondents. It supplied a weekly news service to 360 American newspapers and inspired the preparation of books, pamphlets, and motion pictures to be distributed in the States. This propaganda center was later replaced by the Department of Information and, in 1918, by the Ministry of Propaganda. In June 1917, the British Bureau of Information was established in New York City.

Women Get the Vote

*P*olitics absorbed the attention of many of the women's groups. In 1913, the Congressional Union (later to become the National Woman's party) had been created and had adopted more militant tactics to ensure that women got the vote, much to the disapproval of the National American Woman Suffrage Association. The impetus for women's suffrage after the Civil War had resulted in Wyoming being the first state to grant women the right to limited suffrage, in 1869, usually on bond issues, educational questions, and for municipal elections. When Wyoming was admitted as a state in 1889, that right was continued, and between 1893 and 1914 ten other states followed suit: Kansas, Arizona, Colorado, Utah, Idaho, Washington State, Oregon, California, Alaska Territory, and Illinois (presidential and municipal suffrage).

In 1917, Jeannette Rankin of Montana became the first woman to be elected to Congress, and in 1919, Congress passed the Nineteenth Amendment to the Constitution enfranchising all women nationwide. After its ratification in August 1920, American women were allowed to vote in the presidential election of that year.

Once granted the vote, women were at liberty to join the National Woman's party, the League of Women Voters, and the women's committees of political parties. Women's legislative councils were founded in every state to monitor the progress of acts being considered by state legislators. Congress was lobbied by women's groups in support of the founding of a women's bureau within the national government.

Throughout the years of war, more and more British and American women proved their capabilities in areas outside the traditional world of domesticity. In spite of the discrimination practiced against them, the war offered a unique opportunity to improve their status and position, although the change was not necessarily a permanent one. In 1918, there were more than 1 million British women taking the place of men in industrial employment. At the end of the war, there were between 7.25 and 7.5 million women in paid employment in Great Britain and Ireland, but the government was ready to order their demobilization once hostilities had ceased.

When the armistice was finally signed on 11 November 1918, more than 600,000 British men had been slaughtered and more than 1.6 million mutilated and disabled. In July 1918, the Representation of the People Act had given the franchise to British women over thirty, bringing with it worldwide recognition for the feminist movement. On both sides of the Atlantic, women had played a magnificent part in the war effort, a fact that went a long way toward securing them the vote. The war had not only provided them with a variety of exciting, new experiences, it had also given them the confidence to challenge the bastions of traditional male values and prejudices. For the moment, women had won the battle of emancipation, but they had yet to win the war.

CHAPTER EIGHT

THE INTER-WAR YEARS

From Euphoria to Despair

UNIVERSALLY REGARDED AS A STRUGGLE for the preservation of freedom, World War I had been fought as a noble cause and its end had heralded widespread social and economic changes, all of which had far-reaching effects on women's position in society. "Make Germany Pay" was the general mood of the British people in 1919. However, less than ten years later a different mood prevailed as promises of full employment and a "land fit for heroes" failed to materialize and the Labour Party spread its socialist message. The publication of war memoirs by those who fought on the front lines told of the harsh physical realities of the war, which had been withheld by the British press. The ideology of the "noble cause" was challenged, and the underlying motives of the war began to be questioned as it became apparent to many that Germany was not solely responsible for the war.

The end of the war had brought with it an initial period of prosperity during which prices and wages rose sharply. The boom was short-lived, however, and by the end of 1920 wages were failing to keep pace with rising prices. Gradually, the euphoria of peace gave way to disillusionment and despair. Many ex-soldiers were of the opinion that their commanding generals had been grossly incompetent and that lives had been sacrificed unnecessarily by their bungling tactics. To compound the tragedy, an epidemic of influenza had ravaged the country in the winter of 1918-1919, claiming another 150,000 lives.

During the war years, British industry had lost many of its overseas markets and had over-invested in staples such as iron, steel, coal, and shipbuilding, the products of which were no longer needed in such vast quantities. As a result, regional unemployment spiraled, and in the summer of 1921, the national unemployment level reached over 2 million and did not fall below 1 million during the years leading up to World War II. The national debt, moreover, had reached £7 billion ($10.5 billion), some £850 million of which was owed to the United States.

In Great Britain, while various committees were already looking at ways of reconstructing the country's economic, social, and political affairs, Lloyd George, who regarded himself as the catalyst of victory, called for a general election for 14 December, just over a month after the signing of the armistice. For the moment, the nation supported him.

The British Women's Institutes Flourish

In 1918, the Representation of the People Bill had enfranchised all women over the age of thirty in addition to those who were *ratepayers* (payers of property tax) or *householders* (tenants of a house), or were married to ratepayers or householders. And yet, while the first woman Member of Parliament, Lady Astor, entered Parliament in 1919, it was not until 1928 that all British women received the vote under the same conditions as men (the "Flapper" vote, which gave the vote to all women over twenty-one, without qualification).

Christabel Pankhurst and her mother stepped down from electoral politics in 1919. Unfortunately, Mrs. Pankhurst was to die in 1928 just before the election for the constituency of Whitechapel and St. George's, Stepney, for which she was to stand as Conservative candidate. Christabel, meanwhile, became a traveling evangelist for the religious sect The Second Coming of Christ and in 1936 was made a Dame Commander of the British Empire (DBE) for her work for women's suffrage. She had a great affinity with America, returning in 1940 to Los Angeles, where she lived until her death in 1958.

In 1919, the Sex Disqualification Act dispensed with any lingering barriers regarding female access to the professions and professional associations, although women on both sides of the Atlantic tended to remain firmly ensconced in the traditional feminine occupations, particularly teaching. The majority of women who had taken employment during the war as part of the national effort stepped down in deference to their returning menfolk. For some of them, the role of wife and mother had suddenly become very attractive, while others drifted back to their previous occupations in shops, textiles, and domestic service. It was taken for granted that married women did not work except in special circumstances such as a husband's ill health or unemployment, and in 1921, more than ninety percent of married women were confined to the home. Homemaking continued to be the main female occupation throughout the inter-war years, although new technology was easing the burden of household drudgery and contraceptive practices were precluding the necessity for large families. The main interest of the educated married woman was now her personal appearance, closely followed by homemaking, health, and hygiene.

Suffragette organizations had fallen from grace, to be replaced by co-operative guilds and Labour women's sections, which held a wide range of lectures and discussion groups on topics of interest to working-class women. Women's Institutes (WI's) flourished under the leadership of Lady Denman, with Grace Hadow as vice-chairman, and by the end of 1919 there were 1,405 branches throughout the country. The WI strove to gain self-government and independence, which it achieved by its refusal to be affiliated with other voluntary organizations. Accordingly, when it was suggested that the WI should amalgamate with the Landswomen's Association, the idea was rejected.

While country matters continued to be of paramount importance, the WI started to embroil itself in social issues such as adult education, venereal disease, and the age of consent. It filled a need by tackling both county and national issues and by encouraging village women to take the initiative in matters of concern both to themselves and to the rural community as a whole; family health, child care, better working and housing conditions, and an improvement in the quality of village life were all topics of discussion. And in July 1935, when Princess Alice, Countess of Athlone, opened the Berkshire Federation of Women's Institutes' Exhibition of Handicrafts in Reading, she spoke of the importance of lectures on diet and cooking "especially in these days when the very attractive array of tinned goods tempt inexperienced wives to neglect the cooking of fresh foods so essential for growing children."[1]

By 1939, the WI had a membership of some 300,000 women. Its aim, as always, was to inform, to amuse, and to interest, and experts instructed country women on homemaking and the management of their slender financial resources. There were demonstrations on food preservation, cooking, dressmaking, and gardening, and many branches of the WI organized stalls in the local markets where produce made or grown by their members was sold. The institutes concerned themselves with town and country planning and did a useful job in invigorating both the government and the local authorities into action as they strove to improve the outlook of isolated rural women and to develop and improve the quality of their lives.

Flappers, Prohibition, and the E.R.A.

In the United States, the "Roaring Twenties" were boom years of wealth, affluence, and consumer spending. The nation shifted toward urbanization and mass production. Industrial developments mushroomed, and large corporations continued to expand. Retail credit organizations sprang up, and the installment plan became the answer to buying furniture, domestic appliances, automobiles, and even jewelry. The film and radio-broadcasting industries flourished, helping to form a mass consumer society and fuel the ever-increasing expectations of the ordinary man and woman on the street.

Hollywood inspired the nation's attitude toward materialism by portraying luxury, excitement, and pleasure across the silver screen, and the popular film stars of the day influenced the way women dressed. The so-called "S-bend" style was replaced by the "flapper" look. Old ways and ingrained morals were discarded by these energetic young women as they imitated men as far as they were able. With their short skirts, bobbed or shingled hair, and shapeless dresses, concealing sylph-like figures brought about by dieting, the flappers took part in all kinds of manly sports and pastimes, wielding tennis racquets and driving fast sports cars. The mood was one of frivolity and pleasure as these "bright young things" danced the nights away, and by 1925, they were frequenting the illegal speak-easies, smoking in public, and flaunting their independence in lax morals and easy manners. While the divorce rate in America nearly doubled, the enactment of the Nineteenth Amendment inspired these bold young women to seek greater outlets for their unbridled hedonism and to become even more determined to live life to the fullest.

But the "new woman," or the "flapper," accounted for just a small, young, rich, and privileged minority of females. Most women were content to lead lives of quiet domesticity. They continued to marry and raise children, and some of them were in paid employment, although they found it difficult to combine a career and a family. Nevertheless, increasing numbers of them started to become the sole breadwinner while their husbands went to college. The feminist factions, however, viewed this as a step backwards, maintaining that these women should be enrolling at colleges themselves.

Wages were high at this time, unlike those in Great Britain, and American women, like their British sisters, found that life was made easier by the new technology that brought them such items as washing machines, vacuum cleaners, and ice boxes/refrigerators. These appliances were in great demand, and if a family had insufficient cash to buy them, they could be bought on credit. This was all part of the "American dream," the dream that was only fleetingly dimmed during the years 1929-1932.

While American feminists failed to prioritize their aims for the new era, male disapproval and economic and legal barriers remained firmly entrenched. Established women's groups saw a return to the concerns of women and children. Feminists continued to pursue old causes in addition to developing fresh ideas and to work in existing organizations as well as founding new ones. The problems for women of combining a career and a family persisted. Unemployment at the end of the First World War was low, working hours were shortened, and holidays with pay were being introduced in some industries. Women were determined to gain economic and social freedom. And yet, while their independence increased—they had the right to vote, worked outside the home, and were property owners—few of them attained positions of power in either business or politics.

Large numbers of women voted in the 1920 presidential election, but few of them ran for public office and many of them voted for their husband's choice of candidate. Many suffragists believed that the battle was won, but radical feminists discerned the reality of the situation. Accordingly, total equality was demanded by the National Woman's party, the members of which considered the protective legislation governing the working hours and conditions of women to be discriminatory. This stance, in turn, led to a split with the socialist feminists, who believed that women and children should be protected by such legislation. As a result, more and more women joined the League of Women Voters, a more moderate association that sought support for a variety of reforms, some of which had no bearing on the women's cause.

The National American Women's Suffrage Association had become the League of Women Voters, thereafter devoting itself to educating women on their political roles and responsibilities. In 1923, the Women's Party, under the leadership of Alice Paul, instituted the introduction into Congress of The Equal Rights Amendment (E.R.A.). The equal rights feminists, meanwhile, continued their crusade to free women from oppression by pressing for the abolition of the traditional female roles with which the social feminists ("welfare feminists") concerned themselves, although they, too, adhered to the ideology of separate spheres for women. Although the battle for the Equal Rights Amendment would continue through the 1930s, it was a lost cause. World peace would again be threatened and the momentum of the feminist movement diminished.

Meanwhile, neither the enactment of the Eighteenth Amendment, which forbade Americans to make, sell, or transport any intoxicating liquor, nor the Volstead Act, passed to enforce the Eighteenth Amendment, persuaded all women, and in particular the flappers, to support Prohibition. On the contrary, more and more women increasingly became the fashionable drinkers of illicit liquor.

The feminists wanted to help the prohibitionists, or the "dries," as they were called, because the Prohibition party was the first major organization to endorse suffrage for women. The eleven states that had adopted female enfranchisement before 1917 were all in the West, and, of those states, seven were dry. Accordingly, a woman's vote was considered to be one for Prohibition, and it was generally believed that the female vote would also support reform governments that set out to rid cities of crime. The success of the feminist movement, therefore, became increasingly dependent on the help and support of the dries.

With the closing of the saloons came an increase in illegal liquor such as moonshine, illicit wine, and imported alcohol as well as bootleggers and speakeasies. Females drinking in public became a familiar sight and was even considered respectable in

the large cities. The women who chose to drink began to organize themselves into a movement for the repeal of Prohibition.
Their organization was founded in 1929 by Mrs. Charles H.
Sabin and had as its members the leaders of New York society.
Suddenly, the repeal of Prohibition became the smartest social
movement for American women, and to be looked upon as one
of the "Sabine Women"—as Mrs. Sabin's supporters were
called—guaranteed one's social acceptance and success.

Not surprisingly, the dries reacted strongly to this new movement, vowing to out-do and out-vote its advocates. But the damage had been done. As long as the various women's associations
and clubs had remained adamant in their stance against liquor,
then no politician dared to act in any way that would give
offense. But the prohibitionists wrongly assumed that the
Eighteenth Amendment and Prohibition could not be successfully challenged. Prohibition was, in fact, difficult to enforce
even though the government appointed federal agents to destroy
all supplies of liquor and arrest those breaking the law.

In 1933, with the repeal of the Eighteenth Amendment and
the enactment of the Twenty-first, Prohibition finally came to an
end. The saloons were open once again, although now
euphemistically called bars, taverns, clubs, and cafes, and were
controlled by regulations that varied from state to state. Some
states, for example, prohibited saloons and put liquor stores in
their place, while others demanded that customers be visible
from the streets. Nevertheless, whatever the rules and regulations, the liquor trade had been revived and national Prohibition
ceased.

Female Farm Laborers in Britain

During the inter-war years, British agricultural laborers continued to exist on below the average income, earning 31s.
8d. ($2.37) a week in 1929 and 34s. 7d. ($2.60) in 1938, with
women being paid about half those amounts. Because they were
cheap to employ, female laborers could often find work more easily than men, usually at the traditional hiring fairs that continued to survive until the 1940s in some of the more remote rural
areas. Farmers with small holdings often used their wives and
daughters on the land, while on larger establishments, the wives

and daughters of farmworkers were employed during the corn harvest and for seasonal work such as fruit and potato picking.

Throughout the agricultural depression of the 1920s, the casual labor rate for women was just 6d. (4¢) an hour at a time when new machinery was beginning to replace manpower and combine harvesters and tractors started to appear on rural landscapes. In 1919, the War Agricultural Committees began selling wartime machinery, and many farmers took advantage of the opportunity of owning their own tractors.

British farmers had made substantial profits during the war, but after the passing of the Agriculture Act of 1920, prices began to fall until the autumn of 1922 when they were checked. The Agricultural Wages Board was abolished in September 1921, but not before it had reduced the national minimum wage for men to £2 1s. ($3.07) for a fifty-hour week in the summer and forty-eight hours in the winter, although, by the end of 1922, wages for ordinary farmworkers were down to £1 4s. ($1.80), bringing a return of pre-war poverty to rural districts. From 1929 onwards, with a renewed fall in prices, fewer workers were being employed, and in 1933, the number of agricultural laborers fell below 600,000.

Throughout the appalling poverty and unemployment of the 1920s, economic circumstances forced many country women to seek paid employment. Some of them undertook domestic work for local farmers, others toiled on the land alongside the men. At harvest time women helped with the hay making, standing up stooks of corn and gleaning after the reaping. They tackled the strenuous task of picking up potatoes that had been lifted from the ground, placing the potatoes in large willow baskets, and emptying the baskets into waiting carts. Women were also used to pick up fruit tree prunings, which they afterwards piled into heaps and burned. Blossom thinning was another tedious task given to casual female laborers, as was the laying of straw around strawberry plants, and later in the season, teams of women picked, packed, and crated the strawberry harvest before loading it into lorries.

In October 1932, the British Union of Fascists was formed, under the leadership of Sir Oswald Mosley, and in 1933, Adolf Hitler was catapulted to power by the National Socialist Party in Germany. Both Hitler and Mosley wanted to solve the male unemployment crisis by eliminating women from the labor market. However, as the thirties witnessed the growing cult of domesticity, a trend incidentally that was fully endorsed by many feminists of the time, including M.P. Eleanour Rathbone, female workers made up only a small part of the total labor force.

In previous years British married women had stayed at home to rear large families and cope with the heavy burden of housework. A comfortable home had always meant hard work on the part of the woman, and the home had always been viewed as a woman's special domain whether she was married or not. The development of a variety of household gadgets suddenly eased that burden, giving more women a certain amount of independence and the freedom to choose whether or not they worked outside the home.

The Wall Street Crash

The total income of American farmers dropped from $22 billion in 1919 to $13 billion in 1928. Throughout World War I, the United States had shipped millions of tons of grain to Europe, and when the war was over this market was lost. Added to which, the population of the country was decreasing at this time, Canada was producing large amounts of wheat, and America was overproducing, which led to surpluses of U.S. wheat for which there were no buyers.

By 1929, the United States was the richest nation in the world, but American farmers were suffering. Prices fell because of overproduction, and many farmers were evicted from their homes because they could not pay their rents. They were unable to sell their crops to overseas countries because of the high customs duties on foreign imports, imposed by the Fordney-McCumber tariff introduced in 1922, which resulted in foreign countries having fewer American dollars with which to buy American produce. The farming community accounted for around thirty-three percent of the population during the 1920s, but times were hard, prices were low, and by 1930, 1.5 million people had left the land for the cities.

On 24 October 1929, the post-war bubble burst as billions of dollars were wiped off the market value of leading American companies. On Tuesday, 29 October, the bottom fell out of the market. Many people lost vast fortunes as a result of the Wall

Street Crash, which triggered a crisis in the world economic structure and threatened the political stability of Europe. Unemployment rose to record levels as the global gloom of the Great Depression began to settle.

After the Wall Street Crash, the government sought to strengthen agriculture, passing the Agricultural Adjustment Act in 1933 to encourage farmers to reduce their output, thereby decreasing any surpluses and consequently pushing up the price of their produce. The 1933 act brought in its wake the Agricultural Adjustment Administration (AAA), which was empowered to control the amounts of cotton, wheat, corn, and rice by offering cash subsidies to those farmers who voluntarily reduced the acreage they planted. The AAA also imposed taxes on such people as millers and meat packers, the revenue from these taxes being used to pay the subsidies. Farmers were also given cash payments to plant grasses on waste land to prevent dust storms.

The Farm Credit Administration (FCA) gave loans to farmers for marketing and production, and the Frazier-Lemke Farm Bankruptcy Act (June 1934) postponed the foreclosure of farm mortgages for a five-year period. This was later amended to three years by the second Frazier-Lemke Act of August 1935. In 1933, the AAA was declared unconstitutional and Congress passed a second act in February 1938 in an effort to increase agricultural prices and decrease surpluses. As in 1933, subsidies were again paid to the farmers.

The National Pastime

*A*t the end of World War I, a large percentage of the British population was badly housed. To address the problem, just over 1.5 million council houses and 2.5 million private houses were built during the following twenty years. A pattern of ribbon development spread across the land, and there was a tremendous upsurge in suburban expansion as new semi-detached houses with bathrooms, garages, and gardens sprang up to meet a largely middle-class demand and to satisfy the rising affluence of salaried managers, teachers, and civil servants. These houses could be bought for as little as £350-£450 ($525-$675), and with mortgage rates set at an average of 4.5 percent, they were well within the range of both the middle and upper classes.

The whole of suburbia became "garden-minded," and the garden came to be regarded as an extension of the house. Privacy was considered an important feature, the site was treated as a coherent whole, and the modern fashion for balanced planning, arrangement of vistas, and seasonal rotation was strictly adhered to. According to the prevalent view of the 1930s, "the connection between house and garden should be intimate; there should be inviting views from the windows and from the garden door one should step out into the scent and colour of the garden."[2] Women were advised by the gardening magazines of the day that when "your garden is looking its loveliest with the roses in bloom, the lawn like velvet, and the trees cool and inviting, *then* is the time to give a garden party and show your friends how beautiful everything looks."[3]

Middle-class women spent much of their time in their gardens and were actively encouraged to tend the formal flower beds set amidst neatly manicured lawns, which were bordered and disected by a "crazy paving path." These paths were made from small, irregular-sized pieces of stone or concrete that were fitted together to give a "jigsaw" type of effect. The lady of the house sowed flowers for cutting in small borders specially reserved for them, the favorite ones being coreopsis, cornflower, marigold, larkspur, mignonette, sweet peas, godetia, and single China asters. As regards dress, housewives were advised that "a smock is such a pretty thing to wear in the garden!...You can slip it on over your frock in a second when you want to go out and do the watering, weeding, or perhaps mow the grass."

The small modern gardens of the day reflected the taste, style, and needs of their owners; well-known landscape architects and nurserymen of the time advocated the need for less grass and hedging, for example, and the need for more shrubs, fewer herbaceous borders, more stone work, more specialized garden themes, and fewer paths and curves. In larger gardens, tennis courts and garden games were much in vogue, and other features of the layout might include a kitchen garden, an orchard, and a rose garden. Interestingly, during the early thirties there was a craze for brightly colored garden gnomes, but it was quickly abandoned as inappropriate, particularly when the organizers of the Chelsea Flower Show refused to allow gnomes of any description to be included in exhibits.

Although George VI would be crowned on 12 May 1937 following his brother's abdication on 11 December 1936, earlier in 1936, the nation was preparing to celebrate the forthcoming coronation of Edward VIII. Gardeners were urged to plant "Coronation Flower Beds," and in July the Coronation Planting Committee, with Lord Lothian as its chairman, was established at the Garden Club on Curzon Street in London. In September of that year, the Committee began its work and "decided to encourage in every possible way the conversion of derelict churchyards into pleasant gardens for the public, and the beautifying of the ground around hospitals, churches and other public buildings; to invite the railway companies to further the planting of stations and railway embankments, to urge that the planting of Coronation avenues leading into country towns and villages should be undertaken by competent authorities, in which children should be encouraged to help by planting seeds, acorns etc."[4] In addition, the committee was to organize a competition between English villages for the "greatest transformation toward beauty that can be effected by May of next year."

Gardening magazines showed housewives how to achieve a glorious display of flowers for the following spring and gave them ideas for planting schemes not only in a variety of bright colors but also in red, white, and blue. It was suggested in *Good Gardening* that bulbs, the mainstay of the spring garden, should be selected and planted in October, following the diagrams in the journal, and that each design was admirably suited to both large and small gardens.

FLOWER BEDS FOR THE SPRING AND THE CORONATION

First of all, the flower beds had to be prepared, each one being carefully dug and all weeds and debris removed. Poor soil was to receive a dressing of decayed manure, light soil made firm by treading before planting, and all soils required the benefit of a dressing of bone meal applied at the rate of 2 oz. per sq. yd. Tulips and hyacinths were chosen as the principal bulbs in beds and borders of formal design, complemented by wallflowers in rich and varied colors—the vivid orange *Cheiranthus allionii* (Siberian wallflower); myosotis (forget-me-nots) in white, pink, and shades of blue; and large-flowered double daisies in white, pink,

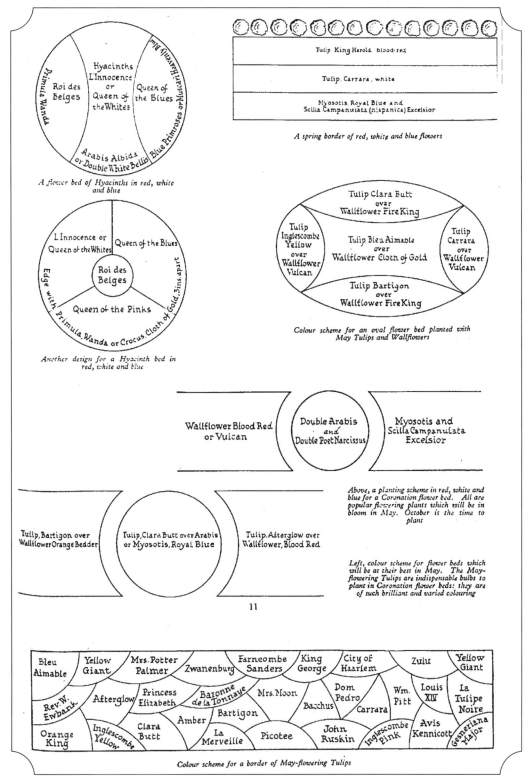

A flower bed of Hyacinths in red, white and blue

A spring border of red, white and blue flowers

Another design for a Hyacinth bed in red, white and blue

Colour scheme for an oval flower bed planted with May Tulips and Wallflowers

Above, a planting scheme in red, white and blue for a Coronation flower bed. All are popular flowering plants which will be in bloom in May. October is the time to plant

Left, colour scheme for flower beds which will be at their best in May. The May-flowering Tulips are indispensable bulbs to plant in Coronation flower beds: they are of such brilliant and varied colouring

11

Colour scheme for a border of May-flowering Tulips

Flower beds for the spring and for the coronation of Edward VIII in 1937 (from Good Gardening, *Vol. 11, No. 20, October 1936).*

and red in addition to red and white miniature "Dresden China" daisies, polyanthus, primroses, and violas in a variety of shades.

As hyacinths bloom in April, it was suggested that bulbs of the second size be planted during October, 4 in. (10 cm.) deep from the top of the bulb and 8 in. (20 cm.) apart. Those recommended were the white "L'Innocence" and "Queen of the Whites," the porcelain-blue "Grand Maitre," and the deeper blue "Bismarck," with the dark blue "King of the Blues," primrose yellow "City of Haarlem," "Queen of the Pinks," and the carmine-red "Roi des Belges." Tulips were also advocated for the stunning effect that could be achieved, commencing with the early flowering singles and doubles, used separately or combined, which could be given an edging of dwarf forget-me-nots such as "Royal blue." Suggestions for the early single varieties included white and rose "Cottage Maid" and crimson-scarlet "Couleur Cardinal"; and of the early double varieties: "Vuurbaak scarlet," "Murillo pink" and "Murillo white," and "Peach Blossom," rose-pink, and white. To achieve the required effect, it was necessary to plant early tulips close together: 5 in. (12.5 cm.) apart for singles and 6 in. (15 cm.) for doubles in soil 5 in. deep from the top of the bulb if the soil was light, and 4 in. (10 cm.) deep in soil that was heavy.

It was also suggested that in a series of beds on the lawn, "Tulip Afterglow" over a groundwork of wallflower, "Blood Red," and "Clara Butt" over a groundwork of double white arabis or white, pink, or blue forget-me-nots of the dwarf *Myosotis dissitiflora* would look quite delightful, and that blue forget-me-nots would form an attractive groundwork for the white "Cottage Tulip Carrara." Housewives were reminded that, in all cases, groundwork and edging plants had to be set out first, planted alternately in rows 12 in. (30 cm.) apart, after which the tulip bulbs could then be randomly placed at a distance of about 10 in. (25 cm.) apart.

Gardening quickly established itself as a national pastime, and Flower Lovers Travel Tours became very popular during the 1930s. The tours, which varied in duration, were organized by Dr. Hugh Roger Smith, the honorary secretary of the Alpine Garden Society, and Mrs. Robert Lukin, a member of the Society. They were arranged by Thos. Cook & Son Ltd. of Berkeley Street, London, who provided an illustrated brochure and full particulars upon request. The tours not only gave keen gardeners, both male and female, the chance to observe the flora of foreign countries but allowed them to collect certain plants and ship them back to England, provided that they had obtained the necessary permit from the Ministry of Agriculture. Not all countries would allow the decimation of their natural flora, however; in Switzerland, for example, the digging up of certain specified plants was forbidden.

On 5-7 May 1936, enthusiasts from all over the world attended an "Alpine Conference and Show" at Westminster, sponsored by the Royal Horticultural Society and the Alpine Garden Society. Flower shows were extremely popular throughout the country, with horticultural societies being established in many towns and villages, the objectives of which were "to extend interest in gardening, to improve the standard of cultivation by friendly rivalry, and to bring to public notice new and improved plants, flowers, fruits, and vegetables."

Garden guilds existed in many parts of Great Britain to encourage tenants to grow flowers, however small their plot of land might be, and to show people who had only window boxes how to plant them so that they would look attractive and bright. This was achieved by holding competitions, by lectures on horticultural subjects, and by the provision of free compost and seeds for those who could not afford to buy them. The medal winner in 1937 was a Ms. Margaret Huish for her entry in the London garden competition. Many of the garden guilds were affiliated with the National Gardens Guild in High Holborn, London, of which Queen Mary was the patroness.

In London, the first ambitious roof garden was planted in the early 1920s on the roof of Adelaide House, overlooking London Bridge, while the most frequented roof garden was that above Selfridge's Oxford Street store. Around Fleet Street, several roofs were set out with evergreen and flowering shrubs, and tubs and boxes, planted first with bulbs and then with bedding-out material, filled shady corners. During Jubilee Year, moreover, householders were encouraged to fit window boxes and fill them with bright, colorful plants such as geraniums, and for those who had balconies, it was suggested that vines be planted, either the common fruiting type or the purple leaved *Vitis purpurea*.

As in America, gardening schools for women became ever more popular. The Pusey School of Horticulture for Women, founded in 1929, developed into the Waterperry Horticultural School in 1932. In 1935, Swanley offered, in addition to its universally recognized three-year diploma course, a three-year course designed to prepare students for the London University degree in horticulture. Swanley diploma students were therafter qualified "for such interesting occupations as private gardening, advisory work, including garden planning, care of the gardens and grounds in schools, and in training colleges, and various aspects of commercial horticulture."[5]

Swanley courses at this time varied from one to three years, with trial courses of twelve weeks, and fees ranged from £40-£50 ($60-$75) per year for tuition, with an additional £60-£80 ($90-$120) for residence. A scholarship examination was held annually in May, and various scholarships, county grants, and bursaries were awarded according to the results achieved. Upon the completion of a course, diploma students could expect to earn £1 ($1.50) a week plus board and lodging in a country district, while degree holders could command remuneration of about £3 ($4.50) a week, which would eventually rise to £300 ($450) a year.

The inter-war years also attested the success of many British women gardeners. It was a time when herb gardening was revived on both sides of the Atlantic and was considered a suitable career for emancipated young ladies. Mrs. Hilda Leyel opened the first Culpeper Shop in London on St. Valentine's Day 1927. The Culpepper Shop supplied the British public with simple herbal remedies, natural perfumes, and pure cosmetics.

One of the most scholarly and best-known herb gardeners was Eleanour Sinclair Rohde; her first book, *A Garden of Herbs*, was published in 1920, followed in 1922 by *The Old English Herbals* and, in 1936, by *Herbs and Herb Gardening*. She lived most of her life at Cranham Lodge in Reigate, Surrey, and her knowledge of herbs, their history, lore, and scents is legion. "How strange it seems," she wrote in 1935, "that knot gardens which were such a popular feature in Elizabethan gardens, but unknown in modern gardens until recently, are once more becoming fashionable."[6] She was also knowledgeable about and interested in flowers and their perfumes, confiding that "My Favourites are the Flowers that were commonly Grown in Cottage Gardens and have remained almost Unchanged through the Centuries."[7]

Vita Sackville-West was another indefatigable gardener and prolific writer. In May 1930, she and her husband, Sir Harold

Nicolson, bought Sissinghurst Castle in Kent, which comprised four squalid buildings and a flat, overgrown garden of seven acres. Together they planned and planted a garden that was mysterious, romantic, and private, formal in structure, and that had focal points approached by long vistas. Vita Sackville-West was greatly influenced by William Robinson, and many of his ideas were adopted by the Nicolsons: roses were grouped and underplanted; creepers and ramblers adorned the walls; sweetbriar and honeysuckle flourished; and borders were filled with a succession of bulbs and flowers.

During 1930-1932, the Nicolsons made a plan of the garden and planted a few vital trees and the most important avenues and hedges, with Sir Harold Nicolson as the landscape architect and his wife as plantswoman. Vita Sackville-West loved lavishness and profusion and used bold mixtures and thick, dense plantings throughout the garden. Her first book on flowers, *Some Flowers*, was published in 1937. Vita's unconventional marriage and lesbian affairs added to the mystique of Sissinghurst and helped to make it into the celebrated garden that it is today.

The global depression of the 1930s witnessed the decline of many of England's country estates, the owners of which could no longer afford the maintenance of elaborate flower beds and borders and lavish kitchen gardens. Modernism, with its shift toward simplification, acquired prominence and was the dominant factor in garden design both in the United States and in Europe, although the work of Gertrude Jekyll enjoyed a resurgence of popularity in the U.S. as the Americans rediscovered the joys of herbaceous plantings.

In Great Britain, commercial flower growers were adapting themselves to a greater and wider choice of cut blooms. The flower industry obtained its supplies from three sources: the open field, under glass in England and Wales, and from overseas markets. Exported flowers from the Scilly Isles rose from 250 tons in 1921 to more than 1,000 tons in 1933. In 1925, the area devoted to flower crops was an estimated 1,400 acres, and the flowers were valued at £400,000 ($600,000). Flower crops under glass were valued at £1,350,000, giving a total value for British flower crops of £1,750,000. By 1931, the acreage of outdoor flowers had increased by 1,000, and the value of crops under glass had reached £2,290,000.

The popular gardening magazines of the day encouraged housewives to have a continuous succession of floral displays in their homes throughout the year. Eleanour Sinclair Rohde disregarded the feminine preference for brightly colored indoor blooms, suggesting instead that "anyone wanting an uncommon and effective arrangement could scarcely use anything better than green flowers." She recommended the Snakeshead Iris (Iris tuberosa), the green hellebores, and Garrya elliptica for early spring arrangements, and Ornithogalum nutans, Solomon's Seal, and wild orchids for early summer. She also noted that "every florist's shop of importance displays bunches of the Snakeshead Iris in early spring and it is curious to notice how much attention they attract even from people who are not interested in flowers."[8]

Women were also advised that mixing flowers was now permitted, given the disappearance of the flower table, and that a selection of vases, not only of plain glass, should be used. A blue pottery vase, for example, was commended as an ideal container for mauve irises and pale yellow narcissus, while chrysanthemums in large, black Oriental vases were considered the height of fashion. Wherever possible, though, roses continued to be displayed in old cut glass and always in uncolored glass. Goldfish bowls were also suggested as a novel receptacle for a variety of cut flowers. And, not only was the housewife regaled with such gadgets as "the FIXEASY Adjustable Plant Support" to make flower arranging less tedious, but she was also encouraged to use devices such as the "Harpoon" weed extractor and the "Mystic" bulb and potato planter to help ease the drudgery of everyday gardening.

Famous name seed and plant catalogues were available on request. The 1936 *Bees Catalogue* offered, in addition to its range of miscellaneous bulbs, asters, sweet peas, and lilies, a novelty vegetable, "a new Pea of which the pod is eaten as well as the Pea." During the same year, Messrs. James Carter & Co. were honored with the Royal Warrant of Appointment as seedsmen to H.R.H. the Prince of Wales, while the *Ryder's Catalogue* offered the latest fashion in asters, "Aurora Golden Sheaf," as well as a new cosmos, "Orange Flare," and a new godetia, "Sweet Lavender." Messrs. Sutton & Sons, on the other hand, were beguiling housewives with four new novelties in sweet peas, a giant-flowered cyclamen named "Triumph," a unique colored pansy called "Fire Beacon," and a primula malacoides named "Royalty." Interestingly, all of these varieties give a fascinating insight into the gardening trends and fashions of the day from both a practical and a visual point of view.

America's Female Landscape Architects

*I*n America, garden clubs sprang up in large numbers and were amalgamated, in 1924, into Federated Garden Clubs throughout the various states. The Garden Club of America pursued its ever-increasing feminist character under the presidency of Mrs. J. Willis Martin of Chestnut Hill, Philadelphia, expanding its scope from gardening at home to include civic responsibilities. The Garden Club's bulletin of 1920 stated: "The objects of this association shall be: to stimulate the knowledge and love of gardening among amateurs; to share the advantages of association through conference and correspondence in this country and abroad; to aid in the protection of native plants and birds; and to encourage civic planting."[9]

At a meeting of the Council of the Woman's National Farm and Garden Association in New York on 5 February of the same year, the Land Service Committee reported that thirty-six agricultural scholarships had been awarded since September 1918 and that it was now seriously contemplating an exchange scholarship with Great Britain. The Association was also considering publishing a list for distribution among its members that would give details of all producing members as a means of helping women who had produce to sell and women who wished to buy it, and special plant societies were encouraged to advertise in their newsletter.

Among the speakers at the conference of the Midwest branch of the Association held on 22-23 March was Mrs. Francis King, who talked about "Lilacs and Other Spring Flowers," while Mrs. Bertram J. Kahn spoke on "Flower Arrangement" and Miss Lena May McCauley on "Gardening of the Community." There were also papers on such subjects as "Succession of Bloom," from Mrs. F. W. Harnwell, and "Small Gardens," by Mrs W. R. Corlett.

In America, as in Great Britain, gardening reached even higher levels of enthusiasm as the economy expanded, suburbs

mushroomed, and a vast number of the population began to purchase automobiles. Everywhere, more and more people were
starting gardens. Mrs. Francis King wrote several books directed
at the owners of the new, smaller houses: *The Little Garden*
(1921), *Variety in the Little Garden* (1923), and *The Beginner's
Garden* (1927). Women were urged not to wait "until you can
spare a half - or even a quarter - of a day to devote to the garden
work, but [to] get in the habit of putting in that extra fifteen
minutes before lunch."[10]

The 1920s were the golden years of American female landscape architects and heralded the establishment of large and
lucrative offices headed by women. Annette Hoyt Flanders
employed dozens of female staff in her successful New York firm,
which she opened in 1923, and in 1929, Marjorie Sewell Cautley
was one of eleven women who controlled their own practices in
the area of New York City. While many of these women specialized in estate work, Marjorie Sewell Cautley's interests lay in city
planning and low-cost housing in urban areas, prompting her to
work on the radical Radburn, an urban housing development in
New Jersey. Sadly, however, the Wall Street Crash resulted in
many of these women being unable to continue in their practices, and very few, largely those who were well established, sur-
vived the depression of the thirties.

In 1929, landscape architects Elizabeth Lord and Edith
Schryver were asked to design a garden at Deepwood in Salem,
Oregon. Clifford Brown and his wife Alice had purchased the
property with its 5 1/2-acre site in 1925, and Alice Brown was
one of the first clients of this female landscape architectural firm.
Elizabeth Lord came from a wealthy upper-class Oregon family,
and Edith Schryver, who was of Dutch extraction, had spent her
childhood in Kingston, New York. Studying landscape architecture in the 1920s was difficult for women, and any professional
opportunities open to them were often generated by other
women.

Both Elizabeth Lord and Edith Schryver studied at the
Lowthorpe School of Landscape Architecture for Women in
Groton, Massachusetts, where they pursued a three-year course
in horticulture, although at different times. After graduating,
Edith Schryver worked for five years in Ellen Shipman's New
York office, during which time she designed several residential

estates. She met Elizabeth Lord on a European tour, after which the two women decided to set up a practice together in Salem, Oregon's capital city. Edith Schryver was responsible for laying out the overall designs and construction details, and Elizabeth Lord took charge of the plantings.

Their practice prospered as they demonstrated by example the necessity of good garden design. They lectured throughout the Pacific Northwest, mainly to garden clubs where women were anxious to put into practice what they had heard, and at every lecture they recommended landscape architecture as a profession to their female audiences. Deepwood is now owned by the City of Salem and is being lovingly restored with the help of volunteers who work in the garden for three or four hours a week.

In both Great Britain and the United States, roof gardens became very fashionable features during the 1930s. Eleven stories above street level, the huge roof space on the RCA building in Rockefeller Center in New York was divided into thirteen separate gardens, described by their creator, Ralph Hancock, as "Gardens of the Nation."

In Virginia during this period, box hedging could be discovered in virtually every garden, along with hydrangeas and azaleas, and apple, pear, and cherry trees. Wild lilies of the valley, orchids, pinks, phlox subulata, monkshood, and meadowrue flourished in the meadowlands, and in the woods, hepatica, anemones, and columbines could be spotted beneath Judas trees and white dogwood. In an effort to enhance the Virginia countryside, the ladies of the American Garden Club, with their characteristic energy and zeal, promoted a campaign to "Cover the State with Dogwood—a million Dogwood by 1935!"

Rumblings of War

*T*he optimism of the early twenties was lost in the gloom of the unemployment and depression of the 1930s, and by 1936, the European political situation had become tense as rumblings of war echoed ever louder. The emancipation of British women became an increasingly diminishing priority, and gardens that were bright with flower beds and shrubs were destined to be turned into vegetable patches as the country struggled to feed itself.

British society during the 1930s was still hierarchical with tremendous inequalities of wealth and privilege. The rich upper classes jealously guarded their high social prestige, while the middle classes defended their privileges and status against the working class and the rising socialism of the time. People generally "knew their place" in the rigid order of society and were very aware of their social position. However, class status and the privileges that went with it were soon to diminish, although, even after World War II, class continued to determine opportunity.

Women, freed from domestic drudgery by modern, labor-saving devices, were to relinquish the mantle of domesticity with which they had enveloped themselves during the inter-war years. Once again, they would couple their role as homemaker with that of breadwinner, leaving behind the comfortable, convenient, middle-class lifestyle that many had secured for themselves. As the clouds of war gathered, the new crises that faced Great Britain were uppermost in the minds of its people as the nation united once again to face the threat of German hostility for the second time in just over twenty years.

CHAPTER NINE

WORLD WAR II

British Women Take On War Work

ON 3 SEPTEMBER 1939, BRITAIN was again at war. For the first time in history, British women were exposed to its horrors as citizens in their own right and were expected to contribute to the war effort and "do their bit" for the common cause. The government, aware of the crucial role women had played in the 1914-1918 conflict, was quick to capitalize, urging them to volunteer immediately for war work. Women rallied in the thousands, but not without an initial show of reluctance voiced by women's groups such as the Women's Freedom League, which appealed to the government to take action to avert a state of war.

The plea was in vain, and, once resigned to the inevitability of war, women began to offer their services for war work in which they were to prove themselves more than competent in many of the former male strongholds. Their attitudes toward war work varied; for many, the extra money was a bonus, while others discovered a newfound independence and the chance to escape from the boredom of domesticity. With unflagging energy they tackled jobs in industry and on the land, many of them joining the Red Cross, the Women's Voluntary Service (WVS), and the armed forces, as, united by air raids and rationing, government regulations, and food shortages, they strove to address the Nazi threat.

The Control of Employment Orders of 1939 and 1943 allowed the government to send workers wherever they were needed. Women with children under the age of fourteen, or who were pregnant, or who had heavy domestic responsibilities, were exempt. Women up to the age of forty were placed in "mobile" and "immobile" groups, many of them directed into work to which they were totally unsuited, which prompted the Women's Freedom League to complain that the government was not utilizing womanpower to the fullest.

This was not the only grievance. A Ministry of Labour Survey in October 1941 revealed a deficit of 2 million forces and munitions workers. The National Service (No. 2) Act became law on 18 December 1941, and the British government brought into force the conscription of unmarried women between the ages of twenty and thirty (nineteen-year-olds were brought in in early 1942), the first country ever to do so. After December 1941, widows and childless women could be conscripted in a non-combatant role into the armed forces, and by the end of 1943, forty-six percent of all women between fourteen and fifty-nine years of age were undertaking some form of national service.

Feminists of the day believed that the introduction of conscription would result in equal pay for women. However, the government refused to consider such a measure, arguing that it could result in confrontation with male workers in addition to burdening an already beleaguered nation with crippling financial costs. That response, coupled with the government's reluctance to provide adequate nursery provision for working mothers and equal compensation for injuries received in the work place and in bombing raids, prompted the women's groups to lay aside their differences, unite, and revive the flagging spirit of feminism that had reached an all-time low during the previous decade.

In 1939, Britain imported two-thirds of its food from the Commonwealth, Argentina, and the United States, which made heavy demands on shipping space. In addition, merchant ships were under constant attack from German U-boats (Britain was to lose 11.4 million tons of shipping during the course of the war). Consequently, in a desperate bid to avoid use of shipping space for food imports, the government launched a massive ploughing-up campaign that resulted in an extra 6 million acres of arable land by 1944. By way of an incentive, the Agricultural Development Act of May 1939 gave farmers a subsidy of two pounds for every acre of grassland ploughed during the first winter of the war, and, by the autumn of 1940, the government had guaranteed prices and markets for all staples grown. In the years 1940-1941, almost 2 million acres of grassland were ploughed up, another 1.5 million between 1941 and 1942, with 1943-1944 seeing a further 600,000 go under the plough. Double British Summer Time, when clocks were put forward two hours at the end of March to give farmers even more daylight in which to plough and harvest, lasted the whole year, and farmers were actively encouraged to plough by night.

The mechanization of farming increased rapidly, the number of farm horses falling by twenty percent and the number of tractors rising from 56,000 in 1939 to 203,000 by 1946. Home output doubled by 1941, and Ford was given a government contract to meet the demand. Imported American Allis Chalmers Crawler tractors were also widely used, although supplies were limited after America's entry into the war in December 1941. "Tractors for Britain" became a familiar wartime slogan; and by 1942, there were some 150,000 farm tractors in service, although in August 1943, rationing was imposed on all new agricultural machinery.

The use of farm land was placed under the control of the County War Agricultural Executive Committees (CWAECs), or the War Ags, as they were known, which acted through district committees (DCs). To these committees fell the task of implementing government policy regarding cultivation, labor, and machinery. Under the Defence Regulations, they were empowered to repossess land and unused machinery, evict unsuitable tenants, classify farms according to efficiency and productivity, organize their own workforce, and allocate machinery, fertilizers, and foodstuffs. The work of these committee members was done on a voluntary basis, and by the end of 1943, the War Ags had control of nearly 400,000 acres of land in England and Wales.

The war brought with it an acute shortage of agricultural labor. More than 30,000 male agricultural workers in England and Wales had been drafted into the armed forces following a deflection from the land during the interwar years of some 10,000 workers per year. With the onset of hostilities, agriculture was, on the one hand, a key industry, and, on the other, severely depressed. There was a steady trickle back to the land by those anxious to avoid conscription (agriculture came under an Essential Work Order in 1941), but it was insufficient to meet the shortfall. If certain targets were to be met, then extra labor had to be forthcoming.

World War II garden tools (from the Royal Horticultural Society, The Vegetable Garden Displayed, 1944, reprinted with permission of the Royal Horticultural Society).

The Women's Land Army and Other Volunteer Programs

*T*he early mobilization of women and the re-forming of the Women's Land Army under the direction of Lady Gertrude Denman, Dame of the British Empire, on 1 June 1939 went a considerable way toward meeting this demand, and by the end of December, 4,544 land girls were already employed.

The "National Service Booklet" (1939) states:

> *In the event of war a Women's Land Army will be organised. This body will be a mobile force consisting of women who are ready to undertake all kinds of farm work in any part of the country. The members will wear uniform, although they will normally be employed and paid by individual farmers and the organisation will supervise their lodging arrangements and their general welfare. There will also be a need for women who are only able to offer their services for work in their home district.*[1]

About one-third of the women who enrolled in the WLA came from large towns and cities. They were from all classes of society and from all walks of life, and many of them had an idealized view of the countryside that was far removed from reality. Initially, they were met by hostile farmers who were reluctant to take them, but male prejudice was evident in every sector of the work place, where resentment often materialized in constant teasing, sexual harassment, and even, in extreme cases, violence.

Chauvinistic attitudes persisted throughout the war. As women tackled physically demanding and sometimes dangerous work previously done only by men, a lot of anti-feminist "little woman" remarks were bandied about. Eventually, however, the general public began to accept working women as a fact of wartime life and farmers started to view the land girls with a grudging admiration.

The WLA, part of the Ministry of Agriculture and Fisheries, was organized and staffed entirely by women. Originally, its general headquarters were at Balcombe Place, the home of Lady Denman, but were transferred in May 1944 to 6 Chesham Street, London S.W.1. In rooms lined with oak paneling could be found desks, typewriters, telephones, and trestle tables. One of the rooms was occupied by the editorial staff of *Land Girl*, the monthly magazine of the WLA, and the garages and stables outside were utilized as warehouses for Land Army uniforms.

Lady Denman and her assistant director, Mrs. Jenkins, CBE (Commander of the British Empire), were supported in their administrative work by seven regional officers who regularly visited the counties in their charge. Every county had its own county office with its own organizing secretary, office staff, chairman, committee, sub-committees, and local representatives. The county offices maintained a close personal contact with the girls they employed, and it was they who were responsible for collating information about each volunteer. Every land girl was interviewed by a minimum of two people, who would ascertain certain facts such as the girl's full name, age, present occupation, experience of country life, if any, and even if she was able to ride a bicycle.

The interviewers then had to decide if the volunteer was suitable; intelligence, physical strength, and health were important criteria that formed the basis of their decision. Upon acceptance, the new recruit had to sign a form of undertaking, promising to make herself available for service on the land wherever she might be needed. The final step was a compulsory medical examination, the fee for which was paid by the Ministry of Agriculture.

The county offices employed district representatives to maintain contact with, and ensure the well-being of, their land girls. To these representatives fell such tasks as resolving difficulties brought to their attention during the course of their monthly visits (the county office dealt with any real problems), introducing their charges into the rural community, and keeping them informed of current correspondence courses, proficiency tests, and clubs that they might wish to join.

The title "Land Army" is probably a misnomer in that land girls were not subject to any disciplinary action other than dismissal; the form of undertaking, signed by each accepted volunteer, was not legally binding. The district representatives, who, incidentally, belonged to "a different class of birth and upbringing, and also...to a different generation,"[2] used all their skills to cajole, encourage and persuade, rather than command, but the turnover of girls was high, many of them unable to stand the heavy work, the long hours, and the Spartan rigors of country life. Nevertheless, by the spring of 1941, there were 20,000 volunteers, rising to more than 80,000 by 1943.

All land girls were given seven days of annual holiday with pay, all public holidays, free Sundays, and a free half-day each week. They were also entitled to one free weekend in four and were paid according to the minimum wage and overtime rates laid down for women agricultural workers by the Agricultural Wages Board for the county of employment. For a working week of fifty hours in summer and forty-eight hours in winter, a land girl of eighteen years or over received a wage of not less than 22s. 6d. ($1.68) after a deduction for board and lodging; seventeen-year-olds received 18s. ($1.35) after the same deduction.

Once recruited, land girls were issued with the following uniform: two green jerseys, two pairs of breeches, two overall coats, two pairs of dungarees, six pairs of stockings, three shirts, one pair of ankle boots, one pair of shoes, one pair of gumboots or boots with leggings, a hat, an overcoat, an oilskin or a mackintosh, an oilskin sou'wester, two towels, a green armband, and a metal badge. A half-diamond was sewn onto the armband after six months of satisfactory service, a special armband was issued after two years' service, and a scarlet armband was given at the end of four years.

About one-third of the land girls lived in hostels, which ranged from castles and manor houses to Ministry of Works hutments and converted chicken houses. In January 1944, there were 696 hostels, of which 475 were run by the Women's Land Army, 146 by the Young Women's Christian Association, and 75 by the War Agricultural Executive Committees, in which approximately 22,000 land girls and 2,300 staff were accommodated.

Others lodged with farmers and their families often in primitive accommodations that came as a culture shock. Many of the girls grumbled, not only about their primeval living conditions but also about the recalcitrance on the part of the farmers in paying them regularly, which made them feel used and exploited. They also believed that the government was treating them as second-class citizens, an issue taken up by some of the voluntary women's groups in 1942. They were allowed none of the perks offered to the other women's services—the Women's Royal

Naval Service, the Auxiliary Territorial Service, and the Women's Auxiliary Air Force—such as canteen privileges, the purchase of cigarettes and chocolate at reduced service rates, and travel warrants, although those working twenty miles or more from their homes were issued a free rail warrant home after each completed six months of satisfactory service.

All land girls had to be mobile and ready and willing to tackle ploughing, hoeing, weeding, lifting, and clamping root crops and all general farmwork. More specialized tasks included the making and laying of thatch, felling timber (the WLA had its own Timber Corps), planting saplings, pulling flax, pruning and spraying fruit trees, and working in both commercial and private gardens, although "at least two-thirds of their time should be devoted to food-production; the other third might be given to the flower-garden, provided the authorities were satisfied that the girl was really replacing a man."[3] There were more than 10,000 land girls in horticultural employment, although most of those in private gardens were removed in 1943 as the farmers' needs became greater.

During harvest time and other seasonal work peaks, land girls were formed into mobile labor gangs, each member of which, stated the June 1942 edition of Land Girl, was expected to "do her share and keep up the reputation of the gang." The girls were also exhorted to "get into the habit of doing the job well; you'll then be proud of your work and, what is more, the farmer will be pleased with you."[4]

Threshing, a dirty, dusty job, offered the only promotion within the WLA. A competent girl could become a charge-hand or forewoman, each of whom was given a special armband to wear during working hours, with a slight increase in wages. While the charge-hand supervised gang labor and was answerable to the forewoman for the quality of work, the forewoman was expected to ensure that every girl did her fair share and that she filled in her weekly time sheets correctly. Time sheets comprised twelve different columns for each day's work; the land girl completed eleven of the columns and the farmer signed the twelfth to confirm that the work had been completed satisfactorily.

Many farmers ultimately came to value the land girls and to respect them for their determination and courage in tackling tough, heavy work, as, despite their disenchantment with country life, many of them remained cheerful and made the best of things. Digging, sorting vegetables, muck spreading, ditching, hedging, and potato picking in the depths of winter and hoeing and harvesting in the sweltering heat of summer, these girls proved themselves indispensable in the battle to feed the nation.

To help cope with seasonal work, the Women's Emergency Land Corps (WELCS) was mobilized. It was made up of village women, who, for 11d. an hour, worked in gangs planting or harvesting. And in 1940, at the request of the Ministry of Agriculture, an appeal went out from Lady Denman for volunteers for short-term land service in the Women's Land Army Auxiliary Force.

By 1942, many women were employed in more than one job, and while they could match or better men in light work such as pulling peas, heavier work, like lifting potatoes, required greater physical strength. Extra muscle power was obviously needed, and farmers were given little choice during seasonal pressure other than relying on prisoners of war and conscientious objectors to provide it.

The much vaunted "Lend a Hand on the Land" scheme was widely supported by numbers of volunteer city and town dwellers who happily gave up evenings, weekends, and annual holidays to help out on the country's farms. Virtually every county had a register of able-bodied citizens who could be called upon at short notice. Female volunteers often helped with pea-pulling and fruit-picking.

By September 1943, a number of flourishing Land Clubs, referred to by the government as "holidays with pay" had evolved. Some patriotic business concerns even "adopted" a farm to which they sent employees, on a week-by-week basis, throughout the summer months. School children spent their holidays at farming camps, and London women continued with the traditional cockney pursuit of hop-picking, which became a holiday for all the family. Women who, for various reasons, were unable to work on the land themselves willingly stepped in and took over the domestic chores of those who could.

The government decided, in 1941, to increase the acreage of flax to replace the dwindling supplies from the Low Countries and the Baltic. Flax was vital to the war effort, as it provided a tough fiber used to make webbing for parachute harnesses, canvas for tents, and fabric for aircraft wings. It also yielded the linseed oil that was added to home-produced animal foodstuff. The crop was harvested by members of the WLA and volunteer women, many of whom had day jobs but who gave up their evenings and weekends to further the war effort.

In March 1942, Mr. Tom Williams, MP, launched a new series of BBC radio programs, "Five to One on the Land." Broadcast each Monday and Wednesday, the series was designed to keep the public informed of the achievements of farmers and farmworkers in growing the nation's food, and those actually doing the job were invited to come along, from all parts of the country, to speak for themselves.

Goods carried by ships, particularly food imports, were costing the lives of sailors because so many ships were being sunk by German U-boats. Great Britain had to become self-supporting to prevent this loss of life. Posters warned that "Cargoes Cost Lives." Although the problems of food production in wartime Britain were immense and land was precious, the government decided that a certain number of parks and gardens should be maintained for rest and recreation. The decision was a popular one.

Kew Gardens

The number of people visiting Kew Gardens in 1940 was 822,928, rising to 825,373 in 1941, despite air raids and evacuation. Many of these visitors were surprised to see women at work in the Gardens. Wearing the familiar clogs and gardeners' aprons, the women were brought in to replace conscripted male students. They were largely employed in the propagating pits, flower and rock gardens, the decorative department, and certain sections of the tropical department. The membership of the Kew Women Gardener's Guild rose to twenty during the seven months following the first arrivals.

Several of the open lawns in front of Kew Palace were ploughed up and planted with vegetables, in addition to an area of about five acres, in 1940-1941, on the Palace and Sundial (1940), Seven Sisters and Bell-tree lawns (1941), two acres of which were planted in 1941 with potatoes: "Majestic," "Red Skin," "Great Scot," "Long Keeper," and "Dunbar Standard." It was noted with interest, moreover, that there was an increased yield on the land where the turf was ploughed in.

On the lawn near the kiosk could be found a ten-rod model allotment cropped in accordance with the cropping plan issued by the Ministry of Agriculture and Fisheries. The Sundial lawn, meanwhile, provided a number of allotments for the staff, male and female, which were of great interest to many of the visitors, who spent their weekends inspecting and discussing the produce.

Kew Gardens also grew a variety of vegetables on areas of thirty rods or more, including carrots, leeks, beets, onions, dwarf beans, swedes, garlic, kohlrabi, and Hubbard squashes. Vegetable marrows were trained up pillars and arches to show the general public how easy it was to save valuable space by using this method in small gardens.

Adverse weather conditions severely hampered planting during 1941, killing off some of the young onions and slowing the growth of others. There was, however, a good cropping of other vegetables, particularly carrots, and some of them were kept for seed for what was probably the first time in the history of Kew.

In the Depot Nursery, crops of *Atropa belladonna* were cultivated to help meet the national demand for medicinal herbs. One and a half tons of tops and fresh leaves were harvested and dispatched to a commercial drug house to be dried. About twenty lbs. of foxglove seeds were collected from thriving plants in various parts of the Gardens, and large numbers of Colchicum corms, gathered by boy scouts in the autumn of 1940, were planted and kept as a reserve until a further supply of these drug-producing plants was obtained the following year.

The "Dig for Victory" Campaign

The aim of the British government was total self-sufficiency, and at the outbreak of war the main home front task for women was to grow and store enough food for their families and themselves for the coming year. Housewives were encouraged to scour hedgerows for "free food": blackberries, rose hips, elderberries, damsons, chestnuts, and wild herbs. Mushrooms suddenly became a "war food crop," and people were asked to grow them in garages, greenhouses, and cellars. Every spare piece of land was dug up and planted with vegetables and herbs, every inch of garden filled with brussels sprouts, carrots, cabbages, cauliflowers, and onions, and tomato plants flourished in window boxes in a patriotic bid to "Dig, Cook and Store."

Anderson shelters, issued free to those with an income of less than £250 ($375) per annum, were sunk three feet into the ground and covered with eighteen inches (45 cm.) of earth. The soil covering was used by enterprising housewives to grow marrows, cucumbers, and nasturtiums. As women gathered seaweed from the shores and grew peas and beans to dry and use as meat substitutes, Ministry of Agriculture posters blazoned down from hoardings reminding them: "Farmers can't grow all your vegetables. You must grow your own."

When rationing was first introduced in January 1940, home food production grew in value and the "Dig for Victory" campaign became perhaps the most famous government scheme of the duration. British women were assisted in their horticultural endeavors by a deluge of government leaflets (10 million were distributed in 1942), by the daily newspaper cartoon characters Mr. Digwell and Adam the Gardener, and by the weekly radio broadcasts of the famous gardener Mr. Middleton. They soon gained the confidence to "Step On It," another government admonition to hurry up and get the garden ready. The Duke of Norfolk, speaking at a meeting in Trowbridge, Wiltshire, in March 1942, announced that "the horticulturist now holds his garden and glasshouses in trust for the nation. Cut flowers and early luxuries must make way for the humbler and more health-giving tomato."[5]

At the beginning of the war, however, seventy-three percent of the population were without gardens, which resulted in the ploughing up of playing fields, village greens, railway embankments, parks, golf courses, and even bomb sites to provide allotments in the national drive to grow more food. Demonstration plots cropped as recommended in the "Dig for Victory" Leaflet No. 1 were established by the Ministry of Agriculture to "serve as practical guides to cultural operations and provide good rendezvous for those who need advice" and where "seasonal demonstrations may be given at advertised times."[6] At the end of World War I, there had been 1,500,000 allotments under cultivation, this number declining to 815,000 by 1939, and rising to 1,400,000 in 1943.

The standard wartime allotment measured approximately 90 ft. x 30 ft. and could provide vegetables all year round if planted according to the Ministry of Agriculture's cropping plan. Those requiring an allotment had to apply to the town clerk, the clerk of the Urban District Council, or the clerk of the Parish Council in their local area. In rural parishes with no council, application had to be made to the chairman of the parish meeting; local allotment associations were requested to contact the secretary. If no plot was available, the applicant could ask to be registered and informed when a vacancy occurred.

Local authorities were required under the Allotments Act to charge a "full fair rent," which varied from county to county but which usually averaged 1s. per rod in big towns and cities. Except where the annual rent was 20s. or less, not more than a quarter's rent was payable in advance.

"Is Your Garden On War Service?" asked the Ministry of Agriculture. Agriculture officials were anxious to encourage gardening as a majority pastime but realized that a lot of help would have to be forthcoming if the population as a whole, and women in particular, were going to tackle, with any degree of success, the numerous tasks and problems facing the novice horticulturist. Accordingly, the Ministry of Agriculture published a variety of practical "Dig for Victory" leaflets at a time when, as stated by the Minister of Food, The Right Honorable Lord Woolton, "The battle on the Kitchen Front cannot be won without help from the Kitchen Garden."

While it was widely appreciated that flowers and ornamental gardens had a worthwhile role to fill during wartime, the reorganization of the garden, entailing a temporary loss of flowers and lawns, was necessary if all gardeners were to grow at least some of the vegetables needed by their families. The Ministry of Agriculture concluded that to provide a family of four or five with a year's supply of all vegetables, other than potatoes, about 240 sq. yd. would have to be cropped, with an additional 170 sq. yd. if potatoes were to be planted. This area would, of course, vary according to the fertility of the soil and would depend on the size of the garden and the labor available.

Large gardens presented no problem, as something of everything could be grown. Small gardens, however, needed careful planning so that carrots and onions and a steady supply of green vegetables, particularly in winter and early spring, could be maintained. These were the crops held by the Ministry of Food to be health-giving because of their vitamin content, taking preference over potatoes, beets, swedes, and turnips, all of which were unlikely to be in short supply.

Many local authorities adopted the government scheme of "Certificates of Merit," introduced in 1940. The certificates, signed by the Minister of Agriculture, were awarded to people who used the Ministry's cropping plan and whose plots were judged to be of a high standard. It was noted by the Ministry, however, that in spite of the information available, "in many areas PRIVATE GARDENS are not contributing to their quota....Where necessary, flowers and lawns should give way to food crops."[7]

A WAR-TIME ALLOTMENT PLAN

When cultivating a garden or allotment, certain simple rules were laid down for the gardener to follow, the first of which was to mark off the plot to be dug with the aid of a line, followed by double digging or bastard trenching. This method allowed the top spit of fertile soil to be retained on the surface and the sub-soil to improve without bringing it to the top. Plots of regular shape were divided lengthwise into two, and a trench, 24 in. wide and 12 in. deep (60 x 30 cm.), taken out across the end of one section. The excavated soil was then removed to the same end of the second section where the digging would finish, after which, the exposed sub-soil was forked to a depth of 10 in. (25 cm.) and the turfs taken from the next 18 in.(45 cm.) width of ground and placed on it, grass-side downwards.

The sod was then chopped up with the spade and the exposed 18 in.(45 cm.) width of top soil dug and thrown forward onto the inverted turf. The process was then repeated along the full length of both the first and second sections, and the task was completed by filling up the working trench with the turf and soil taken from the first trench on the first section.

Newly dug beds were treated with an application of organic manure—hop, animal, or compost—or a chemical fertilizer, such as "National Growmore." A few days before a crop was planted, the ground was given a dressing of fertilizer containing nitrogen, phosphoric acid, and potash, which was also applied during the growing season, particularly after thinning. Well-established leafy plants, such as cabbages, were dressed with "Nitro-Chalk"

MINISTRY OF AGRICULTURE AND FISHERIES' WAR-TIME ALLOTMENT PLAN

Compost Heap	Tool Shed	Seedbed
	Tomatoes, Marrow, Radish, Parsley	

C **MISCELLANEOUS CROPS**	DWARF PEAS .. .. 3 rows 2 ft. 6 in. apart.	Intercrop with Spinach.. 2 rows and follow with, Leeks .. .. .. 4 rows 1 ft. apart.
	DWARF BEANS .. 2 rows 2 ft. 6 in. apart.	
	ONIONS .. .. .. 8 rows 1 ft. apart.	Follow with Spring Cabbage .. 4 rows
	SHALLOTS .. .. 2 rows 1 ft. apart BROAD BEANS .. 1 double row	Follow with Winter Lettuce Intercrop with Summer Lettuce
	RUNNER BEANS .. 1 row	
A **POTATOES AND ROOT CROPS**	PARSNIP .. .. 3 rows 15 in. apart.	
	CARROT (MAINCROP) 5 rows 1 ft. apart.	
	POTATOES (EARLY) .. 3 rows 2 ft. by 1 ft.	Follow with Turnips
	POTATOES (OTHERS) 6 rows 2 ft. by 1 ft. 3 in.	
	SPINACH BEET or SEAKALE BEET .. .. .. 1 row	
		Maincrops CABBAGE (WINTER) 3 rows 2 ft. by 2 ft.
B **WINTER AND SPRING GREEN CROPS**	Intercrop space for Savoys and Brussels Sprouts with Early Carrots 2 rows, and Early Beet, 1 row.	SAVOYS .. .. .. 2 rows 2 ft. by 2 ft. BRUSSELS SPROUTS 2 rows 2 ft. 6 in. by 2 ft. 6 in.
Rotation Diagram	Early Dwarf Peas .. 1 row	SPROUTING BROCCOLI 2 rows 2 ft. by 2 ft. KALE .. .. .. 2 rows 2 ft. by 2 ft. SWEDES .. .. 2 rows 1 ft. 3 in. apart. GLOBE BEET .. .. 2 rows 1 ft. 3 in. apart.

C	B	A
A	C	B
B	A	C

NOTE.—This Cropping Plan is not drawn to scale. The ground dimensions of the whole plot are 30 ft. by 90 ft. Sections A, B and C are each 30 ft. by 28 ft., and the space provided for Seedbed, Tool Shed, etc., is 30 ft. by 6 ft.

A World War II Ministry of Agriculture and Fisheries war-time allotment plan (from the Royal Horticultural Society, The Vegetable Garden Displayed, 1944, reprinted with permission of the Royal Horticultural Society).

at monthly intervals and at the rate of 1/4 oz. to 1/2 oz. per sq. yd.

The Ministry of Agriculture's cropping plan was designed to provide a succession of vegetables throughout the year. For the purpose of crop rotation, the ground was divided into three plots. Plot 1 was used to grow those vegetables requiring the richest soil—onions, leeks, peas, beans, and lettuce. Plot 2 was used for the all-important root crops, carrots, beets, and parsnips, in addition to potatoes, and it was recommended that the ground be dug to a depth of one spit, the sub-soil broken up, and a light dressing of artificial fertilizer applied. Plot 3 contained the green crops that were harvested in the autumn but which continued to provide green vegetables throughout the winter and into the spring. The plan also provided for succession crops, which followed once the land was cleared of the first crop sown.

By December 1940, the "Dig for Victory" campaign had greatly alleviated the food shortage, and well over half the nation's food was home-grown. Members of the Women's Institutes cooperated with the government in preserving surplus produce for later use, and in the summer of that year, a fruit preservation scheme was set up at 2,600 centers throughout the country. Here, armies of volunteer women undertook to save a particularly heavy plum crop in addition to other fruit such as strawberries, raspberries, and black currants, the bulk of which was made into jam, although in some centers the later crops of fruit were bottled and canned as well as being used for jam. The scheme was so successful that it became an annual undertaking, despite the introduction of jam rationing in February 1941.

Throughout the years of war, the Women's Institutes systematically mounted their own war effort. Manned on a voluntary basis by some of the country's 10 million "immobile" women, a large number of whom were middle class, this organization assumed a new and important role. From setting up and running market stalls—there were 319 by 1944—to buying packets of seeds from nurseries at bargain prices and distributing them to women through their local centers, the WIs provided a consistent and valuable service. Since the founding of the Women's Institutes in Canada in 1897, their traditional role had been that of supporting rural communities. This role gradually changed as

the Women's Institutes began to provide a means whereby women who had hitherto shown little or no interest outside the narrow confines of their homes could learn about the wider world beyond domesticity.

This was a tremendous step forward for feminism, as it inspired women's self-confidence and a desire not to leave everything to the men as they had been so used to doing in the past. It also fired these traditionally dependent women with the enthusiasm and courage to make themselves heard in both local and national government, although the old-fashioned male concern for the "weaker sex" continued, as ingrained chauvinistic attitudes refused to die.

The National Federation of Women's Institutes, in conjunction with the Women's Voluntary Service, organized county herb committees for the collection and drying of medicinal herbs from the countryside, so vital to the wartime pharmaceutical industry. Imports of herbs had been severely curtailed for the duration, which created a demand for both home-grown culinary and medicinal plants. Belladonna, foxgloves, aconite, licorice, and valerian were in short supply, and commercial herb growers were given permits to employ labor—mostly female—for their cultivation and harvesting.

A national appeal was made by the Ministry of Supply (Directorate of Medical Supplies) to women, school children, and boy scouts to join land groups organized by the women's voluntary services for the collection of horse chestnuts, which were urgently needed by the pharmaceutical industry. Because this was viewed as vital and valuable war work, 7s. 6d. was paid for every hundredweight of horse chestnuts, without their outer green husks, collected and delivered to the nearest depot. All landowners were urged to encourage collections on their land.

Throughout the long years of war, British food production was sustained under the terms of the American Lend-Lease Bill, signed by President Roosevelt on 12 March 1941. Backed by an initial $7 billion, the bill empowered Roosevelt to provide Great Britain with all it needed on terms he had yet to decide. Shipments of bacon, beans, dried eggs, evaporated milk, lard, canned meat, and cheese crossed the Atlantic in the battle to keep the nation fed.

Before the Lend-Lease program began, however, Britain was required to dispose of all its U.S. capital assets, and while there was no immediate demand for a cash repayment at the end of the war, a large proportion of British export trade was taken over by the United States. By 1943, Britain was dependent on the United States not only for food but also for weapons.

The Americans Mobilize for War

On Sunday, 7 December 1941, Japanese aircraft attacked the U.S. naval base at Pearl Harbor, Hawaii. Reaction in America was one of shock and disbelief as the U.S. government declared war on Germany. The news was catastrophic for Great Britain, whose shipping losses increased dramatically as German U-boats took control of American waters.

Blackout restrictions were imposed in Hawaii and were not lifted until July 1944. Along the West Coast, the blackout was observed with special care because of the possibility of further Japanese aerial attacks. Barrage balloons loomed large above potential enemy targets. Air raid drills were in force throughout the country, and members of the Civil Defense Corps Air Raid Wardens could be found patrolling the streets of towns and cities to make sure that blackout regulations were being observed, regulations, incidentally, that continued throughout the duration.

American civilians prepared themselves for war in much the same way as the British had. Thousands of men and women volunteered as air raid wardens and for civil defense duties. On 13 November 1942, voluntary enlistments were ended and all men between the ages of eighteen and thirty-eight were eligible to be drafted, although industrial and agricultural workers were deferred.

A variety of wartime propaganda posters were printed in the thousands to inspire patriotism and the fight to victory. These ranged from "Make Yours a Victory Home" to "When you ride ALONE you ride with Hitler! Join a Car-Sharing Club TODAY!" They came in many different sizes so they could be displayed in anything from a small window of a house to a billboard. American families also displayed banners in their front room windows with blue stars against a white background and often framed with a red border. The number of stars represented the number of family members in the military services. Sadly, as the war progressed, these blue stars were all too often replaced by gold ones in homes where a loved one had been killed in action.

Ration books were introduced in January 1942, a move which, while it ensured fair shares for all, may have been unnecessary. And, as war progressed, a popular American slogan appeared: "Use it up, wear it out, make it do, or do without."

Defense savings bonds, which were adopted by Congress in 1940, were the brainchild of Henry Morgenthau, then Secretary of the Treasury, but they became known as war bonds after the Japanese attack on Pearl Harbor. War bond rallies and "Victory Loan Drives" were held throughout America, and war bonds were sold everywhere, from banks to street corner booths. Hollywood film stars were enlisted to help promote their sale, and sales were also encouraged with propaganda slogans such as "Back the Attack," which could be seen almost everywhere, from posters to candy wrappers.

The War Industries Board of World War I enabled President Roosevelt, in 1940, to set up the National Defense Advisory Commission, from which came the Office of War Mobilization, the War Production Board, and the Office of Price Administration. This gave the U.S. government control over prices, the allocation of materials, and the rationing of consumer goods. In 1943, war production was at its peak, and by 1944, military goods represented about sixty-five percent of total production, compared with two percent in 1939.

A Temporarily Matriarchal Society

With the conscription of 14 million men into the armed forces between 1942 and 1945, there was a shortfall of workers that led to the employment of some 5 million women during those years. A recruiting campaign was mounted by the government, with war propaganda posters promising "man-sized" jobs with "man-sized" wages, although the American view of women was just as conservative as that of the British.

American women took up jobs for many reasons: economic necessity, patriotism, the desire for excitement in an unknown world, and independence. Life was not easy, as much of the work was heavy and tiring, coupled as it was with male prejudice and, for many, the household chores to contend with at the end of the day. A certain amount of child care was provided by the government, but demand always exceeded supply, making it difficult for women with small children to join the labor force. These wartime nurseries, day-or-night centers, and after-school programs were faced with many practical problems, but they did provide the essential child care that enabled many mothers to go into defense industries. The centers were not permanent, however; the government had set them up as an interim measure to help the war effort, and after VJ (Victory in Japan) Day, they were closed down.

Many women defense workers took to wearing the new, highly fashionable coverall jumpsuits, while other women wore slacks, largely out of necessity but also for convenience at a time when stockings were in short supply (nylon stockings could be found only on the black market at $5 a pair). They tied back their hair under turbans or wore snoods and painted their legs with "liquid stockings." High school girls became known as "bobby soxers" because of the short cotton socks they wore along with Sloppy Joe sweaters, denim jeans, and loafers. They also helped the war effort by doing farm work and by buying 10¢ or 25¢ Defense stamps to put in their savings bond booklets, which, when full, would be exchanged for a savings bond to help defray the cost of the war, estimated at some $315 billion.

Mrs. Eleanor Roosevelt, wife of the president, and Senator Margaret Chase Smith thought that women should play their part in the U.S. war effort, although they met with opposition from those congressmen who firmly believed that a woman's place was in the home. Of the relatively small percentage of women who worked in paid employment, many were black, and the percentage of black women in industry increased while the number who worked on farms and as domestic servants dropped. There was, however, widespread discrimination against blacks, with segregation in many areas of civilian life. A 1941 government executive order forbidding discrimination gave blacks the jobs in defense plants that were earlier refused to them, although their pay was much lower than that of white workers. When black protests occurred, Mrs. Roosevelt lent her support and an end to discrimination was called for by such organizations as the Congress of Racial Equality.

Skilled labor was in short supply, and employers found it necessary to improve working conditions in order to attract and keep the workers they needed. Feminism was given a double boost when, in 1942, the United States allowed women to join the military services in a non-combatant capacity and granted them the same pay as men. In all, around 260,000 women enlisted in the Women's Army Corps (WACs) and in the navy as Women Appointed for Voluntary Emergency Service (WAVEs). These women were largely employed in administrative and clerical work. Along with their defense plant worker counterparts, they were referred to in official U.S. Army posters as "soldiers without guns" or "Dames for Defense." Not surprisingly, there was considerable male resistance to women joining the armed forces, as there was to their employment in industry, both areas having been traditionally dominated by men. It was generally thought that women could not cope with heavy work, but as the demand for labor grew, male prejudice was set aside and many women obtained decently paid jobs for the first time.

While the women in Great Britain were subject to conscription, seventy-one percent of American women over the age of eighteen stayed at home, their menfolk insisting that they were fighting for the right for women to remain in what had always been their traditional domain. Nevertheless, by the end of the war, women made up around thirty-five percent of the labor force.

The dominating role of women in American society gave rise to a great deal of British curiosity and provided excellent material for wartime magazines. Generally speaking, the U.S. feminist movement was at a low ebb, with various organizations losing supporters or disappearing altogether as women's limited impact on policymaking in public life was further eroded. The National Woman's Party, although still very much committed to sexual equality, retained little influence. Still, it appeared that American women were in control. Their tremendous reserves of energy and vitality, their self-confidence, their ability to succeed in business and still retain their femininity were all topics for discussion. Adding to the mystique was their access to consumer goods and luxury items unimaginable to their British sisters. Independent, well-groomed, and liberated, American women made their views felt, knew their "rights," and, what is more, used them in the matriarchal society they had established for themselves.

These same women joined non-military organizations dealing with issues such as agriculture and munitions, in a patriotic bid to bolster their country's war effort. They became involved with the Red Cross, civil defense, servicemen's centers, and salvage drives and various other types of relief work. They were also extremely sympathetic to the British cause. They cared for more than 2,000 evacuated British children, sent items of clothing in their "Bundles for Britain," and provided help for bombed-out families through the English-Speaking Union's War Relief.

Victory Gardens

U.S. farmers became prosperous and mechanization increased along with farm incomes and prices as levels of output rose with the sharp increase of women entering the labor force. World War II was resulting in a booming economy and a move toward state-directed capitalism as America became the "Arsenal of Democracy."

Mobilization itself caused tremendous upheaval as munitions plants sprang up all over the country, creating boom towns in their wake. Thousands of people migrated to these towns seeking employment. Millions more moved around the country, particularly to the Pacific Coast, and newly married "war brides" followed their husbands to training camps. Many people left the land to find work in ship-building and munitions-building centers, resulting in a decrease in the agricultural population of some twenty percent.

The depopulation of the rural landscape might have had serious repercussions by way of a food crisis if it had not been for the "Victory Gardens," which came into being on a purely voluntary basis. Victory Gardens were planted both as a precaution against possible wartime food shortages and out of a sense of patriotic duty. In the early 1940s, city rooftop gardens and backyard gardens started to spring up as many American families cultivated their own Victory Gardens. In some parts of the country, food cooperatives were formed and the gardens worked on a fixed order of rotation, with the produce grown being given to the needy.

The U.S. Department of Agriculture issued instruction booklets on how to plant and tend these gardens, and wartime gardening books such as *Gardening for Victory* could be purchased at bookstores. Magazine articles encouraged people, particularly women, to make their own Victory Gardens, as did some of the film stars of the day who were often pictured in their own "Victory vegetable plots." Some Victory Gardens even boasted scarecrows that bore a close resemblance to enemy war leaders Hitler, Hirohito, and Mussolini. Everyone dug for "vitamins and victory."

There were other important efforts, such as the Farm Security Administration's "An Acre for a Soldier" project, whereby the proceeds from the sale of crops grown on an acre of land would be donated to, among other things, canteens for the troops. But it was the Victory Gardens that had the greatest impact. In fact, the gardens proved so vital to the war effort that by 1942 the Secretary of Agriculture was asking for 18 million of them to be planted to prevent a food shortage. American citizens rose to the challenge, and by 1943 there were 20 million, providing one-third of the fresh vegetables available in the country.

The War Takes Its Toll

*A*merican consumer purchases increased between 1941 and 1943. Woman power in the workforce was still at a premium, and factories introduced piped in music, coffee breaks, and achievement awards as incentives. But as the war progressed, even the cheerful and efficient women of the United States began to feel the effects. By 1943 their dresses had become drabber and their shoes more sensible as restrictions were applied to consumer goods.

By 1945, traditional values were badly shaken on both sides of the Atlantic; morals were lax, and family life almost non-existent. In Britain, consumer purchases had dropped by twenty percent since 1939. British women, who had been told repeatedly that it was their patriotic duty to look their best and keep smiling, were finding it increasingly difficult to do so as sheer exhaustion threatened to overcome them. For these shabby, war-weary women, who labored under tremendous physical and psychological strain to juggle homes, families, and jobs, there was to be little respite as they became ever more dispirited and dejected. The dual burden they carried was unavoidable, but a combination of tiredness, food queues, and the blackout, coupled with continual anxiety and absent menfolk, took its inevitable toll. Women's wartime experiences were to affect their future lives long after the war, for which they had sacrificed so much, had finally ended.

CHAPTER TEN

THE POST-WAR YEARS
TO THE PRESENT

British Women's Impact on the Labor Market

When the war with Germany ended in May 1945, post-war British society welcomed peace with an overwhelming sense of relief, but Great Britain, her wealth and energies exhausted, faced innumerable problems. Although their nation was no longer a great world power, the war-weary British people were nevertheless optimistic and saw it as the duty of Prime Minister Attlee's post-war government to pursue certain economic policies that would guarantee a brighter future with full employment, an expansion in exports, and fair wage agreements for all workers.

An endless round of conferences took place between the various war-torn nations to discuss the precarious economic situation. The Bretton Woods Agreement of 1944 had set up an international monetary fund to help countries in their post-war reconstruction, but, upon the cessation of hostilities with Japan in August 1945, America withdrew its lend-lease agreement, leaving Great Britain to pay in full for all necessary food, raw materials, and essential items vital to the re-equipping and renewal of its industries. Important sectors of the economy were nationalized by the Labour government, which contributed to economic recovery, as did Marshall Aid, an American program that, after 1947, gave help to all western European countries.

In the years 1945-1951, when Aneurin Bevan, Minister of Health, was responsible for housing, the country was in need of virtually 1 million new houses to replace wartime damage and older properties in a state of decay. The immediate, interim solution was the construction of around 160,000 prefabricated houses ("prefabs") while permanent homes were being built. During 1948, approximately 250,000 new council houses were being built for all classes of society, not just for the poor, and rent control was continued by the government to protect tenants of both private landlords and local councils. The New Towns Act of 1946 aimed to rehouse people in communities that would give them easy access to both work and leisure facilities, while under the terms of the Town and Country Planning Act of 1947, local authorities were committed to drawing up development plans, controlling the use of land, and preserving historic buildings.

For women, the end of the war brought even more profound relief. Many of them wanted to return as quickly as possible to the normalcy of family life. Others preferred to remain in paid employment, although, as in 1918, they deferred to their returning menfolk and were subsequently demoted from their wartime positions into the low-level employment that was traditionally considered "women's work." The transition from war to peacetime, however, was achieved far more smoothly than after World War I. By the end of 1946, nearly 8 million men and women had been demobilized, and virtually all of those who wished to, quickly found civilian employment. Although ingrained attitudes remained, women's position in the labor force was maintained and indeed strengthened during the next ten years.

While homemaking and motherhood were still upheld as the ideal, the shortage of workers, 1.3 million in 1946, forced the government to try to entice women back into the labor market in a bid to raise industrial output. The loan from the United States was beginning to run out, and the balance of payment deficit was some £443 million ($664.5 million) by 1947. Women's earnings, however, were regarded as a secondary income, and wives' dependence on their husbands as breadwinners was taken for granted. There was no real or radical change in women's position; nor was any political importance attached to what had effectively been, during the war, an equality of gender. While woman's role still lay within the area of domesticity, by 1951, 43 percent of working women were married. And with the demise of the domestic servant and the increase of mechanized domestic gadgetry, it became acceptable for the first time for middle-class housewives to do their own housework.

In Great Britain, rationing continued until 1954, with bread going on ration for the first time in 1946. British agriculture was in a healthier state than it had been for seventy-five years and, with American aid, was better equipped than other European countries. The work of the county "War Ags" was continued by the newly established National Agricultural Advisory Service (NAAS), which encouraged farmers to strive for higher standards of husbandry. The 1947 Agriculture Act ensured a guaranteed minimum return for produce and gave farmers a wide range of subsidies on such things as equipment, fertilizers, and buildings. Tractors came off the ration, leading *Country Life* to observe in 1948 that "it is good news that six of the most popular tractors can now be bought without the paraphernalia of permits and licences."[1] In 1948, the farmers' cooperative societies were steadily gaining strength and were supported by both the Ministry of Agriculture and the National Farmers Union (NFU). These societies, while charging fixed market prices, gave their members a rebate of 5 percent, more in some cases, on the amount of trade done throughout the year.

The role of women in British agriculture continued, although between 1950, when the Women's Land Army was disbanded, and 1978, the number of full-time workers fell by 71 percent, from 52,100 to 14,900, while the number of part-time and casual women workers increased by about 25 percent over the same period. This increase of women in the casual labor market was accelerated by the Equal Pay Act (1970), nursed through Parliament by Barbara Castle and which came into force in agriculture in 1975.

Women had certain physical advantages for tasks such as thinning fruit and were considered more adaptable and more patient than men. Accordingly, they were employed for seasonal fruit-picking, in greenhouses, and on poultry farms. Some women ran their own farms or horticultural businesses, although, in 1975, only around 3 percent were actually farmer-occupiers in their own right and were associated in the main with cattle rearing, dairying, poultry farming, and horticulture on farms that tended to be smaller than those controlled by men.

In spite of the Women's Liberation Movement, division of labor by gender continued, with women helping at harvest time, carting and stacking bails, operating the grain-drier, hauling grain, and tedding hay. Some farmers' wives drove tractors and managed the "Pick Your Own" fruit-growing acreage, while female farmers spent more of their time in clerical, supervisory, and administrative capacities than did their male counterparts.

Initiatives of the Women's Institute

*I*n 1946, Lady Denman retired as chairman of the Women's Institute, and in the same year an appeal was launched to raise £60,000 ($90,000) to open a Women's Institute College of Education. In honor of its first chairman, it was to be called Denman College and was opened in 1948 at Marcham Park near Abingdon. The Ministry of Education gave its first grant "for the development of liberal education for women." The first course offered in the late Georgian house set amidst 100 acres was "The Education of the Countrywoman through the WIs."[2] By 1976, there were 175 weekend and five-day courses covering subjects ranging from painting in water colors to weather reporting and market gardening.

Throughout the years, the Women's Institute has been quick to face any problem and any challenge. In 1954, it launched the "Keep Britain Tidy" campaign, an effort to prevent the desecration of the countryside with litter, and also expressed in the press its abhorrence of violence. During the 1960s the movement waged war on unnecessary noise, supported the Five-Year Freedom from Hunger Campaign, and concerned itself with the Divorce Reform Bill. The 1970s witnessed, among other things, the WI protest about rural rates (local property taxes), battered wives, rape, national insurance, and women's lack of equal opportunity.

In recent years, the movement has embroiled its collective energy in such emotive national issues as the export of live animals, organ donations, and pensions equality. As always, it continues to operate its legendary market stalls and to promote its wealth of no-nonsense common sense and its democratic ideal. By using reasoned arguments and a constant application of pressure, it encourages women to take pride in themselves and their environment and to involve themselves in broader issues.

Americans Focus on Home and Family

*A*fter World War II, the need to settle down and raise a family was paramount to returning veterans and to their wives or sweethearts. Large families became commonplace. While pediatrician Benjamin Spock's widely read childrearing book *Baby and Child Care* stressed the importance of loving care, the

U.S. government encouraged people to have families by offering tax deductions and by the Minimum Wage Act of 1949, which increased the minimum hourly wage from 40 to 75 cents. In 1955, the Minimum Wage Act again increased hourly rates from 75 cents to $1. Families were further assisted by the Housing Act of 1949, which provided $2.8 billion for low-rent housing projects and slum clearance.

American women became much more home and family centered, and the birthrate rose steadily with a baby boom that lasted until 1960. During the fifties, the population of America increased by 28 million, and the fashion for large families spread to four, even six children. Even college-educated women were marrying at a young age (in 1950, the average marrying age was twenty), devoting their most productive years to childrearing and homemaking, and having their children early. American women became less career-minded, although some would return to the job market once their children were in high school. Woman's social role as hostess was re-instituted in the new affluence of the 1950s as wives provided their husbands with domestic comforts and adopted a supportive and subordinate role both in the home and in society.

Although around 65 percent of women who had taken paid employment during the war remained after hostilities had ceased, this relatively small number of women who continued to work did so largely because they wanted to purchase some of the consumer goods on offer in the booming economy of an affluent society. Pressures against career women at this time were enormous, as they often were viewed in a negative light, while the role of wife and mother was considered one of fulfillment; it was seen as comfortable, safe, and satisfying. "Togetherness" was the fashionable word in 1954, with the husband helping with the household chores as well as with the care of the children.

British Gardens Become Personalized

*T*he gardens of post-war Britain were hard-working extensions of the house; food production had been given priority during the war years and ornamental gardening had all but disappeared. Even the country houses that had not been requisitioned had lost their vital labor force as men were called into the armed services, leaving day-to-day maintenance an impossibility.

As a result these gardens had fallen into decay, many of them being taken over by the National Trust once peace was declared. Large gardens were no longer practicable, even with the advent of mechanization; gardening staff were both expensive and difficult to come by, forcing owners to re-determine and reappraise the layout of their gardens.

With a lack of hired labor, women worked more and more in the garden, although there were still "some charming ladies who, in these hard times, have secured the services of that nearly obsolete species—a gardener." With the rapid increase in the number of smaller estate houses, a large new class of gardener evolved, with mechanization assisting him and his wife in the management of their plot, although lawn mowers were not to everyone's taste. "SIR, during the next few years we may expect to see a great increase in the number of motor cultivators and similar machines in medium-sized gardens," wrote one disgruntled reader to the editor of *Country Life* in 1949. "The noise of one of these machines in one's neighbour's garden can be most annoying, and peace of mind, which is one of the choicest gifts of gardening, can be utterly destroyed by it."[3]

During the war years, many women gardening for the first time had discovered that they actually enjoyed growing vegetables and that it was a short step from cultivating produce to growing flowers and shrubs. The British public was no longer taking Nature for granted but beginning to appreciate all that it had to offer. Accordingly, gardening once again became fashionable, particularly in the late 1950s when prosperity finally began to take the place of austerity. The simple pleasures of life assumed a new importance, with people buying more and more gardening magazines to help them enjoy the rediscovery of a satisfying recreational pursuit.

Amateur Gardening Magazine, which was especially popular, printed regular indoor flower arrangement features for ladies. Violet Stevenson wrote in the *Amateur Gardening Annual* of 1955: "Since up-to-date flower arrangement embraces all kinds of plant material from the leaf to seed-pod, flower to berry, or bark to fungi, it is not surprising that many arrangers are rediscovering the decorative value and beauty of many grasses, both fresh and dried, native and imported." She goes on to say that "one of our cleverest arrangers of such material is, in my opinion,

Mrs. Adele Gotobed, of Hounslow. Her arrangements have brought joy and stirred admiration in many of us. Her selection of containers, often of rough wood or bark, is a lesson to all."[4]

After 1945, gardens started to become more personalized, more actively planned, and less labor-intensive, embracing a variety of past styles. They also housed swings, sand-pits, patios, and concrete areas and, in some instances, swimming pools and tennis courts. People also found inspiration in the gardens of others. For example, Vita Sackville-West called the paying visitors to Sissinghurst Castle "shillingses," and the National Gardens Scheme, founded in 1927, managed virtually all gardens open to the public, just over 1,000 in 1950, giving the proceeds to help retired or needy district nurses.

In the summer of 1951, the Festival of Britain was held on the South Bank in London with the Pleasure Gardens in Battersea Park. A combination of surrealism, fantasy, and imagination, it exemplified the pleasures of a garden setting. For the British public, the Festival provided an opportunity to see plants in an urban setting rather than in the familiar bedding-out schemes of seaside towns. So inspired were the visitors to this extravaganza that gardening became more popular than ever. The charm of the English garden was defined by the mixture of styles adopted and the types of plants used to achieve them.

The goals of the National Gardens Guild, with which the Prison Gardening Association was incorporated, were "to grow flowers and vegetables in urban areas and villages; to plant waste spots and waysides with flowers; and to unite all classes in restoring living beauty through gardening." Queen Mary was the Guild's patroness. The Guild published a magazine which, in January/February 1953, urged its readers to make a special effort to plant their front gardens in a display of color for the coronation of Queen Elizabeth II the following June: "Our Royal Family has always taken a keen interest in Horticulture in general and in the gardens of the public wherever their duties have taken them, and we should try and make the roadsides of our country, not only on the Coronation route but everywhere, a blaze of beauty from May to September at least."[5]

As the sale of roses accelerated, so did their fame in other countries. For example, on the outskirts of Newark, New York, a semi-public rose garden drew thousands of visitors from all over the country. In 1957, it was estimated that crowds of between one-half to three-quarters of a million would travel to Newark to view the rose display that had achieved worldwide renown. The seventeen-acre garden contained more than 36,000 rose plants, displaying the top varieties of roses available to gardeners and showing how roses should be grown and used in the landscape. It was an inspiration to many amateur horticulturists, prompting them to return home eager to grow roses as perfectly and to display them as artistically.

In Great Britain in 1957, The National Rose Society acquired 11,526 new members, male and female, bringing the total membership to 56,000. The Society, which accomplished valuable work on its trial grounds, was founded on 7 December 1876 and had as its patron, in 1958, HRH the Princess Royal. In the Society's Summer Show held in 1956, Miss J. E. Fulford from the West Country won three of the four trophies in division B, showing the best bloom in the amateurs' section and bringing the salmon-pink and yellow rose, "Gay Crusader," into prominence. Mrs. A. K. Wort won second place in the "Decorative Basket" and "Decorative Arrangement" classes, while in the amateur open classes, Mrs. Seymour Heatley was the winner of both the "One Bowl of Floribunda Roses" and the "Three Vases of Floribunda Roses."

Most of the rose books written in the 1950s recommended that amateur growers concentrate on beds of one variety only and specified certain cultivars as particularly effective for bedding. However, most hybrid teas and possibly all hybrid polyanthas were considered suitable by some horticulturists of the day, who were also of the opinion that it was of little importance whether the habit of the chosen species was tall, bushy, or spreading, provided that the plant was relatively free-flowering.

DESIGNING AND PLANTING A ROSE GARDEN

The following 1955 scheme from *Amateur Gardening Annual*, "Designing and Planting a Rose Garden," was specifically targeted at a small area, where the rose garden could be made a feature separate from the rest of the garden. This could be achieved by beginning with rose beds at the end of the lawn or by surrounding the rose garden with a hedge of evergreen

Chamaecyparis Lawsoniana Allumii. According to the magazine, while early autumn is usually the best time for planting rose bushes, especially on light soils, it may not be possible to carry out the task until spring, and a November/December planting on heavy ground will often have to be abandoned because of the autumn rains. Those advocates of early spring planting, however, believe that March is the ideal month, because at this time the sap begins to rise and the trees do not suffer the ill-effects, such as die-back, of those planted in December or January, a period of dormancy. It must be remembered, moreover, that an ample supply of moisture in the sub-soil is essential if the bushes are to survive and that any exposed roots will soon dry up in the cold March winds.

Any bushes that cannot be planted immediately should be heeled into the ground, and if the soil is dry, the roots of the roses should be soaked in a container of water for three or four hours before planting. Soil preparation and the method of planting, incidentally, are the same for both autumn and spring, with compost or hop manure being well mixed in with the top spit of soil to conserve moisture rather than being applied as a surface dressing. There are, of course, several good reasons for growing beds containing just one variety: extra strong and moderately vigorous growers can be kept in separate beds; stronger varieties develop extensive root systems that eventually encroach on the roots of the weaker ones; and pruning is less difficult in beds of one variety.

"The question of colour relationships in gardens," states the journal, "is a difficult one. Colour associations are matters of opinion, not fact, and two or more colours which would appear objectionable side by side in a dress material or a wallpaper may not be displeasing in the open." It goes on to say that the outer and some of the center beds should be planted with the tallest-growing bushes; standards of the same varieties can then be planted either as specimens or in the center of circular, crescent-shaped, oblong, or square flower beds. Unnecessary curves are to be avoided in the grass areas that should be planted to separate the beds, as they make mowing difficult, and a number of small beds are infinitely preferable to just a few large ones. Also, the width of the bed should be such as to require only the minimum of treading on when tending the rose bushes.

Amateur Gardening Annual then goes on to recommend edgings of ageratum, ajuga, alyssum, catmint, portulaca, sedum, and violas for the rose beds, with a reminder that they are likely to become invasive on light, rich soils. In the suggested plan, the garden is flanked by a hedge of the crimson-scarlet floribunda hybrid polyantha rose "Frensham" in the front and another hedge of hybrid polyantha rose "Kirsten Poulsen" at the back. Six pillar roses trained up larch or oak poles are on either side, and from front to back various roses are arranged as follows: left side, three "Crimson Conquest," one "Albertine," one "Golden Glow," one "Sanders White"; right side, one "Mme. Alfred Carrière," one "Climbing Christine," one "Alberic Barbier," three "Crimson Conquest." Each triangular bed is planted with one variety of hybrid tea bush rose: (1) "Lady Sylvia," (2) "Crimson Glory," (3) "Polly," (4) "Phyllis Gold," (5) "Admiral," (6) "Spek's Yellow," (7) "Ophelia," (8) "Ena Harkness," (9) "Admiral," (10) "Red Ensign," (11) "McGredy's Yellow," (12) "Clarice Goodacre," (13) "Picture," (14) "Golden Dawn," (15) "McGredy's Ivory," (16) "Etoile de Hollande." The focal point in the center of the garden is a weeping standard rose of "Sanders White." A number of these rose varieties are no longer available:

A 1955 plan of a small rose garden enclosed by two rose hedges and pillar roses (from Amateur Gardening Annual, 1955).

"Phyllis Gold," "Admiral," "Red Ensign," and "McGredy's Ivory." "Golden Dawn" and "Etoile de Hollande" are now available only in climbing form.

Amateur post-war gardeners were helped by a deluge of gardening books and magazines, by radio and television, and by the Royal Horticultural Society, the membership of which, after the war, more than doubled to 58,000 in 1960, rising to almost 75,000 six years later. Many women took their place as prominent gardeners. A knowledgeable, distinguished, Swanley-trained horticulturist, Francis Perry was appointed horticultural adviser to Middlesex County Council, later becoming its principal organizer for agricultural and horticultural education. Accolade followed accolade; in 1962, she received an MBE (Member of the British Empire) for her work in horticulture, followed in 1971 by the Victoria Medal of Honour, and in 1973 she was presented with the Sara Frances Chapman Medal by the Garden Club of America. In 1968, she had become the Royal Horticultural Society's first woman Council member and was elected one of its vice-presidents in 1978.

An eminent and respected writer, Francis Perry contributed gardening articles to *The Observer* for twenty-six years and was the author of such books as *Flowers of the World, Beautiful Leaved Plants*, and *Tropical and Sub-tropical Plants*, which was written in conjunction with her second husband, Roy Hay. Having retired as principal of Norwood Hall College for Adult Education in 1967, she traveled the world lecturing on gardening in partnership with her husband. In her book *Collins Guide to Border Plants*, published in 1957, she wrote, "A love of plants and gardens seems to be inherent in most people. In the rush and bustle of modern life, their ever changing pattern spells peace and sanity, whatever the conditions of life and the world around."

Author Beverley Nichols writes of one quite extraordinary elderly lady gardener, Miss May Bruce, whose neglected, overgrown garden in the Cotswolds was the site of her experiments with compost.[6] Within her garden could be found a clump of "Campanula lactiflora," normally about a meter high, that had grown at least three times as tall. And so it was with many other flowers and vegetables, each one growing with a tremendous vigor. Apparently, the formula for the mega-compost in which the plants were growing came to Miss Bruce in a dream, and she woke up with the words "the Divinity within the flower is sufficient of itself" running through her mind. Convinced that its meaning was that life comes from life and that plant life could be strengthened by other plants, she began to experiment with such herbs and weeds as camomile and yarrow, nettle, and dandelion, adding to them infusions of oak bark. Having perfected the formula to her satisfaction, she decided, on the advice of a soil expert, to try it on the compost heap in the proportion of 1 to 10,000. Her activator worked and soon became quite famous, drawing people to her garden to see the effect it was having. Eventually, it was commercially produced and sold as "Q.R." (Quick Results) for a few shillings a bottle.

While the government urged the wartime population of Great Britain to "Dig for Victory," it was equally astute in cajoling peacetime gardeners to continue planting their allotments and to "Dig for Plenty." Inevitably, however, with post-war reconstruction, many allotments were lost as urban and suburban land was used for new housing estates, hospitals, and schools, and wartime emergency sites reverted to their peacetime uses. In 1948, there were 1,117,308 plots; by 1975, that number had dwindled to 471,260. When rationing finally ended, people no longer felt the need, or indeed the desire, to grow their own food and were happy just to enjoy the new affluence that came with the 1960s.

The oil crisis of 1973, however, created a new demand for allotments, and various county councils had huge waiting lists for the first time in years. Work on the allotments was usually done by the men, custom and practice dictating that allotment cultivation was not really "women's work." Nowadays, many women are registered tenants, and even more work alongside their partners and win prizes for their garden produce. The deep-seated view that women actually prefer to cultivate flowers, taking charge of the garden at home while their husbands spend time on the allotment, has been gradually eroded and great inroads made into the traditional division of labor.

In Great Britain, the sociological fluctuations affecting gardening throughout the 1930s were accelerated by World War II, and today amateur gardeners want their ever-decreasing plots to be not only beautiful but also useful. For women, gardening is a means of visually expressing their artistic talents by way of color, design, and arrangement, and it also has a soothing, therapeutic effect, often filling a void in a particular area of their lives. A lack of gardening space, however, has encouraged women to cultivate indoor plants.

Throughout Great Britain, there are societies run by men and women with a passion for gardening, such as the Cottage Garden Society, the British National Carnation Society, and the National Auricula and Primula Society. Gardens have become increasingly personal, and there has been growing interest in organic gardening as the trend toward healthy living, holistic teachings, and protection of the environment has resulted in the use of organics rather than chemicals or pesticides. Women are undertaking every conceivable gardening task, from heavy digging and planting to fence-building and patio-laying, many of them holding certificates not only in such areas as landscape design but also in permaculture design.

Both herb and wildflower gardens are extremely popular, wildflower gardening being a relatively new technique. Today's "environmental" gardens, with their "naturalness" and encouragement of wildlife, are protected by the Control of Pesticide Regulations of 1986, which ruled that, as of 1 January 1988, anyone supplying or selling pesticides required purchasers to "take all reasonable precautions to protect the health of human beings, creatures and plants, to safeguard the environment and in particular to avoid the pollution of water."

In recent years, there has been a resurgence in the popularity of the market garden, engendered by the increasing interest in whole foods and organically produced crops. The demand for produce grown without the use of chemicals has risen sharply, and modern market gardens, so vastly different from their predecessors, now cater to the greatly changing eating and buying habits of the British public.

A Return to Leisure Gardening

*I*n America during the Second World War, Lowthorpe, which in the 1940s was to become part of the Rhode Island School of Design in Providence, and the Cambridge School of Landscape Architecture for Women had closed for the duration. Although Harvard had opened its doors to women to fill the vacancies created by men going to war and had continued to offer degree courses, only five women had graduated from the Landscape Department during that time. Many landscape architectural firms existed in name only, while others soldiered on with just a handful of staff. A few women continued to practice—Geraldine Knight Scott, for instance, who in 1942 was the first woman to be appointed to the Los Angeles Regional Planning Agency, where she worked on low-rent housing projects, schools, industrial zone sites, and a few small parks. Ellen Biddle Shipman, on the other hand, had an income of $23,202.92 in 1941, and in 1945 she was paid an annual retainer of $1,200 by Edgar Stern, for whom she had designed Longue Vue Gardens, a large estate in New Orleans.

By November 1946, more than 2 million American women had been withdrawn from their wartime occupations. Very little protest had been voiced, as they, too, experienced, as the British women had, a sense of relief at being able to return at last to normal family life. In the area of landscape architecture, the years between 1945 and 1975 witnessed a trend toward large corporate offices where women were no longer welcome in the boardroom and where clients discussed the rebuilding of America and showed little interest in residential projects.

Accordingly, most women lost all incentive to enter the profession, and of those who continued to practice, virtually all concentrated on small-scale residential commissions. By the end of the 1960s, there were no women enrolled in schools of architecture, and in 1972, there were no full-time women landscape architecture teachers. By 1970, however, there was a re-awakening interest in the possibility of landscape architecture as a female career, as women were encouraged back into the universities by cumulative ecological issues. Nowadays, half the total enrollment of students at schools of landscape architecture are female.

The Garden Club of America, the membership of which was virtually all female since its inception, officially limited its membership to women in the 1970s, and women still continue to form a large percentage of the do-it-yourself fraternity. It was and still is both expensive and difficult to obtain help in the garden, so people naturally turn to looking after their gardens themselves with the help of modern technology to make it easier—lawnmowers and garden machinery, soil conditioners, weedkillers, and so forth.

In the 1970s, there were about 80 million gardeners in the United States tending gardens that varied, on average, from one-fifth acre to a full acre. Americans found the idea of food growing for self-sufficiency an appealing and novel experience. The dollar was devalued at the end of 1971, prices started to rise, and crime and unemployment began to increase. The upsurge of vegetable growing was accelerated by inflation, brought about by rising oil prices in the mid-seventies. Accordingly, at a time of economic stringency and an increasing crime rate, U.S. citizens tended to spend more time at home and more time planning and looking after their gardens, which were used more and more for leisure activities as well as for food production. In the early 1990s, a new approach to the environment took place in America when a group of feminists who were also environmentalists adopted the name "ecofeminists." These women focused on demonstrating a more caring attitude toward the earth and its communities. This theme is shared by many of today's landscape architects, who, through good design, endeavor to restore to modern culture a renewed sense of connectedness to the planet.

Today, many gardens are planted on the flat roofs of apartment buildings and in tiny plots attached to townhomes and duplexes. Balconies often display a vast and sometimes ingenious range of plants in containers of various shapes and sizes. Bedding plants often are restricted to small flower beds or to ornamental pots arranged on porches or steps.

House plants are now as popular in America as outside gardens. This rise in popularity has in turn seen, with the help of technology, an upsurge in specialized methods of culture such as hydrophonics with indoor conservatories and illumination.

In America, the popularity of "community plots" has risen significantly. Some plots are cultivated by families, some by senior citizens, and others tended by schools and colleges, with almost half of American gardens growing vegetables but less than 20 percent of these cultivating fruit. There has also been a massive increase in the practice of organic gardening motivated by today's emphasis on healthy eating. During the late 1980s, organic gardening came into its own as people realized that growing organically helps to maintain an ecological balance by supporting wildlife, reducing soil erosion, and preventing toxic pollution.

In Lancaster County, Pennsylvania, can be found some of the most fertile soil in eastern America. Pennsylvania was founded by the English Quaker, William Penn, who opened the colony to oppressed religious groups: Swiss Anabaptists, French Huguenots, and German Protestants. By the time of the American War of Independence, there were 10,000 German-speaking settlers in Pennsylvania, and today there are three major German groups: the Old Order or Plain People, the Church, and the Fringe People. Large numbers of the Old Order groups are "pure" German, and the Old Order consists of three major subgroups: the Bethren, the Mennonites, and the Amish.

The Amish people are separate from the other Old Order groups because of the severity of their lifestyle and discipline. Whole families work long hours every day without the use of modern technology. They have no electricity, indoor plumbing, televisions, radios, or tractors. Unemployment is non-existent, and every man, woman, and child has his or her role to play within the dairy and vegetable farming community. Generally wealthy because of the richness of their land and their communal ethics, the Amish people work the soil with an eight-horse plough team and drive the traditional horse-drawn buggies, as their religious laws forbid them to own automobiles. One of their deeply held beliefs is that human beings must be caretakers of the land. They organize annual harvest festivals and community and agricultural fairs, and there are several farmers' markets in Lancaster County where Amish women sell the fresh farm produce they have grown. The lifestyle of these people is simple and spartan and has seen very little change during the past one hundred years. It remains geared to the speed of a horse.

The Second Wave and Beyond

*T*he 1950s witnessed some important developments that contributed to the "Second Wave" of feminism in the late 1960s and 1970s. There was a significant expansion of higher education, a steady increase of women in the labor market, and a growing post-war middle class that demanded a middle-class lifestyle requiring two incomes. By the end of the decade, many women who had stayed at home were discovering that, in actual fact, they were unfulfilled, bored, frustrated, and isolated, with no one to talk to all day except the children. This was especial- ly true of those who were better-educated. Many women began to feel trapped in a role they felt society had forced upon them and to regard themselves as little more than machines programed to cook, clean, and do laundry.

Another event, the development of the contraceptive pill in 1952, would open up the floodgates of feminism and women's liberation. Still, in 1960, there was no women's movement as such, and the few organizations that did exist were focusing their energies on the Equal Rights Amendment.

Then in 1963, Betty Friedan, a suburban housewife, pub- lished a book called *The Feminine Mystique,* which challenged the sanctity of marriage, motherhood, and domesticity. The book was a bestseller, and Friedan became known as the "mother" of the Women's Liberation Movement. The movement appealed to large numbers of women, and they began to move beyond their limited boundaries and their isolation to experience solidarity with other women. For the first time, they began to view women's subjugation as a social ill rather than as an individual problem.

In 1961, when President John F. Kennedy established the President's Commission on the Status of Women to document American women's position in the legal system, the economy, and the family, only one women's activist was appointed. The chairperson was Eleanor Roosevelt. The Commission's findings, presented in 1963, resulted in Congress delaying consideration of the E.R.A.

The 1961 Commission prompted an upturn of activism among women united in their interest in political organization. It was the catalyst that women needed to embark upon organized action. In 1963, President Kennedy ratified the Equal Pay Act, and this was followed in 1964 by the prohibiting of discrimina- tory hiring on the basis of gender under Title VII of the Civil Rights Act.

New women's groups, such as the National Organization for Women (NOW) and the Coalition of Labor Union Women, were formed to address new issues. NOW, consisting of mainly professional, politically moderate women, was formed in 1966 when twenty-eight women, including Betty Friedan, tried to coerce the American government into addressing the problem of sex discrimination and to fight for women's inclusion in public life. These women were unhappy with the failure of the Equal Employment Opportunity Commission to enforce the anti–sex discrimination clause of Title VII of the 1964 Civil Rights Act.

The Women's Liberation Movement in the United States was basically middle class and white, and while it attempted to appeal to black women, its gestures often appeared racist and patronizing. To some black women, the real issues to be addressed were racism and the civil and social inequities blacks were forced to endure. Martin Luther King was attempting to educate both blacks and whites in the movement toward civil rights. In 1955, he had encouraged blacks to boycott bus services when Rosa Parks, a black woman from Montgomery, Alabama, made history by refusing to relinquish her seat on a bus to a white passenger. The repercussions of her act of defiance were far-reaching, and the bus companies in the South lost vast amounts of revenue as blacks chose to walk rather than ride.

In both Great Britain and the United States, the energies of feminism embraced a variety of issues and activities. Among the political radicalism and social unrest of the 1960s, women fought against both sex discrimination and racism and protested against the war in Vietnam. Feminists established a communication network through women's newspapers and magazines, study seminars, bookshops, and political organizations as they fought successfully for equal rights in marriage and divorce, for the right of every woman to have access to contraception, for legal rights for single mothers, and for the legalization of abortion. Rape and other sexual offenses against women were brought to the attention of the general public, and the Equal Pay and Sex Discrimination acts of 1970 and 1975, respectively, considered landmarks of feminism, prohibited discrimination in terms of payment for equal work and prejudice in employment—indeed, in all aspects of life—on the basis of gender.

The revival of feminism in the 1960s heralded a new era for the emancipation of women. By the 1970s, its metamorphosis was complete, with the Women's Liberation Movement becoming a force to be reckoned with.

Lack of identity, dependence, and confinement to the home were familiar female complaints at that time. Large numbers of women began to realize that they wanted a career other than that of homemaker, and they started to protest about the predetermined division of labor, denouncing their dependence upon men as limiting and degrading. "Wages for Housework" became the slogan for their conviction that women's contributions in the home should be more highly valued, and they began to demand job-sharing, part-time work, and equal pay. At the same time, the seventies heralded militant feminism, a rise in single-parent families, and an expansion of consciousness-raising and women's groups. In 1971, the U.S. National Women's Political Caucus was founded, followed in 1973 by the International Feminist Congress. In 1974, Eleanor Grasso became the first woman governor elected in her own right, and the United Nations proclaimed 1975 International Women's Year.

With the 1980s came "power-dressing," or so-called "body armor," when women wore suits with large shoulder pads to produce the effect of status and power, of being in control and independent, and to give a positive, professional image of the female sex. But technology was quickening the pace, and promotions came faster and at younger ages. Career-minded women were seeking recognition for their accomplishments and were making steady gains in the work place. While work came before everything for ambitious women, only a small percentage of them actually reached the top of their professions. Still, women were ensnared in a struggle that demanded ever-increasing amounts of work.

In 1982, Betty Friedan published another book, *The Second Stage*, in which she argued for a return to the more traditional feminine roles, but this apparent retreat was not well received by eighties' feminists. Eleven years later, in 1993, Friedan published *The Fountain of Age*, in which she ignored younger women and turned her attention to older people (both women *and* men), arguing that life does not end with menopause and that women continue to thrive as they age.

It appeared that with the dawn of the 1990s the cause had lost its way, given the increasing reluctance among women to identify themselves with the feminist movement. Large numbers of women remained trapped in low-paying "women's jobs" and continued to be undervalued by society in general. And yet today, feminism is far from dead and in fact is heading in a radical new direction, with women as even more potent catalysts of change. The year 1994 saw the feminist victory over the Church, as women were ordained as priests for the first time. In September 1993 came the launch of the first women's daily newspaper, *Her New York*, complete with city pages giving information about businesses run by women, and by the following year, at least 40 percent of senior American business executives were women.

Molding the History of the Garden

*I*n both the United States and Great Britain, women continue to evaluate their position in society and to juxtapose their roles as homemaker, mother, and career woman. Added to an already heavy workload is their management of the garden.

Women have played an enormous, often unrecognized and undervalued part in fashioning the history of the garden, a turbulent history governed by religious, economic, and political events and influenced by eccentricities in thought and tradition. It seems likely that new houses will continue to be built with ever-decreasing garden plots in which plantings will be further reduced and even more stone and concrete introduced. Enthusiastic and intelligent green-fingered plantswomen will, as always, continue to mold the history of gardening with patience and dedication, pursuing horticultural excellence as they care for the earth and its plants through the as yet unknown, but no doubt equally turbulent, millenia to come.

NOTES

CHAPTER ONE
1. Gen. 2:8.
2. Isa. 32:9-11.
3. Prov. 31:14, 16.
4. Prov. 31:27, 28.
5. Prov. 31:19.
6. Josh. 2:6.
7. See *Jewish Antiquities* X, 11.
8. Clayton & Price, *The Seven Wonders of the Ancient World*, p. 45 (by permission of Routledge).
9. *Ibid.*, p. 46.
10. 1 Kings 4:25.
11. Gen. 21:15.
12. Judg. 4:5.
13. Erman, *Life in Ancient Egypt*, p. 425 (by permission of Dover Publications).
14. Num. 11:5.
15. *Demosthenes Book VI. LIX. 122*, pp. 445, 447 (reprinted by permission of Harvard University Press, Cambridge, Massachusetts).
16. *The Girls Own Paper* (William Clowes and Sons Limited, 1917), p. 42.
17. *Marcus Porcius Cato on Agriculture*, CXLIII, p. 125 (reprinted by permission of Harvard University Press, Cambridge, Massachusetts).
18. *M. T. Varro on Farming*, pp. 38, 39.
19. *Ibid.*, p. 105.
20. Pliny, *Letters II*, Book VII, xix, p. 49 (reprinted by permission of the publishers and the Loeb Classical Library, Harvard University Press, Cambridge, Massachusetts).
21. Loudon, *An Encyclopaedia of Gardening*, p. 15.
22. See Martial, *Epigrams*, Book X, XLVIII, p. 191 (reprinted by permission of the publishers and the Loeb Classical Library, Harvard University Press, Cambridge, Massachusetts).
23. Loudon, *An Encyclopaedia of Gardening*, p. 15.
24. Pliny, *Letters I*, Book V, vi, p. 391 (reprinted by permission of the publishers and the Loeb Classical Library, Harvard University Press, Cambridge, Massachusetts).

CHAPTER TWO
1. Amt, *Women's Lives in Medieval Europe: A Sourcebook*, p. 321.
2. Cited in *Social England*, Vol. III, ed. by H. D. Traill and J. S. Mann, p. 547.
3. Wright, *The Story of Gardening*, p. 259.
4. See Shakespeare, *Love's Labour Lost*, Act 1, Scene 1.

CHAPTER THREE
1. Markham, *The English Huswife* (1615), cited in Christina Hole, *The English Housewife in the Seventeenth Century*, p. 99 (by permission of John Johnson [Authors' Agent] Limited).

2. Bacon, *Essays*, Essay VIII, p. 23 (by permission of Everyman's Library).
3. Hole, *The English Housewife in the Seventeenth Century*, p. 101 (by permission of John Johnson [Authors' Agent] Limited).
4. Cited in Georgiana Hill, *Women In English Life*, Vol. 1, p. 188.
5. Hill, *Women In English Life*, Vol. 1, p. 191.
6. See Surflet, *The Countrie Farme* as cited in Christina Hole, *The English Housewife in the Seventeenth Century*, p. 103.
7. Clode, *Merchant Taylors*, Vol. 1, p. 323.
8. Cited in Alice Clark, *Working Life of Women in The Seventeenth Century*, p. 60.
9. Spender, *The Diary of Elizabeth Pepys*, p. 139.
10. Rohde, *The Story of the Garden*, p. 108 (by permission of the Medici Society Limited).
11. Hill, *Women In English Life*, Vol. I, p. 191.
12. Brown, *The Pilgrim Fathers of New England and Their Puritan Successors*, p. 209.
13. Bishop, *History of Elections in The American Colonies* (Vol. III), Number 1, p. 65.
14. Schlesinger & Fox, *A History of American Life*, Vol. II, p. 303.
15. Rohde, *The Story of the Garden*, p. 244 (by permission of the Medici Society Limited).
16. Schlesinger & Fox, *A History of American Life*, Vol. III, p. 88.
17. Bacon, *Essays*, Essay XLVI, p. 139 (by permission of Everyman's Library).
18. Rohde, *The Story of the Garden*, pp. 106, 107 (by permission of the Medici Society Limited).
19. Morris, *The Illustrated Journeys of Celia Fiennes 1685-c.1712*, p. 117 (by permission of Richard Webb Limited).
20. Markham, *The English Huswife*, cited by Christina Hole in *The English Housewife in the Seventeenth Century*, p. 99 (by permission of John Johnson [Authors' Agent] Limited).

CHAPTER FOUR

1. Austen, *Northanger Abbey and Persuasion*, p. 138.
2. Tims, *Mary Wollstonecraft - A Social Pioneer*, p. 143 (with the author's permission).
3. Cobbett, *Rural Rides*, p. 372.
4. Rohde, *The Story of the Garden*, p. 186 (by permission of the Medici Society Limited).
5. *Ibid.*, p. 258.

CHAPTER FIVE

1. *Womanhood Vol. V11*, March 1902, p. 252.
2. *The Lady's Realm 1897*, p. 332 (by permission of The Fawcett Library, London Guildhall University).
3. *Ibid*.
4. Loudon, *The Ladies Companion to the Flower Garden*, p. 115.
5. Loudon, *Gardening For Ladies*, pp. 8 & 9.

6. *Ibid.*, pp. 133 & 134.
7. Hudson, *MUNBY Man of Two Worlds*, p. 295 (by permission of John Murray Publishers Ltd.).
8. Mrs Beeton, *The Beeton Book of Garden Management*, p. 94.
9. Thompson, *Lark Rise To Candleford*, p. 14 (by permission of Oxford University Press).
10. Hudson, *MUNBY Man of Two Worlds*, p. 288 (by permission of John Murray Publishers Ltd.).
11. *The Illustrated London News*, 8 January 1896, p. 86 (by permission of *The Illustrated London News* Picture Library).
12. Written by Queen Victoria in 1870. Cited in McMillan, *The Way We Were 1900-1914*, p.101.

CHAPTER SIX

1. *Womanhood Vol. VII*, p. 98 (by permission of The Fawcett Library, London Guildhall University).
2. *Womanhood Vol. V*, p. 398 (by permission of The Fawcett Library, London Guildhall University).
3. Massingham, *A Century of Gardeners*, p. 135 (by permission of Adam Massingham).
4. Jekyll, *Colour Schemes For The Flower Garden*, p. 124 (by permission of the Antique Collectors' Club Ltd.).
5. Thompson, *Lark Rise To Candleford*, p. 115 (by permission of Oxford University Press).
6. Jekyll, *Old West Surrey*, p. 271 (by permission of the Antique Collectors' Club Ltd.).
7. *Womanhood Vol. V*, p. 398 (by permission of The Fawcett Library, London Guildhall University).
8. *Every-Woman's Encyclopaedia*, Part 27, p. 3085.
9. Jekyll, *Wood and Garden*. See Introduction (by permission of the Antique Collectors' Club).

CHAPTER SEVEN

1. See *The Handbook of the WLA - Papers of Mrs Mazey* (by permission of Her Majesty's Stationery Office, Norwich).
2. See Board of Agriculture & Fisheries West Kent Women's Agricultural Committee, "Instructions and Advice to Members of the Women's Land Army" (by permission of Imperial War Museum, London).
3. *The Journal of the Kew Guild* (No) 6 1941-50, p. 392 (by permission of the Royal Botanic Gardens, Kew).
4. See R.H.S. pamphlet "Autumn Vegetables From Seeds Sown in July and August," Second Edition, 1916 (by permission of the Royal Horticultural Society).
5. *Journal of the Royal Horticultural Society*, Vol. 48, 1918-1919, p. 384 (by permission of the Royal Horticultural Society).
6. Holmes, "Medicinal Herbs: Their Cultivation and Preparation in Great Britain," *Journal of The Royal Horticultural Society*, 1916, p. 137 (by permission of the Royal Horticultural Society).

7. *The WI Handbook*, p. 13 (by permission of The National Federation of Women's Institutes).
8. *The Constitution* (Newspaper), Atlanta, Georgia, 5 May 1918, p. 3F.
9. *Landscape Architecture Magazine*, Vol. 72, No. 3, May 1982, p. 66.

CHAPTER EIGHT

1. *Good Gardening*, Vol. 1, No. 5, July 1935, p. 54.
2. *Ibid.*, Vol. 1, No. 2, April 1935, p. 23.
3. *Ibid.*, Vol. 1, No. 5, July 1935, p. 50.
4. *Ibid.*, Vol. 11, No. 21, Nov. 1936, p. 40.
5. *Ibid.*, Vol. 1, No. 2, April 1935, p. 53.
6. *Ibid.*, Vol. 1, No. 6, August 1935, p. 46.
7. *Ibid.*, Vol. 4, No. 41, July 1938, p. 5.
8. *Ibid.*, Vol. 1, No. 2, April 1935, p. 22.
9. "Bulletin of the Garden Club of America," May 1920.
10. *Country Life* (USA), May 1921, p. 71.

CHAPTER NINE

1. *National Service HMSO 1939, WOMEN'S LAND ARMY*, p. 24 (by permission of Her Majesty's Stationery Office, Norwich).
2. Sackville-West, *The Women's Land Army*, p. 17 (by permission of Imperial War Museum, London).
3. *Ibid.*, p. 48.
4. *Land Girl*, Vols. 3-6, June 1942 to March 1946. June 1942, "Gang Labour" (by permission of Imperial War Museum, London).
5. *Country Life* (UK), 20 March 1942, p. 556 (with the permission of *Country Life*).
6. Ministry of Agriculture and Fisheries, *Dig for Victory Campaign*, T.P.Y.10321, November 1941, p. 1 (by permission of Imperial War Museum, London).
7. *Ibid.*, p. 1.

CHAPTER TEN

1. *Country Life* (UK), 30 Jan. 1948, p. 244 (with the permission of *Country Life*).
2. Goodenough, *Jam & Jerusalem*, p. 89.
3. *Country Life* (UK), 11 March 1949, p. 552 (with the permission of *Country Life*).
4. *Amateur Gardening Annual 1955*, p. 72 (by permission of the Editor of *Amateur Gardening Magazine*).
5. *The Guild Gardener*, January/February 1953, p. 11.
6. Nichols, *Garden Open Tomorrow*, p. 239, Appendix (by permission of the Beverley Nichols Estate).

BIBLIOGRAPHY

BOOKS

Aldred, Cyril. *The Egyptians* (Thames and Hudson, 1961).

Allason-Jones, Lindsay. *Women in Roman Britain* (British Museum Publications, 1989).

Amherst, Lady Cecilia. *A History of Gardening in England* (London, 1910).

Amt, Emilie, ed. *Women's Lives In Medieval Europe: A Sourcebook* (Routledge, 1993).

Anderson, Bonnie S., and Judith P. Zinsser. *A History of Their Own*. Volume 11 (Penguin Books, 1988).

Andrews, Jonathan, ed. & intro. Anthony Huxley. *The Country Diary Book Of Creating A Wild Flower Garden* (Webb & Bower, Michael Joseph, 1986).

Armstrong, Alan. *Farmworkers: A Social and Economic History 1770 - 1980* (B. T. Batsford Ltd., 1988).

Arter, Elisabeth. *Cottage Garden* (Charles Lett & Co. Ltd., 1992).

Ashley, Maurice. *Life in Stuart England* (B. T. Batsford Ltd., 1964).

Ashley, Maurice. *The People of England: A Short Social and Economic History* (Weidenfeld and Nicolson, 1982).

Austen, Jane. *Northanger Abbey and Persuasion* (Collins, 1953).

Avery, Gillian. *Victorian People* (Collins, 1970).

Bacon, Francis. *Essays*. Re-issue (J. M. Dent & Sons Ltd., 1992).

Baring Gould, S. *Old Country Life* (E. P. Publishing Ltd., 1975).

Barrett, Helena, and John Phillips. *Suburban Style: The British Home, 1840 - 1960* (Macdonald Orbis, 1987).

Beeton, Mrs Isabella. *The Beeton Book of Garden Management: A Facsimile Edition* (Omega Books, 1985).

Birley, Anthony. *Life in Roman Britain*. Fifth impression (B. T. Batsford Ltd., 1976).

Bisgrove, Richard. *The National Trust Book of The English Garden* (Viking, 1990).

Bishop, Alan, ed. *Chronicle of Youth: Vera Brittain's War Diary 1913 - 1917* (Victor Gollanz Ltd., 1981).

Bishop, Cortlandt F. *History of Elections In The American Colonies*, Vol. 111, No. 1 (New York: Columbia College, 1893).

Bishop, James. *The Illustrated London News Social History Of Edwardian Britain* (Angus & Robertson, 1977).

Blum, Jerome, ed. *Our Forgotten Past: Seven Centuries of Life on the Land* (Thames and Hudson, 1982).

Bolt, Christine. *The Women's Movements in the United States and Britain from the 1790s to the 1920s* (Harvester Wheatsheaf, 1993).

Boniface, Priscilla. *The Garden Room* (Her Majesty's Stationery Office, 1982).

Bouchier, David. *The Feminist Challenge* (London: Macmillan Press, 1983).

Branson, Noreen. *Britain In The Nineteen Twenties*. Edited by E. J. Hobsbawn (Weidenfeld and Nicolson, 1975).

Briggs, Asa. *Victorian Things* (Penguin Books, 1990).

Brogan, Hugh. *The Pelican History of the United States of America* (Pelican Books, 1989).

Brown, Jane. *The English Garden in Our Time from Gertrude Jekyll to Geoffrey Jellicoe* (Antique Collectors' Club, 1986).

Brown, John. *The Pilgrim Fathers of New England And Their Puritan Successors* (The Religious Tract Society, 1897).

Brown, R. J. *The English Country Cottage* (Robert Hale, London, 1979).

Bryant, Arthur. *The Age of Elegance: 1812 - 1822* (Collins, 1954).

Bryant, Arthur. *Spirit of England* (Collins, 1982).

Bryson, Bill. *Made in America* (London: Secker & Warburg, 1994).

Burn, A. R., and Mary Burn. *The Living Past of Greece* (The Herbert Press, 1980).

Burton, Elizabeth. *The Early Tudors At Home: 1485 - 1558* (Allen Lane, 1976).

Calder, Angus. *The People's War* (Jonathan Cape, 1969).

Camden, Carroll. *The Elizabethan Woman* (London: Cleaver-Hume Press Limited; New York and Houston: The Elsevier Press, 1952).

Campbell, John, ed. *The Experience of World War II* (Harrap Books Ltd., 1989).

Carr, William. *A History of Germany 1815 - 1990* (Edward Arnold, 1992).

Carter, Tom. *The Victorian Garden* (Bell & Hyman Ltd., 1984).

Cassin-Scott, Jack. *Women at War 1939-45* (Osprey Publishing Ltd., 1980).

Castle, Barbara. *Sylvia and Christabel Pankhurst* (Penguin Books, 1987).

Charvet, John. *Feminism* (J. M. Dent & Sons Ltd., 1982).

Clamp, Hugh. *Landscape Professional Practice* (Gower Technical Press Ltd., 1988).

Clark, Alice. *Working Life of Women In The Seventeenth Century* (George Routledge & Sons Ltd., 1919).

Clayton, Peter, and Martin Price, ed. *The Seven Wonders of the Ancient World* (Routledge, 1988).

Cleeve, Brian. *1938 - A World Vanishing* (London: Buchan & Enright, Publishers, 1982).

Clifford, Derek. *A History of Garden Design* (Faber and Faber, 1962).

Clode, Charles Matthew. *Memorials of the guild of Merchant Taylors of the fraternity of St. John the Baptist, in … London, and of its associated chantries and institutions*. Printed for private circulation (London, 1875).

Cobbett, William. *Cottage Economy* (Cedric Chivers Ltd., 1975). First published in 1822.

Cobbett, William.*The English Gardener or A Treatise*. Published by the author, 1829.

Cobbett, William. *Rural Rides*. Edited by George Woodcock. (Penguin English Library, 1967). First published 1830.

Colville, John. *The New Elizabethans 1952 - 1977* (Collins, 1977).

Cook, Olive. *English Cottages and Farmhouses* (Thames and Hudson, 1984).

Cooke, Dorothy, and Pamela McNicol. *A History of Flower Arranging* (Heinemann Professional Publishing Ltd., 1989).

Croall, Jonathan. *Don't You Know There's A War On? The People's Voice 1939 - 45* (Hutchinson, 1988).

Crouch, David, and Colin Ward. *The Allotment: Its Landscape and Culture* (Faber and Faber, 1988).

Crow, Duncan. *The Edwardian Woman* (George Allen & Unwin, 1978).

Cruickshank, Dan, and Neil Burton. *Life In The Georgian City* (Viking, 1990).

Dakers, Caroline. *The Countryside at War 1914 - 18* (Constable, 1987).

Davies, Jennifer. *The Victorian Flower Garden* (BBC Books, 1991).

Davis, Sheena. *Food Through the Ages* (Reader's Digest Association, 1977).

Demosthenes Book VI. Translated by A. T. Murray (Harvard University Press, William Heinemann Ltd., 1956).

Dodd, A. H. *Elizabethan England* (BCA by arrangement with B. T. Batsford Ltd., 1974).

Donnelly, Peter, ed. *Mrs. Milburn's Diaries* (London: Harrap, 1979).

Dover, Kenneth. *The Greeks* (British Broadcasting Company, 1980).

Drury, Elizabeth, and Philippa Lewis, comp. *The Victorian Garden Album* (Collins & Brown Limited, 1993).

Dudley, Donald. *Roman Society* (Penguin Books, 1975).

Dupont, Florence. *Daily Life in Ancient Rome* (Blackwell, 1994). First published in 1989.

Earle, Peter. *The Making of the English Middle Class* (Methuen, 1989).

Ehrenberg, Victor. *The People of Aristophanes* (Oxford: Basil Blackwell, 1951).

Elphinstone, Margaret, and Julia Langley. *The Organic Gardeners Handbook* (Thorsons, 1990).

Emsley, Clive, Arthur Marwick, and Wendy Simpson, ed. *War, Peace And Social Change: Europe 1900 - 1955* (Open University Press, 1989).

Ensor, R. C. K. *England 1870 - 1914* (Oxford at the Clarendon Press, 1936).

Erman, Adolf. *Life in Ancient Egypt*. Translated by H. M. Tirard (Macmillan & Co., 1894).

Ferrero, Guglielmo. *The Women of the Caesars* (T. Fisher Unwin, 1911).

Filbee, Marjorie. *A Woman's Place* (London: Ebury Press, 1980).

Fleming, Laurence, and Alan Gore. *The English Garden* (Michael Joseph, Ltd., 1979).

Fletcher, H. R. *The Story of The Royal Horticultural Society 1804 - 1968* (Oxford University Press, 1969).

Foner, Eric, and John A. Garraty, ed. *The Readers Companion To American History* (Boston: Houghton Miffin Company, 1991).

Forsell, Mary. *Herbs* (London: Anaya Publishers Ltd., 1990).

France, Peter. *Greek As A Treat* (Penguin Books, 1993).

Fraser, Antonia. *The Weaker Vessel* (London: Weidenfeld and Nicolson, 1984).

Fraser, Flora. *The English Gentlewoman* (Barrie & Jenkins, 1987).

Fulford, Roger. *Votes For Women* (White Lion Publishers, 1976). First published 1957.

Furnas, J. C. *The Americans* (Longman Group Limited, 1969).

Fussell, G. E. *Farming Techniques from Prehistoric to Modern Times* (Pergamon Press, 1966).

Garraty, John A., with Robert A. McCaughey. *The American Nation: A History of the United States*. 7th Edition (HarperCollins Publishers, 1991).

Gasson, Ruth. *The Role of Women in British Agriculture* (The Women's Farm and Garden Association, Jan. 1980).

Genders, Roy. *The Cottage Garden Year* (Croom Helm Ltd., 1986).

Gerard, John. *Great Herbal* (1597).

Gibbons, S. R. *Britain 1945 to 1985* (Blackie & Son Ltd., 1986).

Girling, Richard, ed. *The Making of the English Garden* (London: Macmillan, 1988).

The Girls Own Paper, 1917 & 1918 Bound Volumes.

Goodenough, Simon. *Jam and Jerusalem* (Collins, 1977).

Grant, Michael. *The Classical Greeks* (Weidenfeld and Nicolson Ltd., 1989).

Grant, Michael. *Greeks & Romans: A Social History* (Weidenfeld and Nicolson Ltd., 1992).

Greene, Jack P., and J. R. Pole, ed. *Colonial British America* (Baltimore and London: The Johns Hopkins University Press, 1984).

Guhl, E., and W. Koner. *The Romans* (Senate, 1994).

Gwynn, Robin D. *Huguenot Heritage* (Routledge & Kegan Paul, 1985).

Hadfield, Miles. *A History of British Gardening* (John Murray, 1979).

Hadfield, Miles. *Topiary And Ornamental Hedges* (London: Adam & Charles Black, 1971).

Hall, Carolyn. *The Forties In Vogue* (Octopus Books, 1985).

Halliwell, Brian. *Old Garden Flowers* (Bishopsgate Press, 1987).

Hammerton, Sir John, ed. *The Second Great War* (The Waverley Book Company Ltd., n/d).

The Handbook of the WLA (World War II Papers of Mrs Mazey).

Hardy, Thomas. *Tess of the d'Urbervilles*.Originally written in 1891 (Wadsworth Editions Limited, 1992).

Harrison, J. F. C. *The Common People* (Fontana Press, 1989).

Harriss, John, ed. *The Family: A Social History of the 20th Century* (Harrap London, 1992).

Hart, Roger. *English Life in Chaucer's Day* (Wayland Publishers Ltd., 1973).

Heide, Robert, and John Gilman. *Home Front America* (San Francisco: Chronicle Books, 1995).

Hewlett, Sylvia Ann. *A Lesser Life* (London: Michael Joseph, 1987).

Hibbert, Christopher. *The English: A Social History 1066 - 1945* (Grafton Books, 1987).

Hickman, Peggy. *A Jane Austen Household Book* (David & Charles, 1977).

Hill, C. P. *British Economic and Social History 1700 - 1982*. Fifth Edition (Hodder & Stoughton, 1985).

Hill, Christopher. *The Century of Revolution 1603 - 1714* (Van Nostrand Reinhold [International] Co. Ltd., 1961).

Hill, Georgiana. *Women In English Life*. Vol. 1 (Richard Bentley & Son, 1896).

Hill, Thomas. *The Gardner's Labyrinth* (1577).

Hindley, Geoffrey. *England in the Age of Caxton* (Granada, 1979).

Hobhouse, Penelope. *Borders* (The National Trust Pavilion Books Ltd., 1989).

Hobhouse, Penelope. *Gertrude Jekyll on Gardening* (The National Trust and William Collins, 1983).

Hole, Christina. *The English Housewife in the Seventeenth Century* (Chatto & Windus, 1953).

Holy Bible. Authorized King James Version (London & New York: Collins Clear-Type Press, 1956).

Hooper, William Davis, trans. *Marcus Porcius Cato On Agriculture; Marcus Terentius Varro On Agriculture* (William Heinemann Ltd., Harvard University Press, 1934).

Horn, Pamela. *Ladies of the Manor* (Alan Sutton, 1991).

Horn, Pamela. *Rural Life In England In The First World War* (New York: Gilland MacMillan St. Martin's Press, 1984).

Houlbrooke, Ralph A. *The English Family 1450 - 1700* (Longman Group Limited, 1984).

Hudson, Derek. *MUNBY: Man of Two Worlds* (Abacus Edition, 1974).

Hutchinson, W. M. L., rev. *Pliny Letters 1 & 11*. Trans. by William Melmoth (London: William Heinemann, 1923). First published 1915.

Huxley, Anthony, ed. & intro. *The Country Diary Book Of Creating A Wild Flower Garden* (Webb & Bower Michael Joseph, 1986).

Huxley, Anthony. *An Illustrated History of Gardening* (New York and London: Paddington Press Ltd., 1978).

Ingrams, Richard, ed. & intro. *Cobbett's Country Book* (David & Charles, 1974).

Jackson, Alan A. *The Middle Classes 1900 - 1950* (David St. John Thomas, 1991).

Jacques, David. *Georgian Gardens: The Reign of Nature* (B. T. Batsford, 1983).

Jefferies, Richard. *Landscape & Labour* (Moonraker Press, 1979).

Jekyll, Gertrude. *Colour Schemes For The Flower Garden* (Antique Collectors' Club Ltd., 1982). First published by *Country Life* Ltd./George Newnes Ltd., 1908, entitled *Colour Schemes in the Flower Garden*.

Jekyll, Gertrude. *Old West Surrey* (Longmans, Green And Co., 1904).

Jekyll, Gertrude. *Wood and Garden* (Antique Collectors' Club, c.1981). Originally published London, Longmans, Green, 1899.

Jekyll, Gertrude. *A Gardener's Testament*. Edited by Francis Jekyll and G. C. Taylor. (Papermac, 1984). Originally published by *Country Life*, 1937.

Johnson, Lesley. *The Modern Girl: Girlhood and Growing Up* (Open University Press, 1993).

Johnson, Paul. *Modern Times: A History of the World from the 1920s to the 1990s* (Phoenix paperback edition, 1992).

Johnston, David E. *Roman Villas* (Shire Publications Ltd., 1979).

Jones, Alun. *The New Germany: A Human Geography* (John Wiley & Sons Ltd., 1994).

Jones, Barbara. *Follies & Grottoes*. Revised and enlarged 2nd Edition (Constable & Co. Ltd., 1974). First published 1953.

Joseph, Shirley. *If Their Mothers Only Knew* (Faber & Faber Ltd., 1946).

The Journal of the Kew Guild, No. 5 1931 - 1940. Bound Copy.

The Journal of the Kew Guild, No 6 1941 - 1950. Bound Copy.

Journal of the Royal Horticultural Society, Vol. 43 & 48.

King, Ronald. *Royal Kew* (Constable, 1985).

Krout, John A., and Arnold S. Rice. *United States History From 1865* (HarperCollins Publishers, 1991).

Labarge, Margaret Wade. *Women in Medieval Life* (Hamish Hamilton, 1986).

Lambert, Angela. *1939: The Last Season of Peace* (London: Weidenfeld & Nicolson, 1989).

Lancaster, A. B. *A History of the 20th Century World*. C. P. Hill, gen. ed. (Edward Arnold [Publishers] Ltd., 1984).

Langley, Batty. *New Principles of Gardening* (1728).

Langley, Batty. *The City and Country Builder's and Workman's Treasury of Designs* (London, 1750).

Lawson, William. *The Country House-wife's Garden* (1617) (The Cresset Press Ltd., 1927). Previously *A New Orchard and Garden* (1618).

Le Strange, Richard. *A History of Herbal Plants* (Angus and Robertson Publishers, 1977).

Lee, Sir Sidney, and C. T. Onions. *Shakespeare's England*, Vol. 1 (Oxford: Clarendon Press, 1916).

Lerner, Gerda. *The Creation of Feminist Consciousness* (Oxford University Press, 1993).

Lewenhak, Sheila. *Women and Trade Unions* (Ernest Benn, 1977).

Lindsay, Jack. *Cleopatra* (Constable & Company Ltd., 1971).

Lloyd, Christopher. *The Cottage Garden* (Dorling Kindersley Limited, 1990).

Lofts, Norah. *Domestic Life in England* (London: Weidenfeld and Nicolson, 1976).

Longmate, Norman. *How We Lived Then* (Hutchinson & Co., 1971).

Lord Ernle. *English Farming Past and Present*. New (Sixth) Edition (Heinemann, 1961). First published Longmans, Green & Co. Ltd., 1912.

Loudon, J. C. *An Encyclopaedia of Gardening*. London Fifth Edition (London: printed for Longman, Rees, Orme, Brown and Green, 1827).

Loudon, Mrs. *Gardening For Ladies*. Seventh Edition (London: John Murray, 1846).

Loudon, Mrs. *The Ladies Companion To The Flower Garden*. Fifth Edition (London: William Smith, 1849).

Lovendaski, Joni. *Women And European Politics* (Wheatsheaf Books Ltd., 1986).

Mackie, J. D. *The Earlier Tudors 1485 - 1558* (Oxford: Clarendon Press, 1978).

MacLeod, Dawn. *Down To Earth Women* (Edinburgh: William Blackwood, 1982).

Maddy, Ursula. *Waterperry: A dream fulfilled* (Braunton Devon: Merlin Books Ltd., 1990).

Maltby, Richard, ed. *Dreams for Sale* (London: Harrap, 1989).

Margetson, Stella. *Victorian High Society* (B. T. Batsford, 1980).

Martial. *Epigrams*. Revised edition. Translated by Walter C. A. Ker (Harvard University Press, William Heinemann Ltd., 1968).

Martin, Brian P. *Tales of the Old Countrymen* (David & Charles, 1992).

Martin, Howard. *Britain Since 1800: Towards The Welfare State* (Macmillan Education Ltd., 1988).

Marwick, Arthur. *British Society Since 1945* (Penguin Books, 1990).

Marwick, Arthur. *Women At War 1914 - 1918* (Croom Helm Ltd., 1977).

Massingham, Betty. *A Century of Gardeners* (Faber & Faber Limited, 1982).

Mawe, T., and J. Abercrombie. *Every Man His Own Gardener*. The Nineteenth Edition (London, 1809).

McLeod, Kirsty. *Drums And Trumpets* (Andre Deutsch, 1977).

McMillan, James. *The Way It Changed* (London: William Kimber, 1987).

McMillan, James. *The Way We Were 1900 - 1914* (William Kimber & Co. Limited, 1978).

Miles, Rosalind. *The Women's History of the World* (Paladin [imprint of Harper Collins], 1989).

Mingay, G. E. *Rural Life in Victorian England* (Alan Sutton, 1990).

Minns, Raynes. *Bombers and Mash* (Virago Press, 1980).

Mitchell, David. *Queen Christabel* (Macdonald and Jane's, 1977).

More, Sir Thomas. *Utopia* (1519).

Morgan, Kenneth O., ed. *The Oxford History of Britain* (Oxford University Press, 1988).

Morrill, John, ed. *The Impact of the English Civil War* (Collins & Brown Limited, 1991).

Morris, Christopher, ed. *The Illustrated Journeys of Celia Fiennes 1685 - c.1712* (Macdonald & Co. Ltd., 1982).

Moynihan, Michael, ed. *People At War* (David & Charles, 1973).

Nelson, G. K. *Countrywomen on the Land: Memories of Rural Life in the 1920s and '30s* (Alan Sutton, 1992).

Newby, Howard. *Country Life: A Social History of Rural England* (London: Weidenfeld and Nicolson, 1987).

Nichols, Beverley. *Garden Open Tomorrow* (Newton Abbot: Country Book Club, 1972).

Nicholson, Graham, and Jane Fawcett. *The Village In History* (George Weidenfeld & Nicolson Ltd., 1988).

Noakes, Jeremy, ed. *The Civilian In War* (University of Exeter Press, 1992).

Oakley, Ann. *Housewife* (Penguin Books, 1990).

Park, Bertram, ed. *The Rose Annual 1957* (produced by The Publications Committee of the National Rose Society of Great Britain).

Parkinson, John. *Paradisi In Sole Paradisus Terrestris* (1629) (Methuen & Co., 1904). Reprinted from the edition of 1629.

Pearce, Robert. *British Domestic Politics 1918 - 39* (Hodder & Stoughton, 1992).

Perry, Frances. *Collins Guide to Border Plants* (Collins, 1957).

Perry, Frances. *The Water Garden* (Ward Lock Limited, 1981).

Phillips, Janet, and Peter Phillips. *Victorians At Home And Away* (Croom Helm Ltd., 1978).

Pike, E. Royston. *Pioneers of Social Change* (Barrie & Rockcliff [Barrie Books Ltd.], 1963).

Plumb, J. H. *The First Four Georges* (B. T. Batsford Ltd., 1956).

Plumb, J. H. *Georgian Delights* (Weidenfeld & Nicolson, 1980).

Plumptre, George. *The Latest Country Gardens* (London: The Bodley Head, 1988).

Pool, Mary Jane, ed. *20th Century Decorating, Architecture & Gardens* (Weidenfeld & Nicolson, 1978).

Porter, Roy. *English Society In The Eighteenth Century* (Allen Lane, 1982).

Poulson, Barry W. *Economic History of the United States* (New York: Macmillan, 1981).

Power, Eileen. *Medieval Women*. Ed. M. M. Postan (Cambridge University Press, 1975).

Prior, Mary, ed. *Women in English Society 1500 - 1800* (Methuen & Co. Ltd., 1985).

Pugh, Martin. *Women and the Women's Movement in Britain 1914 - 1959* (MacMillan Education Ltd., 1992).

Raeburn, Antonia. *The Suffragette View* (David & Charles, 1976).

Ramm, Agatha. *Europe In The Twentieth Century 1905 - 1970*. Vol. 2. 7th Ed. (Longman Group UK Ltd., 1984).

Read, Donald. *Edwardian England 1901 - 15* (George Harrap & Co. Ltd., 1972).

Reader, W. J. *Life In Victorian England* (B. T. Batsford Ltd., 1985).

Reader, W. J. *Victorian England* (B. T. Batsford Ltd., 1964).

Reed, Michael. *The Georgian Triumph 1700 - 1830* (Routledge & Kegan Paul, 1983).

Reid, Richard. *The Georgian House and Its Details* (Bishopsgate Press, 1989).

Rendall, Jane. *The Origins of Modern Feminism: Women in Britain, France and the United States, 1780 - 1860* (MacMillan Publishers Ltd., 1985).

Rice, Arnold S., and John A. Krout. *United States History From 1865* (HarperCollins Publishers, 1991).

Ridley, Jasper. *The Tudor Age* (London: Constable, 1988).

Robinson, John Martin. *The English Country Estate* (Century, 1988).

Robinson, William. *The Wild Garden*. Intro. by Robin Lane Fox (Yorkshire: Scolar Press, 1977).

Rohde, Eleanour Sinclair, intro. *The Garden Book of Sir Thomas Hanmer Bart* (London: Gerald Howe, 1933).

Rohde, Eleanour Sinclair. *The Story of the Garden* (The Medici Society, 1989). First published 1932 by the Medici Society.

Roland, Charles P. *An American Iliad* (McGraw-Hill Inc., 1991).

Rooke, Patrick. *Women's Rights* (London: Wayland Publishers, 1972).

Rose, Graham. *The Traditional Garden Book* (Dorling Kindersley, 1989).

Rose, Philip, ed. *Social Trends 23, 1993 Edition* (H.M.S.O., 1993).

Rosen, Andrew. *Rise Up Women!* (Routledge & Kegan Paul, 1974).

Rowbotham, Sheila. *Hidden from History: 300 Years of Women's Oppression and the Fight Against It*. 3rd Edition (Pluto Press, 1977).

Rowbotham, Sheila. *The Past Before Us: Feminism in Action Since the 1960s* (Pandora Press, 1989).

Rowse, A. L. *The Expansion of Elizabethan England* (Macmillan and Co. Ltd., 1955).

Royal Horticultural Society. *Autumn Vegetables From Seeds Sown in July and August*. Second Edition (Royal Horticultural Society, 1916).

Royal Horticultural Society. *The Vegetable Garden Displayed* (London: Royal Horticultural Society, 1944).

Ryder, A. J. *Twentieth Century Germany from Bismarck to Brandt* (Macmillan, 1973).

Ryder, Judith, and Harold Silver. *Modern English Society*. 3rd Edition (Methuen, 1985).

Sackville-West, Vita. *The Women's Land Army* (Michael Joseph Ltd., 1944).

Saunders, Beatrice. *Our Ancestors of the Eighteenth Century* (The Book Guild Limited, 1982).

Sauvain, Philip. *British Economic and Social History* (Stanley Thornes [Publishers] Ltd., 1987).

Sauvain, Philip. *A Modern World History 1919 Onwards* (Hulton Educational Publications, 1985).

Schlesinger, Arthur M., and Dixon Ryan Fox, ed. *A History of American Life*, Vol. II & Vol. III. (New York: The Macmillan Company, 1927).

Scott, Joe. *The World Since 1914* (Heinemann Educational, 1989).

Scott-James, Anne. *The Cottage Garden* (Allen Lane, 1981).

Scullard, H. H. *A History of the Roman World 753 to 146 BC.*, 4th Edition (Routledge, 1980).

Seaman, L. C. B. *Life in Britain Between the Wars* (B. T. Batsford, 1970).

Sellers, Charles, Henry May, and Neil McMillen. *A Synopsis of American History*. Seventh Edition (Chicago: Ivan R. Dee, 1992).

Shakespeare, William. Intro and glossary by B. Hodek. *The Complete Works of William Shakespeare* (London: Spring Books, n.d.).

Shewell-Cooper, W. E. *God Planted A Garden* (Arthur James Ltd., 1977).

Short, Brian, ed. *The English Rural Community: Image and Analysis* (Cambridge University Press, 1992).

Sieveking, Alan Forbes, intro. *Essays on Gardens* (London, 1908).

Spender, Dale, ed. *The Diary of Elizabeth Pepys* (Grafton, 1991).

Spring Rice, Margery. *Working-Class Wives* (Pelican Books, 1939).

Staines, Ric. *Market Gardening* (The Crowood Press, 1990).

Stamp, A. H. A *Social and Economic History of England from 1700 to 1970* (Research Publishing Company, 1979).

Stanley Holton, Sandra. *Suffrage Days* (London and New York: Routledge, 1996).

Stead, Miriam. *Egyptian Life* (British Museum Publications Ltd., 1986).

Steigerwald, David. *The Sixties and the End of Modern America* (New York: St. Martin's Press, 1995).

Stevens, David. *Pergolas, Arbours Gazebos Follies* (Ward Lock Limited, 1987).

Stevenson, John. *The Pelican Social History of Britain British Society 1914 - 45* (Allen Lane, 1984).

Stobart, J. C. *The Glory That Was Greece*. 4th Edition (London: Sidgwick and Jackson, 1987). First published 1912.

Storr-Best, Lloyd. Translated by M. A. Lond. *M. T. Varro On Farming* (G. Bell and Sons Ltd., 1912).

Stratton, J. M. *Agricultural Records AD 220 -1977* (John Baker, 1969).

Strong, Roy. *A Celebration of Gardens* (HarperCollins, 1991).

Stuart, David. *The Garden Triumphant* (Viking, 1988).

Stuart, David, and James Sutherland. *Plants from the Past* (Penguin Books, 1989).

Stuart, David C. *Georgian Gardens* (London: Robert Hale, 1979).

Sunlight Year Book (1898).

Tankard, Judith B., and Michael R. Van Valkenburgh. *Gertrude Jekyll: A Vision of Garden and Wood* (John Murray, 1989).

Terry, Roy. *Women in Khaki* (Columbus Books Ltd., 1988).

Thacker, Christopher. *The History of Gardens* (London: Croom Helm, 1979).

Thirsk, Joan, gen. ed. *The Agrarian History of England and Wales*. Vol. VIII 1914 - 1939 (Cambridge University Press, 1978).

Thirsk, Joan, ed. *Chapters from The Agrarian History of England and Wales 1500 - 1750*. Vol. 3, *Agricultural Change: Policy and Practice 1500 - 1750* (Cambridge University Press, 1990).

Thomas, Graham Stuart. *Gardens Of The National Trust* (The National Trust/Weidenfeld and Nicolson, 1979).

Thompson, Flora. *Lark Rise to Candleford* (London: Oxford University Press, 1973).

Thompson, Paul. *The Edwardians* (Weidenfeld and Nicolson, 1984).

Thorne, Richard. *Covent Garden Market: Its History and Restoration* (London: The Architectural Press, 1980).

Thorpe, Andrew. *Britain in the 1930s* (Blackwell, 1992).

Tims, Margaret. *Mary Wollstonecraft: A Social Pioneer* (Millington Books Ltd., 1976).

Traill, H. D., and J. S. Mann, ed. *Social England* Vol. II & Vol. III (Cassell and Company Ltd., 1902).

Trueman, John. *The Romantic Story of Scent* (Aldus Books Limited, 1975).

Truslow Adams, James, ed-in-chief, and R. V. Coleman, Man. Ed. *Dictionary of American History*, Vols. II, III. & V (Charles Scribner's Sons, 1940).

Turner, E. S. *Dear Old Blighty* (Michael Joseph, 1980).

Tusser, Thomas. *Five Hundred Points of Good Husbandry* (1573).

Twinch, Carol. *Women on the Land* (Cambridge: The Lutterworth Press, 1990).

Verey, Rosemary. *Classic Garden Design* (Viking, 1984).

Verey, Rosemary. *The Scented Garden* (London: Michael Joseph, Mermaid Books, 1982).

Verney, Peter, and Michael Dunne. *The Genius of the Garden* (Webb & Bower, 1989).

Wacher, John. *Roman Britain* (J. M. Dent & Sons Ltd., 1978).

Waller, June, and Michael Vaughan-Rees. *Women in Wartime* (Macdonald Optima, 1987).

Walsh, Noelle, and Glyn Davies. *Ragtime to Wartime: The Best of Good Housekeeping 1922 - 1939* (Ebury Press, 1986).

Walton, John. *Late Georgian And Victorian Britain* (George Philip, The National Trust, 1989).

Ward, Jennifer, trans. & ed. *Women of the English Nobility and Gentry* (Manchester University Press, 1995).

Ward, Sadie. *War in the Countryside 1939 - 45* (Cameron Books in association with David & Charles, 1988).

Warwick, Edward, Henry C. Pitz, and Alexander Wyckoff. *Early American Dress* (New York: Benjamin Bloom, 1965).

Watson, Jack B. *Success In British History Since 1945* (John Murray, 1989).

Watson, Jack B. *Success In World History Since 1914* (John Murray, 1983).

Webber, Ronald. *Covent Garden Mud-salad market* (J. M. Dent & Sons Limited, 1969).

Whetham, Edith H. *The Agrarian History of England And Wales*, Vol. VIII (Cambridge University Press, 1978).

White, Julia. *The Inkpen Saga* (The Book Guild, 1985).

Whiten, Faith, and Geoff Whiten. *The Chelsea Flower Show* (Elm Tree Books London/Hamish Hamilton Ltd., 1982).

Whitlock, Ralph. *A Short History of Farming in Britain* (E. P. Publishing Ltd., 1977).

The WI Handbook. Fifth Edition (WI Books Ltd., May 1982).

Wilkinson, L. P. *The Roman Experience* (London: Paul Elek, 1975).

Williams, Thomas. *Life In England from Victoria To Elizabeth II* (Sussex: The Book Guild Ltd., 1987).

Winter, Gordon. *The Golden Years 1903 - 1913* (David & Charles, 1975).

Wissinger, Joanna. *Victorian Details* (Virgin, 1990).

Woodman, Marian. *Food And Cookery in Roman Britain* (Corinium Museum, 1976).

Wright, Louis B. *Everyday Life In Colonial America* (New York: G. P. Putnam's Sons; London: B. T. Batsford Ltd., 1965).

Wright, Richardson. *The Story of Gardening* (Garden City Publishing Company, Inc., 1938).

Amateur Gardening Annual 1955 (UK).

American Horticulturist (USA), October 1991.

Board of Agriculture & Fisheries. "West Kent Women's Agricultural
    Committee Instructions and Advice To Members of the Women's
    Land Army."

"Bulletin No. 90 of the Ministry of Agriculture and Fisheries"
    (H.M.S.O. 1939).

"Bulletin of the Garden Club of America," March 1920 & May 1920.

The Century Magazine (USA), May 1906.

The Constitution (U.S. newspaper), 5 May 1918.

Country Life (USA), May 1921.

Country Life (UK), 20 March 1942, 24 September 1948, 30 January
    1948, 11 March 1949, 1 July 1949.

"Dig for Victory" Leaflets 1 - 23. Issued by the Ministry of
    Agriculture.

Every-Woman's Encyclopaedia, Part 27 (UK). Amalgamated Press,
    Ltd., n.d.

The Garden (UK), Journal of the Royal Horticultural Society, January
    1994.

Garden Design (USA), Autumn 1988.

Good Gardening (UK), Vols. 1 - 5.

The Guild Gardener (UK), January/February 1953.

"Herb Growing & Collecting." Notes from the National Herb
    Growing Association. Taken from "Women's Employment," 1917.

Home & Country (UK), Journal of the National Federation of
    Women's Institutes, June 1994.

House & Garden (USA), August 1984.

The Illustrated London News (UK), 8 January 1896.

The Lady's Realm (UK), 1897.

Land Girl (UK), Vols. 3 - 6.

Landscape Architecture Magazine (USA), May 1982.

The Magazine Antiques (USA), July 1982, April 1985.

Ministry of Agriculture and Fisheries. "Dig for Victory Campaign"
    (T.P.Y. 10321, November 1941).

"National Service" (H.M.S.O., 1939).

Royal Horticultural Society pamphlets.

Suburban Life (USA), March 1914.

War Gardening Leaflet No. 2, January 1940. "War And Your Garden"
    (Issued by Yalding, Kent: Plant Protection Ltd.).

Womanhood (UK), Vols. II, VI, VII.

Women's Studies (USA), Vol. 14, No. 4, 1988.

INDEX

Page references in italics indicate illustrations. Subentries have been arranged in chronological order where appropriate.